Praise for *The New Feminist Agenda*

"In this important new book, Madeleine Kunin argues that empowering women to succeed at home and at work is both good economics and good social policy. She presents a convincing roadmap for how we achieve that vision, and calls on all of us to be part of a brighter future."

—President Bill Clinton

"Women's social and economic gains over the past thirty years have been staggering—but equally staggering is how little America has changed in response. What's needed is a new feminist agenda to bring the country up to date. Madeleine Kunin, one of the nation's foremost leaders, has stepped up to the plate and delivered us a home run. The agenda she advocates is powerful, relevant, and necessary."

—Robert B. Reich, author, *Aftershock*,
former US Secretary of Labor

"*The New Feminist Agenda* is singing our song! It is time for us to take the next leap forward for women and families. When we get rid of the huge bias against mothers in hiring, wages, and advancement, we will have more women in leadership, far fewer children living in poverty, and a better future."

—Joan Blades, cofounder,
MoveOn.org and MomsRising.org

"As one of the first woman governors, Madeleine Kunin knows how to make history and chart a positive course for women."

—Ellen Malcolm, founder, Emily's List

"Madeleine Kunin reinvigorates the feminist movement, bringing the discussion of women's rights to a new generation and into our new social paradigm. This fresh look at the woman of today—balancing work and family—raises questions about how far we have really come and inspires a new advocacy agenda for women and families."

—Rosa L. DeLauro, US Representative

"Madeleine Kunin wants feminists to focus on the family. We've made great strides—nearly two-thirds of women are primary breadwinners for their families or share that responsibility with a partner—but this leaves more work to be done as full-time, stay-at-home caregivers become increasingly rare. Thank you, Madeleine, for pointing the way forward for 21st-century feminists."

—Heather Boushey, senior economist,
Center for American Progress

"Despite the substantial gains made by women in my lifetime, women and families need more. Governor Kunin has defined the new agenda for women—and like-minded men—leading the fight for progress in business, government, education, and society in the years ahead."

—Carolyn B. Maloney, US Representative

"Madeleine Kunin has long recognized that women hold the potential to transform companies, countries, and the global economy as a whole. In *The New Feminist Agenda*, she convinces us that it will be the smart organizations and governments that embrace this reality and create the change necessary for all women to reach their full potential and to make their full contribution."

—James H. Wall, Deloitte

"Madeleine Kunin draws from her vast experience to craft a sweeping yet highly realistic plan for how all of us can contribute to a more-just world that will benefit women *and* men—and their families. She offers a timely prescription for much of what ails our business and political cultures."

—Brad Harrington, executive director,
Center for Work & Family, Boston College

"*The New Feminist Agenda* is a powerful declaration of family values. With clarity and conviction, Madeleine Kunin presents a strong case for the economics and ethics of equality at home, in the workplace, and in government. There are no shortcuts to social change: action, imagination, and optimism—starting right now."

—Barbara Lee, president and founder,
Barbara Lee Family Foundation

THE NEW **FEMINIST** AGENDA

THE NEW FEMINIST AGENDA

Defining the Next Revolution for Women, Work, and Family

MADELEINE M. KUNIN

Chelsea Green Publishing
White River Junction, Vermont

Project Manager: Patricia Stone
Developmental Editor: Joni Praded
Copy Editor: Nancy Ringer
Proofreader: Helen Walden
Indexer: Shana Milkie
Designer: Melissa Jacobson

Printed in the United States of America
First printing March, 2012
10 9 8 7 6 5 4 3 2 1   12 13 14 15 16

Our Commitment to Green Publishing

Chelsea Green sees publishing as a tool for cultural change and ecological stewardship. We strive to align our book manufacturing practices with our editorial mission and to reduce the impact of our business enterprise in the environment. We print our books and catalogs on chlorine-free recycled paper, using vegetable-based inks whenever possible. This book may cost slightly more because it was printed on paper that contains recycled fiber, and we hope you'll agree that it's worth it. Chelsea Green is a member of the Green Press Initiative (www.greenpressinitiative.org), a nonprofit coalition of publishers, manufacturers, and authors working to protect the world's endangered forests and conserve natural resources. *The New Feminist Agenda* was printed on FSC®-certified paper supplied by Thomson-Shore that contains at least 30% postconsumer recycled fiber.

Library of Congress Cataloging-in-Publication Data

Kunin, Madeleine.
The new feminist agenda : defining the next revolution for women, work, and family / Madeleine M. Kunin.
p. cm.
Includes bibliographical references and index.
ISBN 978-1-60358-425-8 (hardcover) — ISBN 978-1-60358-291-9 (pbk.) — ISBN 978-1-60358-368-8 (ebook)
1. Work and family—United States. 2. Working women—United States. 3. Feminism—United States.
I. Title.

HD4904.25.K865 2012
306.3'6--dc23

2012001372

Chelsea Green Publishing
85 North Main Street, Suite 120
White River Junction, VT 05001
(802) 295-6300
www.chelseagreen.com

For John, my first reader, editor,
constant supporter, and also—a feminist

CONTENTS

ACKNOWLEDGMENTS

I thank the people who have worked on family and work issues over the years and who generously agreed to be interviewed for this book.

Every writer needs a room of her own. The University of Vermont provided me a quiet, uninterrupted office which I occupied in my capacity as a Marsh Professor at Large. I am grateful to members of the university staff who solved several computer mysteries for me, who printed out many versions of each chapter, and cheered me on. In particular, I thank Dencie L. Mitchell, Denise M. Marrero, Lisa A.Young, Laura D. Smith, and the computer guys, Philip J. Plourde and Roger Bombardier.

I thank my interview transcriber, Linda Birkenbach, for her diligent work.

Two University of Vermont work-study students provided assistance. Camille Fordy did some early research, and Monica Johnson provided critical technical assistance during the editing process.

I thank my family and friends for their ongoing support.

CHAPTER 1

Time for a New Revolution

Five of us were meeting for lunch and reminiscing about the women's movement. "I was never one of those angry women," one said. "I'm still angry," I blurted. My reaction surprised both me and my friends. Where did that come from? A source I hadn't tapped before. Upon reflection, I realized that I'm not angry enough to carry a placard down hot macadam streets in front of the nation's Capitol, like I did in my thirties when I marched for women's rights. But now in my seventies I'm still dissatisfied with the status quo and harbor a passion for change. Old age allows me the luxury of being impatient—there is not so much time left—and it permits me to say what I think, to be demanding, and, best of all, to imagine a different world where there is true gender equality in the workplace, the home, and the political arena.

Why the anger? What did I expect?

I expected that the women's movement of the 1970s would give me a good answer to the question my students regularly asked: how do you manage to have a family *and* a career?

I expected that affordable, quality child care would be widely available, that paid family leave would be the law, and that equal pay for equal work would be a reality. I did not expect that women would still make 77 cents for every dollar that men earn.

I expected that one-third to one-half of our Congress, governors, state legislatures, and mayors would be female. I did not expect that in 2010 that number would be 17 percent in the Congress, and the United States would be tied at 69th place in the percentage of women in parliaments, out of 178 countries.

I expected that one-third to one-half of corporate board members would be women. I did not expect to see that proportion stuck at 17 percent.

I expected that a high percentage of the Fortune 500 companies would be led by women. I did not expect that figure to be 3 percent.

I expected that misogyny, rape, and other acts of violence against women would be widely condemned and sharply reduced. I did not expect that a female journalist could be sexually abused in the middle of Cairo's Tahrir Square and then blamed for bringing it on herself, as Lara Logan of CBS News experienced in February 2011.

I expected that *Roe v. Wade* would remain the law of the land. I did not expect that it would be eroded, state by state.

I expected that by the year 2011 grandmothers like myself would be able to tell their grandchildren of how life used to be "long ago," when families had to figure out for themselves how to be both wage earners and caregivers.

Some changes occurred that I had not expected and could not have imagined: that women would comprise nearly 60 percent of college undergraduates, that women would comprise half of the medical and law students, that women would enter the workforce in record numbers, and that the traditional family supported by the father would be overtaken by the two-wage-earner family.

That's the good news. The bad news is that many women who have careers that we never could have imagined for ourselves are still flummoxed by the most age-old problem: how to have a job and take care of the children, the elderly, the sick, and the disabled. Until we find a way to sort out how to share these responsibilities—between spouses, partners, employers, and governments—gender equality will remain an elusive goal. Progress for women will remain stalled. But it's not only about gender anymore. As I write, Italy is in an economic crisis, in danger of defaulting on its government debt. One reason given for its economic woes is that it has the lowest percentage of women in the workforce in all of Europe. Why? Whether because of the country's macho culture or lack of family support programs, Italy offers little in the way of encouragement or assistance for working families.

Time for Change, Again

The countries that do support working families benefit from greater productivity and social well-being. It is time for another social revolution, not for the benefit of women alone, but for the most traditional of reasons: for the sake of the family. We need to reweave the fabric of society to provide the love and care necessary for the more fragile members of our families. The workplace must be reconfigured to harmonize with these responsibilities. The urgency for change is felt by families at all income levels, even those who are able to negotiate flexibility for themselves and can afford to pay for quality child care. Middle- and low-income employees are most starkly affected by today's work/life stress. They cannot make ends meet, financially or emotionally. They experience a severe time deficit that does not allow them to give enough of themselves at work or at home. These frustrations are commonplace. If the kitchen table, the water cooler, or Twitter could talk, these stories would overwhelm all other conversation. If one family's text messages about who is picking up the children or shopping for dinner were gathered in a book over a few years, it would be too heavy to lift.

The question families ponder is: how can we be better parents and employees without neglecting either our families or our jobs? We are beginning to understand the individual cost that the schism between work and family exacts. We have not added up the national cost. Our reluctance, or outright refusal, to enact policies that would bridge the gap between family and work has contributed to disturbing national statistics: alarmingly high child poverty rates, declining college graduation rates and test scores, and a growing chasm between the rich, the middle class, and the poor. Our inability—for political, economic, or cultural reasons——to invest in families leaves us vulnerable to being reduced to second-rate status in the global economy. Impossible to measure, but not to be ignored, is the moral cost we pay by depriving so many young Americans of the chance to realize the American Dream.

It is time to mobilize a constituency for change. Who is to be charged with calling a halt to the "push-me, pull-me" tug-of-war game that families are forced to play? The obvious answer is: women, as part of a broad coalition, attending to the unfinished business of feminism.

As *New York Times* columnist Gail Collins concluded in her book *When Everything Changed*, "The feminist movement of the late twentieth century created a new United States in which women ran for president, fought for their country, argued before the Supreme Court, performed heart surgery, directed movies, and flew into space. But it did not resolve the tensions of trying to raise children and hold down a job at the same time. . . . They had not remade the world the way the revolutionaries had hoped."[1]

Do feminists have an obligation to complete their mission of gender equality? Yes, but not single-handedly. The issue of accommodating both work and family has outgrown the parameters of our current perception of feminism. The entire family is affected when women and men cannot find equanimity in their lives: women, men, children, grandparents, and uncles and aunts. The new constituency for work/life policies is inclusive. We have left the female ghetto of family/work issues and moved into every neighborhood.

Women have traditionally led the charge on family issues, in part because of experience: fatigue from too many late-night feedings, red knees from too much scrubbing, and creased brows from too much worrying about where the children are and what they might be doing. Women spoke up because they knew what they were talking about, but more often they were out front because no one else would volunteer. Women remain the key sponsors of legislation affecting women and families, both in Congress and in state legislatures, because they understand the chapters of their own lives. But women alone can no longer complete the mission. We need that other half—men—to march at our sides, linked arm-in-arm as we approach the Capitol steps. What demands will we make? Let's translate the easy rhetoric of "family values" into tough action. Enough sweet talk; we want results that will enable us to be good parents, good caregivers, and good workers.

When women try to figure out the conundrum of finding a good match between work and family, we believe it is only a question of balance. We add an ounce or two on one side of the work/life scale, and subtract an ounce from the other. Perfect——for one moment, but not for the next, when a child gets sick or a new supervisor changes the schedule, or there is an unexpected pregnancy. Suddenly we're out of kilter. And the responsibility for being out of balance is ours and ours alone. We have failed.

We are not alone. When we fall, we bring our families down with us. They bear the consequences of either less income or less care, or both. A minority of highly skilled, highly paid women can negotiate paid family leave and flexible schedules, but the majority cannot because they don't have the power to ask without fear of losing their jobs, and they rightly fear that they are easily replaceable.

One by one, women's and men's requests for policies that support families have been denied. Demands made by a broad and diverse coalition are harder to ignore. This has been the pattern of change throughout history: when the "I" becomes "we," a cause begins to move from the fringe to the center, as has been exemplified by the social changes brought about by movements for disability rights and gay and lesbian civil rights.

Who are "we"? We are the disparate constituencies—children, women (all women, not only those who call themselves feminists, but also those who shudder at the idea of being called feminists), the elderly, the handicapped, the sick—who can give one loud shout out for change. Such a large chorus will increase the volume, but noise is not enough. To build strong bonds among constituencies that have not often worked together, we have to start by redefining ourselves. Can we mobilize under the banner of Feminists for Families?

CHAPTER 2

Back to the Family, After All

It may seem a retrograde step to suggest that feminists like me, who strove to liberate ourselves from the limited roles of wife and mother, have come full circle to focus, once again, on the family. At the start of the feminist revolution, we did not dwell on the question of who would take care of the children. We assumed things would fall into place. Child care centers would spring up like flowers and workplaces would be magically transformed to meet our needs. The catch phrase became "we can have it all." Not everyone agreed. Critics like Phyllis Schlafly, leader of the conservative Eagle Forum, pronounced that if women would stay home and fulfill their proper housewife role of serving their husbands, all would be right with the world. Despite the nascent debate between stay-at-home moms and working moms, not many women heeded Schlafly's advice. The "daddy goes to work and mommy stays home" portrait of the American family is as quaint as a Norman Rockwell *Saturday Evening Post* cover. Just 20 percent of young families fit that model. Half the workforce is comprised of women.

The 1970s exodus of millions of American housewives from their split-level ranch homes was blamed on the seductive powers of feminism, the revolution that destroyed the family. Today, the culprit is no longer feminism; it is economics. Women are streaming into the workplace because their income is essential; 40 percent are either single working mothers or married mothers who earn as much as or more than their spouse.[1] Feminism can still take some of the credit or blame. Without access to education, without a cultural shift in the role of women in society, women today would not be qualified for these jobs.

Feminism shares another responsibility for our present dilemma: once we got out of the house, unlike our European sisters, we failed to make demands of our government for paid family leave laws, workplace flexibility, and quality child care. American feminist groups claim that child care was on their agenda from the start. Others disagree.

In *The Second Stage*, Betty Friedan tried to move feminists to focus on issues that are most important to families, and the balance between work and family was one of them. That message, recall some feminist leaders, did not go over well. "People killed her," remembers Ellen Galinsky, cofounder of the Families and Work Institute, who says she, too, encountered scorn when she raised the issue of child care at feminist conferences.

Some feminists argued that the movement's focus needed to remain narrow for it to succeed. Others simply thought the issue was boring. Says Janet Gornick, who has written widely on family/work questions, "Child care and family leave was ho hum. I heard this said on a thousand occasions, that maternity leave was a middle-class issue, while they were fighting for reproductive freedom and to be free of domestic violence." The irony of this, she points out, is that the lack of child care is what stalled progress in the ensuing years for poor women—especially those removed from public assistance—by preventing them from being integrated into the labor market.

Muriel Fox, a cofounder of the National Organization for Women (NOW), disagrees that the movement deemphasized family issues. "NOW was a leading force in Congress to get a child care bill passed," says Fox, referring to the comprehensive child care bill passed by Congress in 1971 and vetoed by President Richard Nixon. "Don't listen to anyone who perpetuates the myth."

Indeed, NOW's statement of purpose, which Fox calls "one of the great documents of the twentieth century," seems enlightened on this front: "We reject the current assumptions that a man must carry the sole burden of supporting himself, his wife, and family, and that a woman is automatically entitled to lifelong support by a man upon her marriage. . . . We believe that a true partnership between the sexes demands a different concept of marriage, an equitable sharing of the responsibilities of home and children and of the economic burdens of their support. We believe that proper recognition should be given to the economic and social value of homemaking and child-care."

A different perspective comes from Eleanor Smeal, a former president of NOW, who today is head of the Feminist Majority. The feminist agenda has been her work for forty years. She takes pride in its achievements and when I ask her whether feminists have paid sufficient attention to family/work policies, she replies, "I have been working on paid family leave most of my adult life. Hell, I ran a child care center. NOW encouraged chapters to establish child care centers. I provided testimony for those women's groups in the mid-80s." Today, she still mentions paid family leave and paid sick days in her speeches, but, she says, "I can tell you what gets applause and what doesn't. Paid sick days [does] not get the fervor behind it that it should. . . . Every time we do a mailing on paid family leave, child care, sick days, or anything like that, it never gets the support like abortion does. Not even close."

Abortion and violence are the fund-raisers. Paid family leave and child care are not. Until we energize voters on all sides of the political spectrum to open up their checkbooks to advocate for work/family policies, abortion (the most divisive family issue) will continue to eclipse family/work policies (potentially a more unifying one). In order to fulfill the expectations that feminism promised, do we have to jettison the word "feminism" itself?

Efforts to make the word "feminist" less incendiary have not succeeded. For some, it remains radioactive. I naturally identify myself as a feminist because to me the definition is simple: it means equality and that we aren't there yet. But I am made aware of how antiquated my view is whenever I ask a class of young women, "How many of you consider yourselves feminists?" At most one or two brave hands go up. Despite the proliferation of women's studies classes, most of the students who are in them are not prone to rebellion, which seems like a contradiction. At best, they are curious. Kristin Rowe-Finkbeiner, author of *The F-Word*, agrees that "'feminism' now has an outdated, '70s connotation—instead of shifting with the movement, the term has stayed stagnant, becoming one of the many stumbling blocks for a broad-based contemporary women's movement. In fact, a central irony of this rejection of the label is that there is still broad support for the ideals set forth by feminism." She regards the contemporary third-wave women's movement as restricted to academia, not well recognized outside its walls. She asks, "If young women focus only on individual interests, what happens to the broader social issues of poverty, wage inequity, education disparities, parenting, and social hierarchy? And how can electoral action and political change be organized effectively by a sea of individuals who don't identify with common issues?"[2]

I asked Felicia Kornbluh, who teaches gender studies at the University of Vermont, what her students think of feminism. "It's another kind of feminism. It's an anti-violence feminism," she observes. Her students are concerned about interpersonal issues, she says, like "how individual men treat individual women. It takes a lot for them to see that in a social or political context, to see that how families relate can be shaped by whether or not there's affordable child care, or whether there is enforcement of anti-discrimination laws."

This generation is not the first to distance itself from the word. It is one of the ironies of our time that every woman in America, regardless of her age, race, earnings, or political beliefs, has been affected by the modern feminist movement—whether she is a supervisor on the factory floor or a physics professor at a university; or whether she is Sarah Palin or Hillary Clinton. Without Title IX, Sarah Palin would probably not have played college basketball and Hillary Clinton may not have been admitted to Yale Law School. Neither one of them would have been able to campaign for president or vice president of the United States. My generation helped make it happen, but we should not expect gratitude. I do not want to become the scold who bemoans how little this generation knows or cares about her years of struggle. Ignorance may be a good thing if we accept that the precepts of feminism have become so deeply embedded that they are taken for granted, no longer worthy of comment. On the downside, such a gap in education can lead to self-satisfaction, obscuring the need for continued action not only to make progress, but to hold on to what we have.

During Secretary of State Hillary Clinton's campaign for the Democratic nomination for the presidency, most of the young women I spoke with on college campuses did not grasp that the election of the first female president would be as historic as that of the first African-American. Neither did they know that it was unique to have a serious female candidate. Can these same women who happily believe the battle for gender equality has been won be mobilized for action on family/work policies? When will they wake up? Will it be when they get their first job? With the arrival of their first baby? Their second? Eleanor Miller, who has taught at the University of Wisconsin in Milwaukee, where students tend to be older, and the University of Vermont, where they tend to be younger, says that her students differed in their perspectives on the family/work balance according to age. The youthful University of Vermont students thought that "combining work and family would be a walk in the park," while the Wisconsin students, many of whom had young children, felt quite differently.

Meanwhile, we continue to balance and juggle—both acrobatic feats. Even Tina Fey, best known for her impersonation of Sarah Palin on *Saturday Night Live*, has to do it. In "Confessions of a Juggler," a piece she wrote for *The New Yorker*, she comments: "The topic of working moms is a tap-dance recital in a minefield. . . . 'How do you juggle it all?' people constantly ask me, with an accusatory look in their eyes. 'You're screwing it all up, aren't you?' My standard answer is that I have the same struggles as any working parent but with the good fortune to be working at my dream job."[3]

Well, not exactly like any working parent; most can't afford good child care and may not have a dream job. Still, the act of juggling is familiar to all working families, including my own when I was a mother of four young children. I thought that if I tossed the balls in the air just right, and was adept enough to catch them, I could *have it all*—career, husband, kids. It was only a matter of time, skill, and practice. Most days I did, some days I didn't. What I and other working mothers didn't know is that when we didn't succeed, it wasn't necessarily our fault; it was a combination of societal expectations and workplace structure.

Work/Family Mismatch

Those steeped in work/family issues point out that the way our nation's workforce took shape and remains organized is at direct odds with the demands of an increasingly diverse workforce. Kathleen E. Christensen, director of the Alfred P. Sloan Foundation's working families program, puts it this way: "The workplace, as we know it, is a one-size-fits-all workplace. It's an artifact of the mid-twentieth century." That workplace, with a smattering of exceptions, continues to adhere to the model of the "ideal male worker"—who works from nine to five, five days a week, and is welcomed home by his beautiful wife, ready with a homemade dinner and cute, clean-faced kids sitting quietly at the table. This ideal worker has what *Unbending Gender* author Joan Williams calls "immunity from family work."[4]

"We have a public policy that's perfectly designed for the work force of 1960," Williams tells me. "We should have a policy designed for a workforce where 70 percent of families with children have all the adults in the labor force. That means shifting the workplace ideals from the old-fashioned ideal worker to the new balanced worker, who has to balance work and family obligations." Williams describes the ideal masculine worker norm as "someone who starts work in early adulthood [and] works full-time for forty years straight, taking no time off for child rearing or child bearing. You penalize almost all women, and you penalize men who don't want that traditional pattern."

Why has this ill-fitting ideal worker not been ushered into history? Because, according to Williams, "we have changed from a society that formerly delegated to women the care of children, the sick, and the elderly to a society that pretends these groups do not exist." As she points out in *Reshaping the Work-Family Debate*, though, mothers and fathers, employees, and employers all ultimately need the same thing: "they need today's workplaces to be designed to reflect the realities of today's family life."[5]

Social Darwinism and the Rise of Childhood Poverty

Ignoring the realities of family/work dilemmas has profoundly impacted our culture. Not only have work/family conflicts increased, but the oversight has spawned a socially Darwinian approach to raising children and caring for the elderly, the sick, and the disabled. One indicator of the price paid for work/family *imbalance* is the increasingly high rate of childhood poverty. The United States has the highest child poverty rate in the developed world, 22 percent and rising.[6] We cannot continue to wait for gradual change to reduce that figure, on either moral or economic grounds. How can a country so rich, by most indices, accept such high poverty rates? One reason is that most people don't see it. We don't have children begging in the streets as in India, though we do have children filling up the beds in homeless shelters.

What must we do to recognize that by impoverishing our children, we are impoverishing our nation—severely today, drastically tomorrow?

We are accustomed to being a throwaway society. Can we afford to discard our children's chances for living a good and productive life in the same way that we dispose of empty bottles and cans, expecting someone else to pick them up? We fail to acknowledge that it is we, the taxpayers, who pick up the cost of our high incarceration rate—nine times higher than Canada's, and yes, highest in the world. We pick up the cost of high school dropouts and of unskilled workers incapable of being employed, and we pick up that impossible-to-measure cost of too many people living miserable lives. We can no longer afford that spendthrift attitude toward disposable *people*—acknowledged as our most precious resource by both the left and the right.

How long can we continue to ask families to improvise, catch as catch can, to cope with family/work conflicts? The do-it-yourself spirit of American independence, which preaches that each of us, woman and man, can pull ourselves up by our bootstraps, is a treasured American credo, hard to give up. We cling to the romance of the self-made man (woman) who succeeds on his (her) own. The idea that government is the problem, not the solution, a legacy of Ronald Reagan, has gained new life with the birth of the Tea Party.

The Horatio Alger stories of those who make it to the top without a helping hand are well known. The stories of the millions who do not are seldom told. It is those millions who don't have the voice, the money, or the time to tell their own stories who are failed by the Darwinian ethos that underlies our culture's work/family struggles.

Women in the Workplace

The influx of large numbers of women into the workplace has begun to change the conversation for both employees and employers. Some family-friendly workplaces pride themselves on implementing policies such as paid family leave and flexible scheduling. They have become magnets for attracting and retaining the most talented and skilled employees. Such companies inspire and motivate other employers by proving that it pays to acknowledge the changing dual responsibilities of those who work for them. Federal and a few state governments have sluggishly moved in that direction as well.

We took the first step in 1978 with the passage of the Pregnancy Discrimination Act of 1978, which prohibits discrimination on the basis of pregnancy, childbirth, or related medical conditions. The law does not always protect pregnant women from being put on unpaid leave or being fired when they ask for special accommodations during pregnancy, like more bathroom breaks, or to be excused from heavy lifting or long periods of standing, contends Dina Bakst, cofounder of A Better Balance, in the *New York Times*.[7] Fifteen years later, in 1993, we passed the federal unpaid Family and Medical Leave Act. It was the first bill to be signed into law by President Bill Clinton, after it had been vetoed twice by President George H. W. Bush on the grounds that it would hurt business. FMLA was to be the first step, expected to be soon followed by a paid family and medical leave law. Eighteen years later, we are still waiting.

Why have expectations not been fulfilled? Why has progress been so slow? Viewed through the lens of women in the workforce, the women's movement sparked changes that far exceeded expectations. When seen through the lens of family/work policies, it has fallen far short. Disappointment may be the pattern of all revolutions, which tend to overpromise. Revolutionary rhetoric is inevitably extravagant in order to rally and retain followers. The outcome is edited by experience, exhaustion, and backlash. Revolutions settle down, revolutionaries die. People forget. Energy gets depleted. Divisive factions rise up. But the spark that ignited the revolution continues to burn at a low flame, reminding us that the mission of gender equality still waits to be fulfilled.

It is time for women, though separated by income, race, and experience, to work together to achieve sensible family/work policies. We must form a new sisterhood among women—and men—of all classes and backgrounds. Each wave of the women's movement has had inclusivity as its goal. The 1990s third-wave women's movement criticized my generation for being too white, too homophobic, and too middle class. They looked at photos of the 1970s second-wave feminists and saw college-educated, upper- and middle-income women whose leaders' names and faces became famous: Betty Friedan, Bella Abzug, and Gloria Steinem. What they missed were the thousands of women who marched behind them, their names and faces unknown. What led these women to leave their homes, get on buses and planes, and drive their own cars to march on Washington?

The threat of taking away the right to a safe and legal abortion brought them there. The ability to control fertility in any form is fundamental to a woman's ability to do more than bear children. Gail Collins explains that soon after the availability of "The Pill," female enrollment in graduate schools soared. Access to legal abortions was threatened in the 1970s, and it is being steadily eroded now by new restrictions adopted by state legislatures.

My own fury rose to the surface when I realized that when men have the power to dictate to women when and whether they should have children, they are exercising ultimate control over women's lives. At the beginning of my political career, when I was lieutenant governor of Vermont, I overheard these words from a huddle of male state senators: "I say keep 'em barefoot and pregnant," followed by laughter. The debate concerned funding for Planned Parenthood. My face turned red. Fortunately, I could answer them back, from the podium. They called the roll. The vote was 15–15. I cast the tie-breaking vote in favor of funding for Planned Parenthood. Little did I dream then that thirty years later the same battle would be fought again in Congress.

The struggle for choice cannot be abandoned, but neither can we continue to make abortion the only issue that motivates women to take to the streets and to write checks. It is too divisive. I felt the visceral divide that separates pro-choice and pro-life women and men when I marched in a pro-choice demonstration in Washington. I encountered women who leaned toward us from the sidewalks, waving pro-life placards and screaming at us with frightening vitriol. I tried to ignore their taunts and kept marching down Pennsylvania Avenue, protectively linking arms with the women to the left and to the right of me. It was easy to demonize the protestors. They were wrong, we were right. But I had to stop and think; why were they so angry, so outraged with our position on abortion? Was it possible for us to have a conversation instead of a confrontation?

I thought we could but became discouraged by the results of Senator Hillary Clinton's speech on the thirty-second anniversary of *Roe v. Wade* in 2005. Testing her diplomatic skills, she suggested that both sides of the abortion debate ask for common ground. "We should be able to agree that we want every child born in this country and around the world to be wanted, cherished, and loved," she said. "The best way to get there is to do more to educate the public about reproductive health, about how to prevent unsafe and unwanted pregnancies." She concluded, "So my hope now, today, is that whatever our disagreements with those in this debate, that we join together to take real action to improve the quality of health care for women and families, to reduce the number of abortions, and to build a healthier, brighter, more hopeful future for women and girls in our country and around the world."[8] She got clobbered by almost everyone, especially those at the far ends of the pro-choice and pro-life scale.

Should we put aside the abortion debate and learn to compartmentalize? We could put the abortion debate in one drawer, close it, and open a new drawer for the family/work debate. Would that work? Can women and men, despite their differences on reproductive choice, unite on sensible and fair family/work issues? Instead of two groups shaking their fists at one other, can we march together for the benefit of fathers, mothers, children, and grandchildren?

Could we hold a march for family/work policies in Washington? Would anybody come? Or would they be too tired, too busy, too scared of losing their jobs to attend? (Child care could be provided.) Of equal importance: would the media cover it, especially if it was peaceful, or would this be another ho-hum event?

How do we set in motion a robust grassroots movement that would galvanize the leadership of our country to enact policies such as paid family leave, workplace flexibility, good child care, and early childhood education? Marches, Tweets, letters, lobbyists—every possible means has to be employed to convince the country that these issues are not only "women's" issues, not only "children's" issues, which can easily be dismissed with a gentle pat on the head. These are gut economic issues. How well we address them today, through government and private action, will determine how well we do as a nation tomorrow.

Anger, Imagination, and Optimism

What does it take for an individual to get up off the sofa and make a phone call, send an e-mail, or write a blog posting or a letter to the editor? I ask you to visualize three boxes floating in front of you. The first box is labeled "Anger." A dose of anger is necessary to become politically engaged. It can be provoked by a global issue such as the war in Afghanistan, or a local issue, like safe streets. My first political act, though I didn't realize it at the time, was to campaign for flashing red lights at a railroad crossing in my neighborhood. My children had to cross the tracks on their way to school. I learned how to gather signatures in the neighborhood for a petition and how to testify before a commission, and to my surprise, I succeeded. My "worried mother syndrome" transformed me into a political activist.

A word of caution: you can't be too angry. As for Goldilocks and the three bears, the portion of anger has to be "just right." If you are too angry, you don't believe the system can be changed—either you become a revolutionary and want to tear the system down, or you become apathetic and conclude, "Why bother? I'm going to stay on the sofa and watch the video."

The second box is labeled "Imagination/Empathy." To create change you have to imagine change; not see things as they are, but as they could be. Empathy, the companion of imagination, is the capacity to walk in someone else's shoes.

The third box is labeled "Optimism." It has been said that pessimists are usually right, but optimists change the world. Without optimism, political change is impossible. Only optimism gives us the courage to take risks. It is not necessarily rational. It requires a leap of faith. If we believe that our words and our actions will make a difference, we will find the strength to speak and to act. It was my belief in the ratification of the Equal Rights Amendment, a hot issue in the 1970s, that enabled me to spring to my feet on the floor of the Vermont House and give my "maiden" speech to urge its passage. My fear of public speaking simply melted away.

If we are to achieve the social revolution that will bring families and their work in closer harmony, we have to join forces and nurture our anger, imagine change, and be optimistic enough to believe that rewards will outweigh the risks.

Joining Forces with Men

Change does not happen without a willingness on the part of some to do battle *for* and *with* others—those who join forces not only out of self-interest, but because they comprehend the common interest. Women no longer have to battle alone for the work/family agenda. Allies can help build a wide and deep constituency for change. The most powerful ally is the most obvious one: men, be they husbands, fathers, brothers, or sons. Men, too, are beginning to express their dissatisfaction with the model of the ideal worker.[9] Men, like women, often have to leave work early—or exactly on time, which is often trouble enough—to pick up children in two-worker families. But they often run into bosses who think that kind of flexibility is a luxury rather than a necessity.

According to polls, nearly all working parents have experienced workplace conflict over family issues, but men experience slightly more.[10] Part of the reason is that more men want to spend more time with their children, and more than ever before, they are pitching in with family care. Because of the large numbers of out-of-work men in a depressed economy, one-third of fathers with working wives are now the caregivers for their children, according to the Census Bureau.[11]

Whether out of choice or necessity, the growing engagement of fathers is good news. The bad news is that working women still put in twice as many hours on housework and child care than their spouses or partners. But the more time men spend at home, the more they appreciate what has been "women's work." With discontent rising from women and men, the likelihood of forming a broader constituency for change also rises. There are still countercurrents: those who believe that a "manly man" should be spending his time at the office making more money, not at home making dinner for his children. The differences in perspective among men tend to be generational; sons look at their fathers and question whether their lifelong sacrifice of family time for the company's demands was worth it.

Men are moving in the right direction, according to longtime feminist Muriel Fox: "We have raised the consciousness of women and girls. Now we have to raise the consciousness of boys and men. It's a huge job. It took us forty years to prove [that] women can do what men can do. Now we have to prove that men can do what women can do."

Building a Coalition

Within the universe of men and women there are specific groups of allies waiting to be tapped: labor, the elderly, the disabled, religious groups, and some businesses, large and small.

These groups can be mobilized if they see that their self-interests coincide with those of larger constituencies who can amplify their voices. For example, AARP played a role in passing paid family leave legislation in New Jersey. The two bookends of life, the young and the old, do not often work together, but it is in both their interests to do so. Together, they have the capacity to expand the constituency for change and transform wishful thinking into action. All members of this new coalition have to do their part to reframe the debate, and that sometimes means giving something up in order to garner larger gains. Family/work advocacy would no longer be an exclusively women's issue, though women have always been at the forefront of the movement and are usually thought of as the primary beneficiaries. Labor would no longer lobby exclusively for better wages and health benefits, and AARP would no longer lobby only for the elderly (though the elderly are among the most successful lobbying groups, as evidenced by the drop in poverty rates for the elderly over the last thirty years, while child poverty rates increased in the same period). Child advocates, who have labored long and hard on their own, would for the first time have an equal voice with the elderly. Intergenerational advocacy is more effective than pitting one constituency against another. It is not a zero-sum equation.

Such a broad coalition for change carries the risk of becoming more amorphous but holds the promise of becoming more powerful. Each member will bring new advocates into a diverse movement—one that is harder to ignore, and more difficult to relegate to "women's issue" status and place it at the bottom of the agenda.

Bridging the Partisan Divide

The most difficult bridge to cross on family/work policies is that which divides liberals, moderates, and conservatives. Can blue states and red states turn purple? Logic tells us that family/work policies provide the infrastructure that upholds family values. The term "family values" has come to define such a broad range of positions—everything from being against gay marriage, pornography, and abortion to being for abstinence, religion in the schools, and gun ownership—that it has lost its meaning. Now is the time to redefine "family values" as values that strengthen families. It will not be easy to find common ground, but it is not impossible. One indicator is the fact that politically conservative states like Georgia and Oklahoma have established, universal voluntary, free preschools, a policy yet to be adopted by more progressive states. Katie Corrigan of Workplace Flexibility 2010 asserts, "This has to be above party, . . . it is too big an issue to be a partisan issue." I agree. We cannot allow policies that strengthen families to be framed as a special interest. Neither, in this atmosphere of vitriolic partisanship, can we give up on building bridges.

Sometimes, though, bipartisanship springs from unexpected places—something I learned as a freshman legislator. The first amendment I proposed on the floor of the Vermont House was to add money to the child care budget. I made the strategic error of asking that the money for child care be taken from the highway budget, which was where I could see the money was. Little did I know that every legislator regards the highway fund as sacrosanct. My amendment was immediately shot down by the chairman of the Appropriations Committee. The next term, I myself was on the Appropriations Committee, and that same Republican chairman helped me get an increase in the budget for child care; his perspective on the issue had changed because his daughter had recently been divorced and had to go back to work and find child care.

Can business and government sit at the same table? Business groups fought fiercely against unpaid family leave, making it unlikely that they would engage in a dialogue on paid family leave. But some business leaders and conservative governors are showing support for early childhood education. More businesses are acknowledging that "the world has changed. They see the demographic shifts of women in the workforce, the aged, and see the shifting attitudes about caregiving. The question is how you meet that challenge," says Katie Corrigan.

She believes that both business and government have to be part of the coalition: "We don't think voluntary policies are the answer alone. Some businesses do." Nor is government alone the answer, she notes. While businesses may be reluctant to engage in dialogue on paid family leave, a business/government dialogue on flexible work policies is possible. The greatest barrier to such a dialogue is not that all businesses oppose such policies, but that their powerful lobbyists—the US Chamber of Commerce and, to a somewhat more moderate degree, the Business Roundtable—do.

Can these well-funded organizations be counterbalanced by the Children's Defense Fund, the Sloan Centers on Working Families, the National Partnership for Women and Families, and other family advocacy organizations? Not likely. A more likely possibility is that male managers and CEOs will learn from the experiences of their daughters and partners and that female managers and CEOs will draw on their work/life conflicts to create family-friendly policies. That's a good start.

Cut Taxes or Invest in Families?

We can no longer afford a standoff between opposing factions: Democrats and Republicans, or business and working families. All groups share an equal commitment to increased prosperity for the United States. The question is, how do we get there? Some have a simple answer: cut taxes. My answer is more complex: invest in families. If men and women were able to make a smoother transition from work to family, and back, more parents would be able to work and increase their incomes, companies would retain talent and, therefore, become more competitive and productive. If quality child care and early education became widely available, all children, and particularly middle- and low-income children, would be less likely to fall behind their classmates even before they start kindergarten. When they reached high school, these same children would be less likely to become high school dropout statistics, and thus less likely as adults to be unemployed, on the streets, or in prison.

Without such early education policies, the United States continues to be embarrassed by its world rankings. In a global test of fifteen-year-olds, the Program for International Student Assessment (PISA) placed the United States below thirty other countries. In reading, the United States came in seventeenth.[12] Singapore was the overall winner. If these numbers are not sufficient cause for concern about the next generation, consider our incarceration rate.

"We're No. 11!" Michael Hirsh notes in *Newsweek Magazine*. "That's where the U.S.A. ranks in Newsweek's list of the 100 best countries in the world, not even in the top 10."[13] These ratings not only make us blush, they cripple our ability to compete with the rest of the world. If we continue to turn a blind eye toward these dismaying figures, there is no way that we can be number one and promise greater prosperity for the next generation.

But how to do we convince Americans to invest in families? Many do not like to single out the poor for special assistance because of the belief that poverty is self-inflicted. Nor do we disapprove of privilege; our earnings gap and tax structure, which favors the wealthy, confirm that. Investing in families is really about fairness, not handouts. And fairness is a theme that may prove more palatable to citizens, as it did in Australia during that nation's successful campaign for paid family leave. In her work at the Families and Work Institute, Ellen Galinsky has come to see that that the work/family agenda has to be reinvented. She would like to see work/life policies used as a "strategic business tool," benefitting all workers, whether they are parents or not, at the top of the pyramid or at the bottom, in a two-worker household or with a stay-at-home parent—not just given to a company's best employees as a perk or a favor.

However, just as the women's movement has historically been fractured by divides between liberals and conservatives and along class and race lines, divides also exist between working moms and stay-at-home moms. In the 1960s, before I became a working mom myself, every member of my book group in Cambridge, Massachusetts, had young children. Our only rule was that we could not discuss babies or recipes. The night we discussed *The Feminine Mystique* by Betty Friedan we were so divided in our opinions that my living room could have had a baby gate running down the middle of it. There were those, like myself, who said, "At last, she is saying what I've been thinking," and those who hated every word. They felt *The Feminine Mystique* demeaned them as housewives and mothers. Little did I suspect that the baby gate would stay put until we became grandmothers. Today, we call this divide the Mommy Wars.

According to Miriam Peskowitz, author of *The Truth Behind the Mommy Wars*, "We need to create a culture that doesn't see parenting and mothering as such an all-or-nothing choice, that gives us more space for interlacing these parts of our lives."[14] The Mommy Wars, she says, pit "women against each other. They take our focus off real social issues and the possibility of making parenting a bit easier, a bit less sacrificial, for all of us."[15]

Is it time for a truce? Can women, whether they are working moms, stay-at-home moms, or not moms at all, unite? How can you convince a childless couple to adjust their schedule so that the family with a new baby can take paid family leave? Elaine McCrate, associate professor of feminist economics at the University of Vermont, has a retort: "Who the heck do you think is going to pay for your social security?" she asks, making the connection between a skilled workforce and family/work policies. That is the long-term perspective. In the short term most moms and non-moms will at some point in their lives be likely to be in the workforce and have caretaking responsibilities, whether for a child, an elderly relative, or an ailing spouse.

Sometimes legislation doesn't pass and political movements fall apart not because the advocates disagree with their enemies, but because they disagree with their friends. Felicia Kornbluh was a staff member for the committee that worked on the child care bill vetoed by President Nixon in 1972. One reason it failed, she concludes, was that different constituencies could not get together. "There were church groups who wanted child care provided in churches, but the ACLU [American Civil Liberties Union] went bananas thinking we were going to create a new large-scale national program that [was] going to have money funneled through sectarian institutions. The NEA [National Education Association] was very concerned that teachers were going to be left out. If they had banded together and really demanded universal child care for everybody, we might really have had something."

Our challenge is not only to enable women to unite, but for family/work institutions and non-government organizations to fit their individual agendas into a cohesive design. Can teachers and their unions, day care providers and their centers, parents and their children, get on the same page on such a seemingly straightforward issue as child care? If not, this group of advocates will continue to be swamped by those on the other side who believe that child care is a family responsibility and that government should keep its hands off.

Many opponents of reforming family/work policies do not understand that if we had a policy that guaranteed paid family leave for all families, those families would not immediately need child care, paid for privately or by the government, upon the birth or adoption of a child. Instead infants would be cared for at home for those first critical months of their lives. That is the common practice in other countries. The realization that the United States is so different is both distressing and encouraging. Distressing, because it is an indicator of how far America has fallen behind in supporting families, but encouraging because it gives us a powerful incentive to demand change.

The impact is felt by a broader swathe of Americans than ever before. "The middle class is in as much trouble as the poor," notes Edward Zigler, professor at Yale University who has been engaged in the campaign for child care for almost fifty years. Despite repeated disappointments, he remains optimistic because he has concluded that the lack of quality child care is seen as a problem by more and more Americans. The first step toward change is to recognize the problem—something that more and more Americans are doing. The second step is to find the solution. We know most, if not all, the answers that would help families achieve their dual goals: to be able to provide for and care for their families. We have some experience with innovative work/family policies in the United States and a great deal of experience coming from other countries. Our problem is not a lack of information; it is a lack of political will. The private sector must play a large role, but experience shows that no country has succeeded in building a supportive infrastructure for working families without enacting legislation. The most powerful argument in favor of a push for dramatic change is that the payback exceeds the cost. Nobel Prize–winning University of Chicago economist James Heckman has made the argument that one dollar invested in early education brings a return of seven dollars. Can we convince political, civic, and business leaders to make a major short-term investment in the American family's well-being in order to enjoy the long-term benefit of a workforce better prepared for the twenty-first century?

The GI Bill of Rights and the Middle Class

The United States made such a huge investment for veterans returning from World War II in 1944. It was called the Servicemen's Readjustment Act, known as the GI Bill of Rights. It has been updated several times, most recently in 2008 for veterans of the wars in Iraq and Afghanistan. Its impact has been beyond measure, creating a new generation of college graduates, homeowners, and entrepreneurs through its generous benefits. The GI Bill of Rights, more than any other piece of legislation, is given credit for creating the American middle class. Its universal acceptance today camouflages the divisive debate it inspired in Congress at the time of its passage. Many believed that hardened war veterans were not capable of attending college or benefiting from higher education, which then was thought to be predominantly the province of the upper classes. Others put forth a familiar argument: we could not afford the expense. The bill inched forward because of the nation's guilty memory of its treatment of World War I veterans. In passing the Bonus Act of 1924, Congress had promised those veterans a payment of $500 for those who served in the United States and $625 for those who served overseas. But veterans were not scheduled to receive any money until twenty years later. In 1932, starving, unemployed, and homeless WWI veterans formed the Bonus Army and protested for months at the capital, until eventually they were brutally routed by US troops.

No one wanted to see a replay of that despicable event. Nevertheless, the vote was so close that ailing Representative John Gibson of Georgia "was rushed in to cast the tie-breaking vote."[16] President Franklin D. Roosevelt signed the GI Bill into law on June 22, 1944. It covered not only tuition costs but also living expenses, including housing, which helped spur a post-war construction boom.

In addition to the efforts of the American Legion, a Republican congresswoman from Massachusetts, Edith Nourse Rogers, who won her seat after her husband's death, became the most effective advocate for the bill. "I hope that everyone will forget that I am a woman as soon as possible," she said after she won 72 percent of the vote in her first election. A difficult command to follow, judging from her official portrait, which portrays her in an elegant fur wrap and a double string of pearls. She was beloved by veterans groups and in 1952 proposed the creation of a Cabinet-level Department of Veterans Affairs, not achieved until 1989.[17]

Once a new law receives a critical number of beneficiaries, like the GI Bill and Social Security it becomes sacrosanct. The stumbling journey to sainthood is soon forgotten. Could we achieve similar comprehensive legislation to address the needs of working families today? Can we in the United States of America, which still has the largest economy in the world, enact policies that make a substantial investment in our future, like the GI Bill? Can we provide Americans with safe, quality child care, preschool education, paid family leave, sick days, and the right to request workplace flexibility? We can do so only if we can envision the benefits. Such an investment in the early years could parallel the GI Bill investment in the college years by once again creating a strong middle class and a well-prepared workforce. We have the capacity to enable all families, regardless of income, to combine caring for their families with bringing home a paycheck to support them. It is not a choice between work and caregiving; most families who seek economic security need to do both. The greatest reward for the next generation—which is now threatened with becoming the first generation to do *less* well than their parents—would be the restoration of the American Dream.

CHAPTER 3

What Can We Learn from the Rest of the World?

If you tally up the barriers that make the United States so different from other countries in terms of work/family policy, the list is long: opposition from the business community, weak labor unions, a feminist movement focused more on abortion and less on the needs of working families, class and economic divisions, extreme partisanship, a growing distrust of government, a belief in American Exceptionalism, and an inability to form broad coalitions for change.

This is what has caused us to fall so far behind other nations—in the developed world and even most of the developing world. Consider the company we keep on paid maternity leave. Only Liberia, Papua New Guinea, Swaziland, and, yes, the United States do not guarantee any form of paid leave for families with newborns.[1] Even in Saudi Arabia, where women can be arrested for getting behind the wheel of a car, laws require employers to provide women four weeks of paid leave before their due date, and six weeks of paid maternity leave after delivery.[2] In contrast, American families felt that they had achieved a major breakthrough when the Congress passed the unpaid Family and Medical Leave Act of 1993. But others are light years ahead of us. So, how does the rest of the world do it?

The Nordic Advantage

If you were an American single parent living in Denmark, you would be reluctant to return to the United States unless you could manage a precipitous drop in income. That is the situation that faces Beth Merit, mother of ten-year-old twins. "As soon as you are pregnant [in Denmark], you can take sick leave from work," she explains. "I took paid leave three months before the twins were born, and then, after they were born, I could take one year off for each child."

How much payment did she receive? "I got the minimum, and it was more than I make at my job." Beth is the owner of a small English-language bookshop that barely turns a profit. "Because I'm a single parent, I got father money also." Father money, says Merit, is provided by the government when there is no father contributing to a child's care. In addition, all parents are eligible for free or highly subsidized child care. Who pays? The government and the unions. No wonder Denmark's citizens are number one in world happiness rankings.[3]

If this seems like heaven to an American single parent or hell to a Tea Party single mother, it is not quite either.

Similar programs are available to one- and two-parent families in all the Nordic countries and have produced some dramatic results. Childhood poverty in the Nordic countries is the lowest in the world—the rate in Denmark, Finland, and Norway is 3 percent (Sweden is at 4 percent), compared to 22 percent in the United States[4]—six times higher![5] This juxtaposition—the United States not measuring up against other countries less wealthy than we are—should arouse a cry of alarm at the highest levels. But Americans may not know what they are missing, or the motivation behind these policies.

"It's all about giving the kids a good life. It's meant for the children," Merit observes. Indeed, the policy has a broad social-justice mission: to promote children's well-being, aid gender equality, advance employment for women, and encourage parenting roles for men.[6]

Do these policies of paid family leave and free or subsidized child care eliminate the stress that two-wage-earner families or single parents feel everywhere? "People still complain. People are stressed," reports Merit. No matter how generous government programs may be, they cannot eradicate all family/work conflicts. But the consequences for families are different, particularly for those in the middle- and low-income brackets: they do not fear homelessness or hunger. Is it a coincidence that a Nordic country, Finland, has the highest test scores in Europe, or is that achievement due in part to universal access to good child care and early education?[7] Recent studies showing the importance of early brain development help explain why Finland's investment in the early years has paid off.

Merit stayed home with her twins for their first year because of the income she received from paid maternity leave. "In the United States most people would put their kids in day care at four months," she says. "Here they had late-night day care, which is open until 8 p.m. I brought my kids in at 11 a.m., they ate lunch and they ate dinner there, and I picked them up when I closed the store at 5:30 and they were fed already. It's reliable good-quality care."

Not all is perfect in Denmark, though. These services depend on a high tax rate—something generally more tolerated in the Nordic countries, where the government pays for or heavily subsidizes services that benefit all citizens, like child care and health care. And though family support services in Denmark have been reduced under a conservative government, no one wishes to do away with them, despite the large influx of immigrants, and a growing anti-immigrant sentiment.

Finland, too, has advanced work/family policies, observes Finnish career woman Elina Kukkonen, who is happily combining her work and family responsibilities. But she also notes that Finland's citizens pay quite high income taxes for these privileges—which include a ten-month maternity leave. Four months of that leave is for the mother alone, and the remaining six months can be shared between both parents. Mothers retain 90 percent of their salaries for the first fifty-six days. Nearly all mothers take maternity leave and 70 percent of fathers take paternity leave, receiving 70 percent of their salaries. The cost is shared by employers and the government. Finnish law also allows a nursing leave of up to three years.[8] "I am a mother of three children—[ages] six, ten, and thirteen—and have been on full maternity leave three times, but never on a nursing leave," says Kukkonen. She returned to work after her children were ten or eleven months and still enjoyed yearly vacations of five weeks on top of maternity leave. "Despite the long leaves I have always been able to return to my same job and even build a career," she notes. Kukkonen heads the marketing department of Kauppalehti, the nation's largest business media company, and is also a member of its executive group. "Today life is quite busy with the vast responsibility at work, and as the mother of a family of five, plus a Labrador retriever," she reports. "A significant house loan will keep us both working for many years to come. But I do not complain. Life feels quite rich."

A Different Political Culture

It is a trade-off: high taxes for high benefits, a notion completely counter to the present political climate in the United States. How did the Nordic countries achieve consensus on making such significant social investments? The answer is that their political culture is dramatically different from ours. The government's role in supporting working families is widely accepted as being good for families and good for business. In Sweden, for instance, the maximum fee for all-day child care, for those who have the highest incomes, is $170 a month. "Then we have an after-school program too, which is subsidized. No political party is proposing changes. It's so established," says Vickie Doom, a Swedish grandmother.

As three-term Norwegian prime minister Gro Harlem Brundtland tells me, "Starting in the mid-1930s the driving force has been to change society so there is greater equality between men and women and rich and poor. We are interested in solidarity."

Brundtland became a cabinet minister for the environment in 1974 when she was thirty-five. "My whole life changed. I hadn't looked to become a politician." Eight months later she became deputy leader of the Labor Party. "How do you make it possible for women to be working and feel secure that their children are well taken care of?" she asks. "We got kindergarten, child care, pregnancy leave, and [leave] to nurse a baby for at least a year."

Business tried to oppose it, but the Labor Party had a majority. "A parliamentary system like ours gives stronger force to political parties," Brundtland explains. "When the Labor Party wins, there are policy debates within the party, a platform is put through, and everyone will vote for it." Unlike American party platforms, which are forgotten soon after they are written, parliamentary systems enable platforms to become law. Neither do special interest groups exert their power as forcefully through campaign contributions. In Norway, Brundtland explains, "Nobody can give you money for anything."

Her own experience as a mother, balancing her political duties with parenting, influenced her advocacy for family/work policies: "I'm sure when you feel convinced by your own experience, you feel more passionate, and I knew what was going on in many women's lives."

Over the years, Norway's maternity leave has been extended and expanded to include father leave. It got off to a slow start, but now 70 percent of fathers take some leave. "We're now debating one-third for each parent, and the last third decided between them. It makes a difference in the career paths of men and women," Brundtland explains. "If there is an excellent woman applying for a job, they might say, 'Better not choose her, she may become pregnant.' If many men take leave, you minimize the difference. Father leave works best when the leave is short and well paid."

What effects have these generous family/work policies had in Norway? Families have had more children, productivity has risen, and more women are now participating in the workforce. In fact, the nation has 75 percent of its women in the workforce—a higher rate than in any other country in the OECD (Organization for Economic Cooperation and Development)—and more than half of them are unionized. A high percentage of women work part-time, which is more encouraged in the Nordic countries than in the United States because part-time workers receive benefits according to the hours worked.

Meeting Labor Shortage Needs

In addition to having a different political culture, the Nordic countries were inspired to enact generous family-friendly policies to meet their labor shortage needs. Policy makers preferred encouraging new mothers to return to the workforce over importing more immigrant labor. "As our need for highly skilled workers may be unmet, that argument will be persuasive, particularly if we recognize the female labor force is a major contributor to economic growth," Brundtland explains.

The Power of Women in Elective Office

Achieving political consensus on taxes and on spending is a challenge for any country. Arguably, it is easier to achieve agreement in small, more homogenous societies like Norway, with a population of just under five million, than in a large, sprawling, diverse country like the United States, with a population of three hundred million.

But all the Nordic countries have something else in common that makes consensus possible: a strong belief in gender equality, which has roots that are deeper than those of the American suffrage movement of the late nineteenth and early twentieth centuries. In 1893 New Zealand became the first country to give women the right to vote, but Finland has the distinction of being the first country to have allowed women to vote and to run for office, in 1907. That same year, these pioneer political women introduced a bill for a compulsory six-week maternity leave. It was granted in 1937, but only to low-income women at first. Since 1949, maternity leave has been provided to every expectant mother and more recently to fathers. By granting benefits to all parents of all income levels, Finland and other Nordic countries have created a 360-degree base of political support.

In the United States, child care subsidies are targeted toward low-income parents. It may be reasonable, when resources are limited, to allocate resources to the few, on the basis of need, to reduce costs, but targeted policies have deprived the United States of a broad, reliable constituency of continued support for work/family policies. In contrast, Social Security and Medicare, which are not focused on the needy, are inscribed in the budget as entitlements. While there has been much debate about reducing entitlements, historically little action has been taken because cutting either program is considered highly risky for politicians. During the partisan 2011 standoff on raising the debt ceiling, Republican House members voted for a "Cut, Cap, and Balance" plan that called for large cuts in domestic spending, including Social Security, Medicare, and Medicaid. The next election will tell whether voters are prepared to accept these cuts, which not only provide a safety net for the poor, the elderly, and children but also give middle- and upper-income Americans a higher level of economic security.

If the US Congress had more women—membership now is 83 percent male—would the debate about budget priorities be different? We'll delve more deeply into the role of female leadership in chapter 9, but a look at the female political leadership in the Nordic countries bolsters this supposition. Finland's history of electing women to Parliament and to top positions—two women have served as prime minister and one as president—had an influence on its enactment of generous work/family policies. What is the result?

Every child under seven can attend free municipal day care, which supports the 70 percent of Finnish women who work outside the home. The government provides the generous leave earlier described by Elina Kukkonen—at about 70% of an average salary—and also generous child allowances.[9] When I asked the former Finnish ambassador to the United States, Pekka Lintu, why Finland was number one in Europe in test scores and why the country enacted such strong laws to support working families, he did not pause for a second: "It was the women."

The significant presence of women in politics, the labor force, and labor unions gave women political legitimacy to a degree that women never have had in the United States. Finland's policies exemplify the strong relationship between the percentage of women in elective office and the likelihood that family/work policies like paid family leave and subsidized day care will become law.

In Sweden, the percentage of women in Parliament is 45 percent; in Norway and in Finland, 40 percent. Even in traditionally patriarchal Germany, the percentage of women in Parliament is 33 percent, almost twice the proportion of women as in the United States, where women are stuck at barely 17 percent.[10] The reason more women in power makes a difference is not complicated: life experience matters. Female leaders, like Brundtland, understand work/family issues in a very specific and personal way. That is why they are often the ones who have the passion and persistence to move these issues to the top of a political agenda, rather than seeing them drop down to a footnote where they can be ignored. That is how laws get passed. And once on the books, it is difficult, even in hard times, for governments to retreat from them.

What happened during Norway's economic downturns? I asked Brundtland. "They never dared to take away anything even when the Conservatives won," she reports. During the oil crisis and the debt crisis of 1986 Norway continued to increase the number of weeks of paid family leave. "The women's movement in Norway pushed hard, including women's groups in the center such as women's clubs. Without the labor union and the labor party, we would not have been able to move forward; we had enough political power," Brundtland concludes.

What Happens to Competitiveness?

A consistent argument by the American business community is that the adoption of family/work policies similar to those of the Nordic countries would shatter our competitiveness. However, a study by researchers at Harvard and McGill universities found that fourteen of the world's fifteen most competitive countries provide paid sick leave, thirteen guarantee paid leave for new mothers, and twelve provide paid leave for new fathers. "The world's most successful and competitive nations are providing the supports the United States lacks, without harming their competitiveness," says Jody Heymann, one of the authors of *Raising the Global Floor*.[11] The World Economic Forum's Global Competitiveness Index for 2010–2011 lists Switzerland—which provides paid maternity leave for 98 days—as number one, and Sweden and Singapore are next. All three are ahead of the United States, which is number four. Finland and Denmark are in the top ten and Norway is number fourteen. The forum also publishes a gender-gap index, a ranking of 134 countries that "examines the gap between men and women in four fundamental categories: economic participation and opportunity; educational attainment, political empowerment and health and survival." Iceland is number one, followed by Norway, Finland, Sweden, and New Zealand. The United States (at nineteen) made it into the top twenty for the first time in the report's five-year history because "of the higher number of women in leading roles in the current administration and improvements in the wage gap," the report states.

According to Klaus Schwab, the Swiss founder and executive chairman of the World Economic Forum, an elite gathering of top global corporate and political leaders held annually in Davos, Switzerland, "Low gender gaps are directly correlated with high economic competitiveness. Women and girls must be treated equally if a country is to grow and prosper. We still need a true gender equality revolution, not only to mobilize a major pool of talent both in terms of volume and quality, but also to create a more compassionate value system within all our institutions."[12]

When I was the US ambassador to Switzerland between 1996 and 1999, I regularly was invited to the World Economic Forum. One year I hosted a breakfast for the few women who had been invited to the forum. Most of the jewel- and fur-bedecked women whom I had spotted in the audiences and happily thought were invitees turned out to be corporate spouses. At breakfast, I raised the question, "How do we get more women involved in top leadership positions?" The organization made little effort then to reach out to women. Today, the World Economic Forum membership is 16 percent women (women are represented at almost the same percentage on corporate boards in the United States and in Congress). The forum itself is asking and answering the question, why are there not more? The changed attitude toward corporate women at the World Economic Forum reflects the evolution in thinking about women's roles worldwide. Karen Hagemann, European and gender history professor at the University of North Carolina, sums it up: "In Germany and elsewhere, once unthinkable notions are now being entertained. All change," Hegemann says, "starts with a change in the head."[13]

One necessary "change in the head" is the American myth that investments in women and families are not cost effective. It will die hard. The United States continues to believe it is exceptional—or simply different from every other country. Can we continue to sustain that belief in a global economy where every other country we compete with has more advanced maternity leave policies?

The French Approach

If policies of the Nordic countries do not seem to be a good fit for the United States, let's take a look at the rest of Europe. France has one of the most effective and universal child care policies of any country. *L'écoles maternelles* ("nursery schools") provide free, quality care for children as soon as they are toilet trained and until they are five years old. Although the program is voluntary, astonishingly, about 90 percent of French children over the age of two are enrolled, full-time or part-time, whether their parents are rich or poor, at home or at work.[14] Instead of asking, "Why are your children not home with you?" the question in France would be, "Why are your children not in *l'école maternelle*?"

Unlike child care workers in our country, French teachers are well paid and are required to have two years of college and two more years of training in early childhood education and development.

Four months of paid maternity leave is provided for all new mothers and 73 percent of French women between the ages of twenty-five and thirty-four work, many of them part-time.[15]

A further impetus to France's universal child care system is the desire to integrate the immigrant community into French culture, including a skill most important to the food-loving French—the teaching of table manners. But as in the Nordic countries and Germany, France's cluster of family-friendly policies exists, in part, to increase the birthrate. During World War I and World War II both France and Germany experienced huge losses on the battlefield. The historic enmity between the two countries produced a population-growth rivalry. As a result, France today has the highest fertility rate in Europe, 1.89, right behind the United States at 2.06. To sustain its population, a country needs a fertility rate of 2.1. Germany, at 1.42, is facing a serious threat of population decline that is forcing it to rethink its family/work policies.[16]

The world officially hit the seven billion population mark on October 31, 2011, so it may seem bizarre to be concerned about fertility rates. But population growth is not uniform. The highest rates are found in developing countries in Africa, Asia, and Latin America, while most of Europe is stagnant or in decline. With these low fertility rates Europeans will be faced with a declining workforce to support their elderly. Immigration is playing a role, but it is also stirring controversy in many countries where right-wing politicians call for closing off borders.

Counterintuitive as it may seem, the countries that have the most traditional attitudes toward gender roles—that mothers should stay home with their children and that fathers should be at work—have the lowest fertility rates. Women in Spain and Italy, for example, not only abstain from the workforce in large numbers; they also seem to reject motherhood if there is no family support system in place to help them manage. Not coincidentally, both countries were teetering on the precipice of an economic meltdown in 2011. The birthrate exception is the United States, which despite the lack of family support programs has a higher fertility rate than all of Europe and Scandinavia. One reason may be the higher fertility rates among immigrants. But the US fertility rate is income sensitive: In the 1970s, during a recession, the rate fell to 1.7. It had increased by 22 percent by 2007, but between 2007 and 2009 the United States had the highest birthrate drop in thirty years, and it continued to fall into 2010.[17]

The United States has another distinction: it ranks number one in the world in teenage pregnancy rates.[18] That factor adds both to our population growth and to a high poverty rate, because 31.6 percent of single mothers are poor, compared to 6.2 percent of married couples.[19] We cannot conclude that American teenagers are more promiscuous than their peers worldwide. The more likely cause is the lack of access to birth control and, in some areas, legal abortion. A recent decision by the Obama administration's secretary of health and human services, Kathleen Sebelius, to eliminate health insurance co-payments for birth control is a promising strategy to reduce both unwanted pregnancies and abortions. Half of US pregnancies are estimated to be unanticipated.

None of these observations fully explains the willingness of Americans to continue to struggle with the challenge of combining their work and family without demanding a change in policy. They assume that it is their responsibility to juggle, to balance, and to get it just right—no one else's, and most certainly not that of the government. This is the way it always has been, and this the way it's always going to be. Perhaps they do not know that having a baby in the United States, especially for a single woman, is the fastest way to fall into poverty. When they look at other families around them, they see just the surface. If my neighbors are able to have two or three kids and manage to get to work, they ask, why can't I do it?

One conclusion seems certain: the need to increase fertility rates is an unlikely selling point for improved family/work policies in the United States. For one thing, our population is already growing faster than any other industrialized nation's—a fact that signals strength to some economists, but that, especially given our high consumption rates, signals peril to those concerned about the planet's finite resources and our nation's huge environmental footprint. For another, conservative groups may argue that by providing paid family leave and affordable child care, immigrants and the poor would be encouraged to have more children in order to receive the benefits, placing a greater tax burden on everyone else.

One goal of family-friendly benefits is greater gender equality. It works in the Nordic countries, but not in France. French women do not do well on the Economic Forum's ranking of the gender gap, where they are in forty-sixth place, in part because of the country's drop in the number of female ministers. "French women are exhausted," Valérie Toranian, editor in chief of *Elle* magazine in France, told the *New York Times*. "We have the right to do what men do—as long as we also care for the children, cook a delicious dinner and look immaculate. We have to be superwoman." The same *Times* article included a photo of Dr. Fleur Cohen, bringing her four children to school and to the child care center (subsidized) on her way to work, smartly dressed, wearing high heels.[20]

The refrain sounds familiar. The maddening multitasking Superwoman was the model in the 1960s when I had young children, and she hasn't gone away. Combining work and family continues to be a highly individual and carefully choreographed dance. Government is not the entire solution; cultural attitudes about the roles of men and women remain paramount. What does not work for some makes all the difference for others.

"Katy de Bresson, a single mother of two, called the enrollment of her son Arthur (in the École Maternelle) a 'mini revolution.' 'Free of all child care costs; I could return to work full time. I am a lot happier and a lot more self-confident since then.'"[21]

How many single mothers in the United States would rejoice to find themselves in a similar situation? It is not likely that the United States is about to emulate the French system. We do not wish to copy the Nordic countries because they are too socialistic. We don't want to use France as a model because—well, it's too French. Remember Freedom Fries? That's when France failed to support the US invasion of Iraq in 2003 and two Republican congressmen decided that all menus listing French Fries in the US House of Representatives dining areas must be changed to "Freedom Fries," a policy later reversed.

What about the German Model?

Changing cultural expectations for gender roles are having a large impact on Germany's work/family policies. For centuries the underpinning of the German social structure has been the three Ks said to define where women belong: *kuche*, *kinder*, and *kirche* (kitchen, children, and church). School hours in Germany, and in neighboring Switzerland and Austria, pose an almost insurmountable barrier to women working. Children usually come home for two hours for lunch; different grades and schools have different hours for each day when school ends. This varies from canton to canton in Switzerland, from city to city in Germany. Unless there is a grandma or nanny to prepare lunch at noon (usually hot) and set out milk and cookies in the afternoon, a parent has to be home when the children come home from school. In Germany, parental duties still largely fall on the mother.

Every mother, regardless of nationality, carries in her maternal DNA the fear of being called a bad mother. In Germany, women who choose to return to work fear being labeled a *Rabenmutter*, a "raven mother" who pushes her chicks out of the nest. That's what happened to Manuela Maier when she signed up her nine-year-old son for school lunch and afternoon classes, so that she could return to work as a teacher. She was "ostracized by other mothers, berated by neighbors and family and screamed at in a local store," she told the *New York Times*. She was asked, "Why do you have children if you can't take care of them?"[22]

Economic necessity is pushing the lever of reform. As in the United States, more families in Germany are dependent on the mother's income. The rigid school system and the lack of support for working families discouraged many educated women from having children. In addition, literacy skills among immigrant children were shockingly low. In response, Germany made a $5.7 billion investment in all day school programs. And since 2003, one-fifth of Germany's schools have instituted afternoon programs. (Similarly, a few cantons in Switzerland are providing school lunches and afternoon programs, for a fee.)

In 2008, 64 percent of German women were in the workforce. But for mothers with children under twelve, that figure fell to 39 percent. Only 6 percent of German mothers return to work full-time after the birth of their second child.[23] Some observers believe Germany has been slow to take up family-friendly policies because such programs remind people of state mandates under the Communists. But most attribute it to the conservative belief that a mother's place is in the home and fear that the social order would collapse if she left the house to go to work.

These fears are receding as a result of policies promoted by labor minister Ursula von der Leyen, strongly supported by Chancellor Angela Merkel. "It was those two who were very strong advocates of child care and parental leave. They could stand down all the conservatives in the

Christian Democratic Party. They fought them off and pushed forward," observes Kimberly Morgan, associate professor of political science at George Washington University. Together they pushed to enact a parental leave policy of fourteen months that pays 67 percent of the parents' salary. The mother and father can apportion their leave as they wish, but the father has to take at least two months, or those two months are lost.

Although Chancellor Merkel has no children, it is likely that her effort to change the mind-set of German traditionalists was influenced by her sensitivity to the struggles of other women, like von der Leyen, who practices what she preaches. She is the mother of seven children aged ten to twenty-two. She has a doctorate in medicine, and talks about how her husband used to work part-time to help with the children. Oddly enough, her inspiration to engage fathers in caregiving and give mothers the opportunity for paid family leave came from a four-year stay in the United States. "It was the first time that I was not criticized as a mother for wanting to work or as a professional for having children," she told the *New York Times*. "It was liberating." So liberating that she subsequently had four more children and went into politics.[24] It sometimes takes an outsider, like the German labor minister, to see what we cannot recognize in our own country. It was a Frenchman, Alexis de Tocqueville, who wrote *Democracy in America*, considered one of the best descriptions of American life. He believed that women and men should not strive for equality, but he concluded:

> As for myself, I do not hesitate to avow that although the women of the United States are confined within the narrow circle of domestic life, and their situation is in some respects one of extreme dependence, I have nowhere seen woman occupying a loftier position; and if I were asked, now that I am drawing to the close of this work, in which I have spoken of so many important things done by the Americans, to what the singular prosperity and growing strength of that people ought mainly to be attributed, I should reply: To the superiority of their women.[25]

De Tocqueville wrote these words in 1840; he continues to be quoted because he saw us with greater clarity than we could see ourselves.

"Liberated" American Women

The United States is liberating for women, compared to traditional gender expectations in countries like Germany, thanks to the 1960s women's liberation movement. Women are not likely to be criticized today for combining work and family. American women are freer than their German and Swiss sisters to make their own choices without being called bad mothers. The downside is that despite their "liberation" they remain captive of the old male model of the ideal worker, as writer Joan Williams has described. They are free to join the workforce, but then they are left on their own to figure out how to make their complicated lives work. A family's ability to cobble together a support system depends on where the parents work and, to a large extent, the size of their paycheck. Some employers have learned that if they are to attract and retain a talented workforce, they have to support working families by implementing family-friendly policies. The landscape is sketchy, it varies greatly, and it is hard to detect a strong trend in a new direction. For those who qualify, the government is providing assistance through child care subsidies and tax credits, Head Start, and the unpaid Family and Medical Leave Act. There is an odd paradox in the United States: the culture encourages women to work, but the social structure is not there to support them, unlike in Germany, where the culture remains more gender stereotyped, but the structure is becoming more accommodating.

Almost all working women, regardless of nationality, have one thing in common: they usually do not have a choice of whether to work or not. We've long outgrown the post–World War II era when men could be the sole support of their families and proudly claim that their wives were homemakers. At that time, being the sole wage earner was the first sign of male respectability and high achievement, a segue into joining the local country club. Though many lower-income wives and single women, particularly African-Americans, had always worked out of economic necessity, when middle- and upper-class women worked, it was considered to be for "pin money," not to help pay the mortgage or the rent. Today, 63.3 percent of women are either co-wage earners or the sole wage earner in their families.[26] Without their earnings, more families would fall into the lower income or poverty class.

Opting Out or Pushed Out?

Despite evidence to the contrary, the belief lingers that when women leave the workforce after the birth of a child, it is because they voluntarily opt out. It is their choice to be a full-time mom. That is true for some women, but not all. In the United States, scholars like Joan Williams and Ellen Galinsky have concluded that the opt-out trend is greatly exaggerated. In reality, opt out means pushed out. Opting out is an option only for women of the top layer of the upper class; their spouse is usually a high earner who can support a growing family on one income. Those who leave the workforce after childbirth are more often pushed out because managers are either unable or unwilling to provide paid family leave, allow for part-time work, or adjust the mother's schedule to allow her to meet her new caregiving responsibilities. Unlike in other countries, where the cost is often shared between the government and the employer, in the United States the employer must pay the total cost of family leave. Many women would return to their jobs after childbirth if they could receive a longer period of paid family leave and, upon return, work out a flexible work schedule, whether by working fewer hours or working remotely.

Jan Blittersdorf, president of NRG Systems, a wind energy company, has encouraged flexible work arrangements for all her employees. "When I told a friend who is a CEO that most of my female workers return after pregnancy," says Blittersdorf, her friend was surprised. "You're so lucky," she told Blittersdorf. "I lose almost everybody." Blittersdorf wasn't particularly lucky; she was smart in permitting her employees to work out schedules that meet the changing needs of their lives. The benefits accrued not only to her employees, but to her company's ability to retain valuable talent. She, and other employers like her, recognize that with the rise of two-income families, employers can no longer play by the old rules if they are to be productive.

The Shriver Report, a study of women in the workplace by Maria Shriver and the Center for American Progress, puts it this way:

> Today, the movement of women into the labor force is not just enduring but certifiably revolutionary—perhaps the greatest social transformation of our time. Women are more likely to work outside the home and their earnings are more important

> to family well-being than ever before in our nation's history. This transformation changes everything. . . . Quite simply, as women go to work, everything changes. Yet, we, as a nation, have not yet digested what this all means and what changes are still to be made. But change we must.[27]

Father Leave

The "digestion" of changing family/work patterns is happening most quickly, and without too much abdominal pain, in the Nordic countries. Fathers in Sweden are doing the "unthinkable" by making father's leave the norm instead of the exception. There, father leave got off to a slow start, with few men taking time off to change diapers when the law was first enacted in 1995. Today, though, 85 percent take advantage of the law, which reserves two of the thirteen months of paid parental leave for fathers. Most Swedish fathers cannot imagine not doing so. As one new father observed, "Everybody does."[28]

How did this social shift take place? Government action helped. In the past, given a choice between mother or father taking time off, mothers stayed home because their pay was usually lower. When the government implemented a "use it or lose it" policy for fathers, more men took advantage of the benefit. For employers, when maternity leave is granted only to women, women are seen as more risky hires because they will take time off after childbirth. If both parents share, that stigma goes away, as former prime minister Brundtland observed in Norway. One consequence, according to the Swedish Institute for Labour Market Policy Evaluation, is that a mother's future earnings have increased on average 7 percent for every month the father takes leave. Fathers' new roles have resulted in a lowering of the divorce rate and, when divorce does occur, an increase in joint custody arrangements.

Has father leave affected the macho Viking image of Nordic men? One woman, a police officer, doesn't think so. She found her husband most attractive, she told the *New York Times*, "when he is in the forest with his rifle over his shoulder and baby on his back."[29]

The generous paid family leave law in Norway is not without controversy. Employers have to adjust work schedules to accommodate parental leave for women and men. Long leaves can be disruptive for both the employer and the employee. But 41 percent of companies in 2006 reported that they encourage fathers to take leave. Some see an advantage in being able to test short-term employees for future employment, and some see that these policies—more than the size of a paycheck—are the best way to attract talent. The most difficult question for fathers who are used to working full-time, are used to being primary wage earners, and have their eyes on the next promotion is: will taking father's leave hurt my chances for success? If both men and women follow a similar pattern of leave, neither are more likely to be penalized.

Implementing such practices in the United States would require a huge cultural shift in thinking about gender roles and established work patterns. Under present conditions, many fathers, and some mothers, do not take maternity or family leave because they fear that taking time off will hurt their careers; they fear that they will be perceived as being less ambitious and less dedicated. In a period of recession, they may fear that if they take advantage of these policies, they will be among the first to be laid off. For similar reasons, many men and women are not eager to ask to work part-time. Face time at work, not quality time at home, is what matters most in the United States. The limited number of employers who provide pro-rated benefits are another reason. But not all countries look at taking time off or working part-time the same way.

The Netherlands: Part-Time for Moms and Dads

The Netherlands is initiating a different trend in part-time work, according to reporter Katrin Bennhold. She gives an example: "Remco Vermaire is ambitious and, at 37, the youngest partner in his law firm. His banker clients expect him on call constantly—except on Fridays, when he looks after his two children. Fourteen of the thirty-three lawyers in Mr. Vermaire's firm work part time, as do many of their high-powered spouses. Some clients work part time, too. . . . Part-time work has ceased being the prerogative of [women] with little career ambition, and become a powerful tool to attract and retain talent—male and female—in a competitive Dutch labor market."[30]

It is not likely to happen here, but American fathers' *desire* to work fewer hours and spend more time with their families surely is comparable to that of Dutch fathers (of whom 65 percent would like to work less, according to one poll).[31] The ability to *fulfill* that desire marks the difference between the two countries. Younger American men are more likely to tailor their work schedules to suit their families' needs than older men, but economic pressures and employers' expectations present powerful barriers. Psychologist and journalist Ellen de Bruin, author of *Dutch Women Don't Get Depressed*, observes that the Dutch rank low on gender equity rankings because so many women work part-time, "but we rank high on happiness."[32] And family-friendly Denmark is considered the "happiest place on earth" (followed by Switzerland, Austria, and Iceland), according to a British study.[33]

The cost of these policies for taxpayers is high. In the Netherlands taxes are 38% of gross domestic product and in Sweden, taxes are 47% of gross domestic product, compared to 27% in the United States. Family benefits account for 3.3 percent of GDP in Sweden, placing it third highest, after France and the United Kingdom; in the United States that figure is 1.3 percent, placing it near the bottom.[34]

Lessons Learned

Looking back over how the Nordic countries, France, and, more recently, Germany have developed the political backing to support their generous family-friendly policies, the specifics vary from country to country. But certain realities stand out. Unlike the United States, these nations appear to have a greater tolerance for taxation, a greater intolerance for wide income disparities, a stronger belief in the social compact, and a weaker sense of rugged individualism.

No doubt achieving political consensus on taxing and spending policies is a challenge for any country. That's particularly true in a shrinking economy, like ours, when the mantra of "No New Taxes," under any circumstances, is engulfing the nation. But though all these other nations have different social and political structures, there are lessons we can learn from them as we construct our family/work agenda. What factors contributed to their success in achieving generous family/work policies?

- A recognition that the needs of families in the workplace are no longer "women's" issues; they are a strategy for overall economic growth and vitality
- Support from labor unions
- Female leadership in government
- A broad grassroots constituency of women and men advocating for change
- Tacit support from the business community to meet skilled labor needs
- A culture of social solidarity that rejects wide disparities between rich and poor

The most optimistic lesson that we can take away from other countries' embrace of family/work policies is that change occurs when economic forces shift. The once universally accepted old-regime assumptions about the separate roles of men and women as wage earners and caregivers become obsolete when women become an essential part of the economy.

Despite all the lessons it has to offer, Europe has rarely been a welcome model for the United States. Possibly like adolescents rebelling against their parents, we want to escape the memories of the "old country." We are quick to point fingers at Europeans and say, God forbid, we don't want to be like Sweden. (Though if the question were posed to working families, the answer would be different. When I asked one working mother what the answer to our work/family problems was, she replied, "Becoming Scandinavian.") During the health care debate we distanced ourselves as far as possible from European and Canadian models, never acknowledging that their provision of universal access to health care has resulted in lower health care costs and better health outcomes. The global debt crises—most acute in Ireland, Spain, Portugal, Greece, and Italy—gave us a further reason to say "no" to Europe. See what happens when you spend too much money on social services to sustain a welfare state? We have not acknowledged that some of the countries with more advanced family/work policies also enjoy greater economic competitiveness than we do.

If we did take a careful look at other countries, what would we see? Less income disparity between rich and poor, lower childhood poverty rates, higher test scores, and more time spent with families. The question we have to ask ourselves is: are higher taxes and more government investment in families' well-being worth the trade-off? It depends how the question is framed. The knee-jerk reaction from many American taxpayers to any tax increase would be negative. But if we could assure the public that their tax dollars are buying better child care and early education, more flexibility at work, and more time with their families without fear of losing their jobs, I believe the answer would be yes.

That has been the response of three English-speaking countries that critics of tax-based social reform would have a hard time labeling welfare or "nanny" states: England, Canada, and Australia.

CHAPTER 4

What Can We Learn from Similar Nations: England, Australia, and Canada?

Could the United States adopt a hybrid policy that breaches the divide between Europe and America and between employers and employees? Many observers say yes. And while countries like Sweden, Denmark, Norway, Finland, and France represent the gold standard on work and child care policy, the United States may find more feasible models in other English-speaking nations—the United Kingdom, Australia, and Canada. These countries are more like ours in that they are not "socialist" and have had both liberal and conservative governments, both of which have supported family/work policies.

Paid Family Leave, British Style

Take the case of the United Kingdom, which was able to expand its paid six-week family leave to a full year, with the right to transfer six months of that to fathers. Parents are paid 90 percent of their earnings for the first six weeks, with no upper limit. After that period, payments are about one-quarter of the median income.

Prior to 1997, "the government did very little for children; there were not even tax credits," notes Kimberly Morgan, associate professor of political science at George Washington University. But by the late 1990s, the British were shocked to discover that they had an extremely high rate of childhood poverty, the highest in Europe. It was the Conservative Party (similar to the US Republican Party) that made the initial push for reforms, not the Labor Party (more like the US Democratic Party). Why? They wanted to garner the women's vote. "The Conservative Party wanted to outmaneuver the liberals by being in tune with the way society was changing, sort of like Nixon in

China," Morgan says. "Policies were framed in a way that addressed national concerns that went beyond the issues of work and family. You could build a wider constituency and frame the policies in ways that were more acceptable. These policies were not always framed in a way that feminists would like; they were not framed in terms of gender equality."

Prime Minister Tony Blair of the Labor Party also felt compelled to address the problem and declared in 1999 that he was on a twenty-year mission to end child poverty forever. Enabling mothers to go back to work, full or part-time, and to have access to child care were viewed as the best strategies both to improve the condition of children and to strengthen the larger economy. The election of more women to Parliament helped push the agenda.

Some Conservatives voiced their opposition by appealing to "family values"—similar to the criticisms heard in the United States. But that theme did not resonate, says Morgan, because people had moved away from the belief that women should continue to be traditional housewives and mothers.

What appealed to the British about paid family leave was that it gave parents the opportunity to care for their children until they were a year old. "I think the idea of family leave soothes the anxieties people might have about mothers' employment and putting small babies in day care because you don't need that if the parent stays home for the first year of a child's life. People feel less nervous about day care when the child is one or two. You're not just pushing women into the labor market right after they have babies," Morgan explains.

What was the reaction of the business community? "Pretty unhappy," she says. That has been particularly true for small businesses. "But both parties largely ignored them."

To Americans who are used to business holding sway on many issues, abetted by well-financed lobbyists, this seems an improbable outcome. How did it happen? As in Norway, the parliamentary system turned out to be a powerful ally. Once these issues were in the party platform, they became law.

Now that Britain has been turned over to a Conservative / Liberal Democrat government coalition and is experiencing drastic budget cuts, it's anticipated that these generous family/work policies could be either scratched or slashed. Not yet. But some are expecting the worst. Conservative Prime Minister David Cameron has reduced eligibility for child tax credits for upper-income families. "The Conservatives are unraveling it all," Professor Jane Lewis of the London School of Economics complains. "They never bought into child care; they have the traditional view of the family that mothers should stay home. We succeeded because of New Labor and the additional number of women members of Parliament."

Others disagree that the Conservative government has abandoned these policies. Jane Waldfogel, author of *Britain's War on Poverty*, believes most of the programs will remain intact. A program that has not had severe cuts at the time of this writing is Sure Start, similar to the US Head Start, but more widespread and comprehensive. It provides fifteen hours of free child care per week for three- and four-year-olds and services for their parents at some 3,600 centers."We are getting slow but steady improvement at the age of five, ⌊in⌋ the poorest kids most quickly, but the gaps are still massive. There's a huge amount of work to level the playing field," notes Naomi Eisenstadt, former director of the Sure Start Unit.

Cameron, who has fathered four children, has portrayed himself as a modern man who supports maternity leave. He is not about to give up that image now, and if he were to do so, retrenchment would be difficult. Family-friendly policies are like any other popular benefit; once it is provided, it's almost impossible to take it away, especially if a program has support among all income groups.

Right to Request Flexibility

When Tony Blair became prime minister in 1997 he brought with him a new contingent of women who were sometimes referred to as "Blair's Babes." Patricia Hewitt was one of them. A member of Parliament (who has recently retired), Hewitt held posts in Blair's Cabinet as minister for women and secretary of state for trade and industry. She then became secretary of health and was a key figure in passing Britain's maternity and father's leave policies, along with a vital feature in the United Kingdom's work/family portfolio—the "right to request flexibility" policy. Under it, workers can ask their employers to consider part-time hours, school hours, flex-time, telecommuting options, job sharing, shift working, and staggered or compressed hours.[1] "The employer can refuse the request," explains Lonnie

Golden, professor of economics and labor studies at Penn State University, but must put the reasons in writing. If differences cannot be worked out, the case is decided by an impartial tribunal. "I think it's sold because it is an individualized approach, not a blanket one-size-fits-all approach. Eighty percent of the requests are granted," says Golden. "It's a compromise between the American and more Scandinavian approach. It has a bit of European flavor but does not go so far as to impose flexibility on employers."

The "right to request" policy has since been adopted by Australia as well, and I spoke to Hewitt just after she returned from there. "It's become a leading example of what the economists call here soft law," she explains. Hewitt doesn't believe that mothers have an absolute right to work part-time after returning from maternity leave:

> It could be completely impractical depending on the nature of the work. [In the United Kingdom,] we created a situation where the employer was forced to talk to the employee. In effect you have the right to make your request, have it listened to properly, and to engage in dialogue with the employer, but it isn't an absolute right to get the hours you want. It's been the most enormous success with a tiny handful of exceptions. Either the employer says yes because the request is a reasonable one, or they talk about it and the employer says, 'I can't do this but I can do something else.' They work out something that is mutually satisfactory. Relatively few cases have ended up in the tribunal. [The right-to-request policy has since been introduced for workers sixty-five or older when the company has a retirement age of sixty-five and the employee wants to continue.]

Hewitt explained that the idea of the "right to request" campaign was initiated in the 2001 UK election with a limited election manifesto (party platform) that stated that a woman coming back from maternity leave could request shorter hours.

> But I wanted to do something more radical. I also knew the only way that I would be able to extend what we had in the manifesto

> was if we could get the business community to accept. So I set up a task force which brought together the Confederation of British Industry, the Trade Union Congress, and the Equal Opportunities Commission. I briefed them all and I said, look, you need to sit down and work something out that is reasonable that gives parents more flexibility when they've got a young child. You've got to reach consensus. The employers were afraid they would have to allow a woman to come back from maternity leave and work part-time. The trade unions were unhappy; it wasn't radical enough. It nearly didn't work. In the end they agreed on the law of the right to request for fathers and mothers of a child under six. So I was able to legislate it.

The law has since been expanded to include workers with children under seventeen, or under eighteen if the child is disabled.

The negotiations sound so delightfully simple, compared to the American way of passing legislation. The dynamic, however, was similar: opposition from employers. Now, though, many of the businesses that once vigorously opposed the bill favor it, because it works well for them, too, according to Waldfogel. "A lot of employers concluded that rather than losing a valuable member of the staff . . . they'd keep them, and maybe when the kids get older, they will come back full-time." About 90 percent of the requests have come from mothers.

Can UK Policies Work in the United States?

Government policies like the "right to request" are not a panacea for guilt or stress for working families. What they provide is less stress and more options—two things many Americans would welcome. A majority of new parents in the United States, according to polls, would prefer to work part-time or have flexible hours if they could work out such arrangements and have sufficient income and benefits. Women comprise 70 percent of part-time workers in the United States. Sixty-eight percent of these women are on a part-time schedule voluntarily, compared to 51 percent of the men.[2] The "right to request" is far different from the possibility to request, which carries with it the threat of retaliation, or worse, dismissal.

Would it be politically feasible to have a "right to request" law in the United States? Some companies already provide flexibility, either on an individual request basis or as company policy. The same reasons for doing so exist here as in Britain: attracting and retaining talent, reducing the cost of training new employees, and providing better balance for families who struggle with finding a happy medium between their work and family lives.

It just might work, although business groups may oppose it, as they first did in England. Consensus building will be a more difficult and lengthy process in America. Some have concluded that such government intervention in business practices will never be tolerated in the United States, even if many employers are already voluntarily putting those practices into effect. I believe it is too soon to reach that conclusion, because several states and municipalities have enacted family-supportive laws despite the opposition of the business community.

And how might US business react to a year-long family leave? That may be harder to build support for, based on the British experience, but still worth fighting for. Says Hewitt, "There are employers who are saying, 'It's too long, it's too expensive, it's too difficult to get a replacement so we're not going to employ women of childbearing age. But the truth is they've been saying that ever since we introduced equal pay laws in the 1970s." Others have argued that it is easier for employers to replace a worker for a full year than for a few months. Experience has shown that the law is working for families by allowing women to combine work and family life.

Following Australia's Lead

A *Newsweek* columnist framed the case for following Australia's lead this way: "Only two countries in the advanced world provide no guarantee for paid leave from work to care for a newborn child. Last spring one of the two, Australia, gave up that dubious distinction by establishing paid family leave starting in 2011. . . . We're now the only wealthy country without such a policy."[3]

How and why did Australia do it? Prime Minister Kevin Rudd of the Labor Party (similar to US Democrats) challenged the opposing Liberal Party (similar to US Republicans), calling the family values culture war "a complete fraud." He said that the Liberal Party talked about family but at the same time supported "corrosive" market forces that resulted in lower wages and less security. Rudd challenged the Conservatives to promote genuine family values. Could that work in the United States? Some have tried, thus far without success, but that does not rule out the possibility of redefining family values as "values that value the family." As of this writing, the Republican Party, most identified with family values, has approved a long list of budget cuts for programs including food stamps, nutrition programs for pregnant mothers and infants, health screening services for women, and subsidies for child care, all of which makes a mockery of "family values."

Australia has historically been motivated by what they call "familism" (defined as "natalism" elsewhere) to encourage women to have more babies, exemplified by the country's "baby bonus" of $5,000 per child. The paid family leave law goes further; it is designed to help working mothers "stay attached to the workplace and remain productive contributors to the economy."[4]

To gain a firsthand perspective on the new law, I talked to Barbara Pocock, director of the Centre for Work + Life at the University of South Australia, a week after the family leave law was passed in June 2010.

How Did the Law Win Passage?

"Let me give you the historical picture," Pocock explains. "Australia has a very masculine tradition. It holds at its core to the ideas of the past 150 years that a full-time worker is a white male, same as in the United States but it also has a strong voice for fairness and we have 20 percent union membership, compared to the United States [7.6 percent in the private sector and 37 percent in the public sector, in 2008]. The struggle to get paid parental leave has been long and bitter. We had a conservative government like the Bush administration with John Howard as prime minister between 1996 and 2007. It's only with the election of the Labor Party in 2007 that we saw action."

Pocock says Australia had an unpaid year-long parental leave policy since 1993. "About one-third of women like me [who work at universities] had three months or longer of paid leave," says Pocock, "but three-fourths of low-paid women had nothing. Now they have eighteen weeks—paid at the minimum wage of about $15 or $16 an hour." The new law's backers were women in the labor unions, Australia's Human Rights Commission, and some members (particularly women) in the parliament. "And we won the support of some men. What has changed is that many men have daughters in the labor market now and are thinking about their babies. The leader of the opposition was Tony Abbott, who is a conservative. Two years ago he said [his] party will not support paid parental leave. Now he's saying it's not good enough; it should be twenty-six weeks. One significant factor is that there has been sufficient research and special reports that show we have an aging workforce and women are needed in the labor market," she explains.

Australia enjoys a stronger economy than the United States. Unemployment was at 5.1 percent in July 2011. Pocock notes that family leave legislation is likely to be adopted only in good economic times, a cautionary note to the United States. But that is not always the case. The Scandinavian countries enacted and retained many of their policies in times of austerity.

And even in Australia's good economic times there were detractors. Business groups that wanted to see the leave policy fail claimed that family leave would be paid for by employers who couldn't afford the burden. Though there had never been any suggestion that employers would pay, their messaging managed to muddy the view. Debate also swirled over if and when mothers should be required to return to work. And there were some women who opposed paid leave because, notes Pocock, they thought, "I did it the tough way; you should too."

Many of these arguments sound familiar to American ears. Australia overcame them by forming a strong coalition of unions, the Labor Party, and female members of parliament. They gained some bipartisan support and received evidence of positive economic results. There are lessons to be learned. In the United States we cannot count on the unions to have a large impact because they are a shrinking constituency. There is a counter trend, however, as more women join unions and an increasing number gain leadership positions. They may succeed in putting family/work issues higher on the union agenda. Male union leaders, too, have become reinvigorated as a result of anti-union legislation efforts in states like Wisconsin.

Another startling difference in the US–Australia comparison is that we do not see any prospect of bipartisanship in the United States. The Republican Party could do the unexpected and place family/work issues on their agenda, following the British strategy of winning the women's vote. That would certainly surprise the Democrats, who would then have to outdo them. However, the United States is likely to make little progress unless more is done to prove to skeptics that investment in families and children provides both short-term and long-term dividends not only for the families themselves, but for the country as a whole. Eileen Trzcinski, professor at the School of Social Work at Wayne State University, observes that in the United States we look at children as "consumption goods. We have children for our own pleasure." Lotte Bailyn, professor of management at MIT's Sloan School of Management, has spent forty years on work/family issues, and agrees that the way we view children puts us far behind other countries. We fall behind, she says, because of our individualism and the fact that we don't view children as a social good. Rather, she says, we assume that "it's an individual decision to have children and therefore an individual responsibility."

How do we get to the point where we value children not only as private commodities but also as public "goods"? We need to understand that when our nation's children succeed as adults, they increase our wealth, and when they fail, we pay the price. Inversely, not investing in families means that we will continue to fall behind other countries on many yardsticks, from having the highest infant mortality rate (forty-seven countries rank better than us) among developed countries, and the highest incarceration rate, to falling to twelth place among thirty-six developed countries in the percentage of college graduates.[5] The sum total of these costs is hard to calculate, but the consequences are obvious—it will be harder to achieve our goal to remain competitive and even more difficult to be "exceptional."

How Canada Does It

In our search for strategies that work, let us turn to our North American neighbor, Canada. The Canadian experience—if geography and language (except for the French-speaking province of Quebec) have anything to do with it—should provide a good model for the United States. But as we learned during the heated debate over health care legislation, Americans do not take kindly to advice from Canada. "Americans have never been exactly riveted by Canadians and they may have to be convinced that they have anything to learn by looking northward," says Michael Ignatieff, a Canadian historian.[6] Nevertheless, given our similarities, the contrast in paid family leave policies between the two countries is dramatic. Why? I asked Maria Hanratty, associate professor at the Humphrey School of Public Affairs at the University of Minnesota. "Canada tends to look at Europe for its models, more than the United States," she explains. Just as we don't look to them, they don't look to us.

Unpaid family leave in Canada is twelve months, in contrast to the US limit of twelve weeks. Canada provides paid maternity leave for the first seventeen weeks, plus up to thirty-seven weeks of unpaid parental leave to be shared between both parents. Workers who are covered by the federal employment insurance program (which covers half the population) are paid 55 percent of their salaries, with a limit of $447 a week. The province of Quebec, which tends to be more liberal because of the influence of the Parti Québécois, has a more generous policy, with paid leave at 70 percent of salary for twenty-five weeks and lesser benefits for an additional twenty-five weeks. In Quebec, almost everyone is covered by unemployment insurance.

Canada initiated its first maternity leave program in 1971, when women's groups and labor unions were strong advocates. The '70s were a period of social activism, when the social structure of health insurance and other safety net programs were built, according to Jane Jenson, professor at the University of Montreal. She notes that Canada, like the Nordic countries, is concerned about having an adequate labor supply. "We fix it with immigration," she says, "but that is not enough."

Enabling women to return to work after they take maternity or parental leave is a motivator for supportive family policies, Jenson says. And labor has played a large role. Explains Martha Friendly, executive director of Canada's Childcare Resource and Research Unit, "The Canadian labor movement has always been more activist than other labor movements, and they work across party lines. There is an acceptance of paid family leave policies. They are afraid if they oppose it they won't be able to find workers; nobody wants to get rid of it."

Despite the similarity between the United States and its northern neighbor, Canada has a different culture. "Canada is a much more benign country. We are not a military power," observes Friendly, who moved to the country as an adult, having grown up in the United States. "We have a different concept of rights. Canada believes in collective rights; the United States in individual rights. There is a different relationship between the state and the individual."

Professor Eileen Trzcinski believes the contrast between the United States and Canada is caused by our belief in "untethered capitalism. We believe that the market provides, despite the evidence that it doesn't." In an article called "No Infant Left Behind," she wrote: "Other countries, particularly those in Western Europe and Canada, have formulated work and family policies to reflect a redefinition of childbearing and childrearing as a contribution to the survival and well-being of society, not merely as a source of personal and individual pleasure."[7]

Could it also be that Canadians trust their government more than Americans do? Or do they believe they get more services in return for their tax dollars? Or are they more willing to accept government participation in people's lives? One reason may be that citizens have more local control because Canada has devolved more power to the provinces than the United States has to the states. Federalism ignites an ongoing argument in our country; we're still trying to sort out who does what.

We may not want to emulate Canada, but we can learn from the Canadian experience: the economy does not appear to have suffered as a result of paid family leave, a claim that American business interests are quick to make.

Must we conclude that only developed countries with labor shortages, strong unions, and welfare state tendencies have enacted paid family leave policies? It's tempting to think so, until we're confronted with a list of 169 countries and discover that ninety-eight of them provide fourteen or more weeks of paid leave. Developing countries that provide at least fourteen weeks of paid leave at 100 percent of wages include Benin, Cameroon, Congo, Cote d'Ivoire, Gabon, Guinea, Mali, Mauritania, Niger, Senegal, Seychelles, and Togo, among others.[8] It is hard to know how well these laws are enforced, but we do know that there was a political constituency strong enough to put them in place, despite the reality that most of these countries are struggling with overwhelming poverty.

We are not only different from Europe and Canada, but also from Latin America. Argentina, which ranks twelfth in the world in the percentage of women in its parliament (38.5 percent), passed legislation mandating "a nursing mother shall be entitled to two breaks of half an hour during working hours to nurse her child and shall enjoy such entitlement for a period not exceeding one year." Women in the United States celebrated a great victory when Congress included a section in the new health care law that requires employers with fifty or more employees "(A) a reasonable break time for an employee to express breast milk for her nursing child for one year after the child's birth; and (B) a place, other than a bathroom, that is shielded from view and free from intrusion from co-workers and the public, which may be used by an employee to express breast milk." (Employers are not required to pay employees while they take a breast-feeding break.)

Soon after the law was adopted, the so-called breast feeding war began. When First Lady Michelle Obama started a campaign for breast feeding (only 40 percent of black women breast-feed, compared to 70 percent of white women and 72 percent of Hispanic women) to reduce obesity by suggesting a tax break for breast pumps, controversy broke out. Republican congresswoman and former presidential candidate Michele Bachmann weighed in with, "To think that government has to go out and buy my breast pump—you want to talk about nanny state, I think we just got a definition." (In fact, under First Lady Obama's plan, government would not "buy" your breast pump, it would make it tax-free.) Sarah Palin could not resist chiming in with: "No wonder Michelle Obama is telling everybody 'You better breast-feed your baby' . . . because the price of milk is so high right now." The negative response was not limited to Republicans. Women who could not breast-feed for a variety of reasons felt guilty. "Holy mackerel, I might have to agree with Michele Bachmann on this one," wrote a blogger.[9]

It is hard to come up with a complete answer as to why the US government has the uncomfortable distinction of being so steadfastly opposed to policies that would help families to be both wage earners and caregivers. Is it our system of government, which, unlike parliamentary systems, makes it difficult for party platforms to be translated into law? Are our elected officials unduly influenced by campaign contributions from business organizations, like the US Chamber of Commerce? Or has the polarization between the major parties scrubbed away any possibility of dialogue and compromise? Is our weak labor movement, which only recently has begun to pay attention to family/work questions, at fault for not speaking out sooner and louder?

Can we blame feminists who did not put family issues first in the 1970s and '80s, when many other countries did? Or is it a matter of culture? Paid family leave is the norm in most of the world. Why is that not the case in the United States?

CHAPTER 5

American Exceptionalism, Political Divisions, and the States

Perhaps we are too caught up in American Exceptionalism—the belief that we are extraordinary, different from and better than everyone else, unwilling to admit that we have a problem, and therefore blind to the need for a solution.

"We don't 'see' the problem. We don't see a collapsing care system because we don't see care as a system to begin with," Mona Harrington writes in *Care and Equality*. "We see individuals making private decisions about who takes care of the children or helps an arthritis-plagued elderly parent. We see families using the private market for services they don't have time to provide themselves—day care, housecleaning, fast food. We don't add all of this up and call it a system that is working well or badly."[1]

Neither do we see abandoned babies sprawled on street corners or crying toddlers wandering about by themselves. Somebody, often anybody, from a ten-year-old sister to a seventy-year-old grandparent, keeps them out of sight. It is easy to ignore the problem that has no poster child and no name. We can remain self-satisfied in the belief that we are number one.

The Exceptionalist argument, favored by Republicans and the Tea Party, is so intent on flag waving that it has not stopped to analyze why so many middle-class American families are in trouble, unable to take time off after having a baby or to take care of an elderly parent because they live in fear of losing their jobs. Exceptionalism carried to the extreme shields us from the need to improve, because damn the statistics, we know we are the best. If extreme conservatives acknowledged there was a family/work problem, their answer likely would be not *more* government in the form of better child care and paid family leave, but rather *less* government, to keep the government out of our lives. If there is a villain in the room, for them, it is government itself.

"For thirty years we have witnessed a downward spiral of eroding public trust in government," according to Michael Lipsky, research professor at the Georgetown Public Policy Institute and Dianne Stewart, director at Public Works, an advocacy organization for low income families.[2] Confidence in government hit a new low in October 2011, when a New York Times/CBS poll reported that 89 percent of Americans distrusted their government to do the right thing. Support for Congress plummeted to 9 percent.[3] The best way to restore faith in government is to demonstrate that government programs improve people's lives. Family/work policies, like paid family leave and affordable quality child care, present an *opportunity* to do precisely that.

Parallel with the Horatio Alger "pull yourself up by your bootstraps" credo, Americans share another belief: "help thy neighbor." Consistently in our culture, friends and neighbors pitch in to help someone in need. Before there was a national welfare system, Vermont towns had an "Overseer of the Poor," in the mid 19th to mid 20th centuries who provided help to needy neighbors. Some communities had poor farms for people who, today, would be homeless. Assistance may have been meager, and uneven, but small towns would not let someone freeze to death when fuel ran out. If a farmer's barn burned down to the ground, neighbors would get together for a "barn raising," bringing lumber, saws, hammers, and nails, and with one heave-ho they'd raise high the roof beams. Women sat together by the fire stitching patchwork at quilting bees, each one adding a square or a triangle to become part of the geometric design. Families who headed out West when the fever of westward expansionism gripped the nation could only survive by, when hard times beset them, neighbor helping neighbor.

That spirit of neighborliness remains very much alive today. I witnessed that phenomenon in my home state recently, when the disastrous 2011 flood left 175 Vermont roads closed, several towns stranded, hundreds of buildings destroyed, and many acres of farmland ruined. The outpouring of help from friends and strangers was so moving that many recipients wiped away tears.

The United States ranks, with Australia and New Zealand, among the most charitable countries in the world, according to the World Giving Index. The American tradition of compassion and caring is strong. The question is not *do* we want to help our neighbors, but rather *how* do we help our neighbors? Should we rely on our individual generous instincts, which may benefit some, but never all those in need, or should we share the responsibility? Neighborliness, for all its virtues, has limitations. It is fickle. It is unreliable. It leaves a lot of people out. Not everyone receives according to his or her need. Neither does everyone give according to his or her capacity. When I was charged with overseeing the campaign for United Way at the US Department of Education, I was surprised to learn that those at the low end of the wage scale contributed a substantially higher percentage of their earnings than those at the top.

Charity may be too personal, but government may be too impersonal. To be evenhanded, government must by necessity be blind to the very personal circumstances that describe each person's need. The anonymity this brings to the process makes it easy to rail against public assistance; that anonymity enables those who need help to be easily castigated as the "other," often the equivalent to the "undeserving." How do we resurrect a sense of community when, in this digital age, we spend more time face-to-face with electronics than with our neighbors? Can we try, as all religions teach, to walk in their shoes? Americans are skilled at independence; can we rediscover our interdependence, one person to another, one generation to another? The cliché remains true: by helping others, we help ourselves. A neighbor will help put out his neighbor's fire because the sparks might fly next door and incinerate his own home. Or because the next time, it might be his barn that's burning down. Or out of simple altruism, because he cares. The thread of community has to be respooled if we are to enact policies, private and public, that will enable our families to thrive, and in doing so, fulfill the most important task we have been given for our time on earth: to prepare those who come after us to lead happy, productive lives.

The moral argument for investing in families and children has become a political cliché. "We cannot leave our children and grandchildren with a huge deficit," we hear over and over. At a gathering of former governors of Vermont, Republican Jim Douglas told the audience how proud he was to be a new grandfather. He described gazing at the newborn in the hospital bassinet and quipped, "His share of the deficit is $50,000." What he did not say was that for 22 percent of America's children, their share of the deficit will be a life of hopeless poverty.

Moral arguments for change, we have learned, have their limitations. They may appeal to the heart, for the short term, but how do we change what leaders really think?

Nobel Prize–winning economist James Heckman, who has studied early childhood education, has given us dollars-and-cents evidence that investing in children and families pays, and that the lack of such investment exacts a terrible cost. Yet the argument does not hold sufficient sway in government circles.

Will Change Come from the White House?

The prospect for federal legislation on paid family leave, paid sick days, and flexible work schedules and more funding for child care and early child education, as of this writing, looks dim. The budget-slashing pendulum is swinging in the opposite direction. The only hopeful sign is that the Obama White House has put workplace flexibility on the table. On March 11, 2009, President Obama created the White House Council on Women and Girls, stating, "I want to be clear that issues like equal pay, family leave, child care and others are not just women's issues, they are family issues and economic issues. Our progress in these areas is an important measure of whether we are truly fulfilling the promise of our democracy for all our people."[4]

President Obama and his wife, Michelle, are supportive of these issues because of their own experience raising two daughters, even while they remain cognizant of their personal advantages. Once, during a meeting with congressional Democratic leaders in the White House on health care, Obama skipped out to listen to his daughter Malia play the flute. "There are certain things that are sacrosanct on his schedule—kids' recitals, soccer games, basketball games, school meetings," says David Axelrod. According to Anita Dunn, former communications director, "Not only does [President Obama] have no problem saying, 'I have to do this, this is my priority,' but it gives people who work for him the space to say, 'I'm sorry, I can't be at that meeting, because my child has an honor roll assembly.'"[5]

As part of their commitment to family issues, the President and Michelle Obama sponsored a White House conference on workplace flexibility. The US Department of Labor's Women's Bureau and the White House Council on Women and Girls followed up with the National Dialogue on Workplace Flexibility program, which resulted in several regional conferences. "We hope to get the conversation started and keep it going," explains Avra Siegel, deputy director of the White House Council on Women and Girls, who says the council's main task is to "integrate issues of importance to women and girls into the DNA of how we [the government] do business."

The conversation on flexibility may be a necessary step to highlight public awareness, but it is a far cry from proposing legislation, a move the White House does not support. They fear that during a prolonged recession such legislation would have no chance of passage; it would be framed as a "job killer," believes Avra. More likely, though, it would have the opposite effect—becoming a job creator by enabling more people to work flexibly or part-time instead of being laid off. This is the practice in Germany: instead of large lay-offs, workers agree to shorter hours. Germany's economy is the strongest in Europe.

Will the President take note of the British experience that laws that help families combine caregiving and work are essential not only to children's well-being, but also to building and sustaining a strong, productive economy? That message has to come from the top. Only the President can speak from the bully pulpit. President Obama has taken some modest steps, such as proposing to include in the FY 2012 budget $23 million (last year it was $50 million) for a state paid leave fund that would provide grants to states to help cover planning and start-up costs for paid family and medical leave programs. He has also proposed doubling the Child and Dependent Care Tax Credit rate for middle-class families. These small steps, while sending an important message, fail to address the larger challenge: why do these proposals get summarily rejected? It is time for the President to make a strong case for a cluster of family/work policies by putting them high on his agenda. The result would be twofold: stronger families and a stronger economy.

Political Will and Public Opinion

Politicians are generous with lip service, but stingy with action. Some reasons are obvious: the current tidal wave favoring domestic budget cuts is hard to escape, but even in good economic times, scant attention has been paid to the needs of working families. Business groups, like the US Chamber of Commerce, contribute more generously to conservative Republican candidates than to Democrats. It is the gorilla who pounces on any bill that smacks of government intrusion into business practices. The Chamber fought fiercely against the unpaid Family and Medical Leave Act for the same reasons that it has habitually opposed an increase in the minimum wage. As governor, when I supported (and won) a modest increase in the minimum wage, I learned how fiercely business groups put up a fight. Why? They hate mandates. Any business mandate is framed as a job killer.

Should we give up on the federal government? Has Congress built an impenetrable wall that family/work policies can't scale? Persistent high unemployment gives elected officials the opportunity to claim that any increased cost to employers, regardless of the long-term benefits, should not be incurred during an economic downturn. How can this stranglehold on legislation be loosened? In a democracy, there is a proven political strategy: build a constituency equal in power to that of the opponent's. But we must not dismiss the entire business community. There are individuals and companies who are supportive of these policies and are willing to go public. We must identify them and ask them to join a family/work coalition.

The biggest hurdle for family-friendly coalitions is money spent on lobbying and financing campaigns. Family advocacy groups have always been greatly outspent by business organizations. The playing field is tilting even further to their side as a result of a recent US Supreme Court decision, *Citizens United v. Federal Election Commission*, that declared most restrictions on corporate giving unconstitutional. Family/work advocacy groups, however, have a stealth weapon—public opinion. A majority of the public understands that working families are under severe stress. They are ready to support paid family and medical leave by a significant majority. When asked, "Would you favor or oppose expanding the Family and Medical Leave Act to offer *paid* family and medical leave for a set number of weeks paid by both the employer and the employee in taxes, at an average cost of $1 for the employer per week and an average cost of $1 for the employee per week?" 61 percent of women and 53 percent of men said they "strongly favored" paid leave, and an additional 18 percent of women and 20 percent of men favored it "not so strongly."[6] As might be expected, women with children voiced the strongest support—73 percent—but even 55 percent of men without children and 54 percent of women without children expressed "strong support."

In another poll, liberal and conservative groups were asked whether they strongly or somewhat agreed with this statement: "Business should be required to provide paid family and medical leave for every worker that needs it." All respondents agreed with the statement by 77 percent; liberals by 85 percent; moderates by 81 percent; conservatives by 64 percent, and Evangelicals by 74 percent.[7] (It is interesting to note that the numbers are higher for Evangelicals than for conservatives.)

Public support is strong even when there is a price tag is attached, paid by both employees and employers. That is encouraging. How can we translate that public support into action?

There has been no action on the federal level since the passage of the Family and Medical Leave Act in 1993, which provides twelve weeks of unpaid leave, with job guarantees for those who work for companies that employ more than fifty people and who have worked at least 1,250 hours during the past year. The leave can be taken for an employee's own illness, for care of a newborn, adopted, or foster child, or for care of a family member with a serious health condition. It covers approximately 50 percent of the workforce, and a lesser percentage of low-wage workers because many work part-time or cannot afford to take any unpaid leave.

Signs of Hope from the States

Should we turn to the states, which have historically been the laboratories of change for nationwide policies? Women's suffrage was granted by fifteen states before the ratification of the Nineteenth Amendment. A number of (mostly western) states had already granted limited suffrage, for either municipal or presidential elections. Women's groups were sharply divided on whether to take the state-by-state route to suffrage or concentrate on a constitutional amendment. Looking back, state action built momentum for the passage of the Nineteenth Amendment, which had become a hundred-year struggle.

Paid family leave laws have been adopted in three states—California, Washington, and New Jersey. That's not enough to achieve momentum, but it is enough to gather some views on how it can be done.

California

California passed its law in 2002 and implemented it in 2004. The California Paid Family Leave Act provides up to six weeks of partial pay (generally 55 percent) with a maximum of $882 a week as of 2007 "to care for a child, parent, spouse or registered domestic partner with a serious health condition (or to bond with a newborn baby or newly adopted or foster child)."[8]

How did California succeed in passing this legislation? I spoke with former state senator and assemblywoman Sheila James Kuehl, the prime sponsor of the law, to find out.

"There was a coalition of women in the labor movement and the Legal Aid Society of San Francisco and they pushed their brothers, so the state labor federation agreed to sponsor the bill, but no one had much confidence that the bill would go through," Kuehl recalls. She had thought she would have to "bring a bill [and] have it shot down, and then eventually, like gay marriage, it would make sense to people and you'd get that extra vote."

To her surprise, the bill was passed the year it was introduced. "I had a good record for getting bills through," Kuehl says, notwithstanding "the wild-eyed ones which I always brought in to throw overboard as ballast." What made California uniquely ready for this legislation, she notes,

> is that we had a state disability insurance system that comes out of every worker's check [except state employees, who had a different system]. First we tried to develop a system where the employer and the employee each paid half. [But some legislators] simply would not vote for anything that would cost employers one more dime. So we changed it and made it fully funded by the employees, who would pay a small additional tax, whether they were beneficiaries or not. Employers still lobbied heavily against it. The tactic they took was that letting an employee take paid time off to take care of family members would cost them money because they would have to replace them with temporary workers and retrain them.

Kuehl had to accept a lot of compromises, like losing the guarantee that returning workers would still have their job: "I took a sort of Teddy Kennedy approach, which he learned from playing football: take the yardage when you can, plant the ball, and start from there." She had hoped the law could be improved over time, but that has not happened, she laments.

Kuehl, who was also the first openly gay legislator in California, had not predicted that California's law would set the standard for states attempting to follow suit. "What made you run for office?" I ask out of curiosity. She replies, "I was engaged in the fledgling women's movement in the early '70s and became a feminist attorney and founded the California Women's Law Center. I went to Sacramento to testify on domestic violence issues, and of course, if you sit and watch the legislators, you say 'Hell, I could do that.'"

I ask her if she thinks women legislators, regardless of party, are more likely to support legislation like paid family leave.

"Regardless of party? No. They won't vote across party lines. But women do have more authenticity. They can say that, 'This is what it's like for women in the world and I want to fix it.'" She adds, "The men were very good about being coauthors on bills."

Kuehl got the votes to pass the bill in just one year, she says, because she "arm-wrestled everybody on every amendment" that would weaken the bill. "I would tell people that John So-and-So wants to undermine the bill and here's his phone number." If someone was going to try to kill the bill, she let his or her district know.

The legislation had the support of Democratic governor Gray Davis, which made a big difference. Several organizations, too, threw broad support at the bill. The end result has been a new policy that has few detractors.

"The truth is, I don't think most employers have found it noticeable, much less burdensome," notes Kuehl. Nor have workers complained about money coming out of their paychecks—which may be due to the fact that relatively few people are aware of the law. A survey revealed that only 29.5 percent of Californians knew about the law, compared to 55 percent who knew about the federal Family and Medical Leave Act.

As of 2007, the vast majority of claims—almost 90 percent—had been for bonding with a new child, according to a report from the California Senate Office of Research. "Workers who earned less than $12,000 per year filed claims at a lower rate than higher-wage earners," according to the report, and those who worked "for large employers (1,000 or more employees) accounted for nearly half of all paid family leave claims."[9]

There has been little effort to inform the public about California's law, in contrast to how similar legislation is publicized in England and Canada. Both countries have simple and clear websites that spell out precisely how an employee may apply and what the benefits are. In the United States, government may not wish to spend tax dollars on informing the public. Another theory is that families are so accustomed to the status quo—that if you have a baby, you're on your own—that they do not expect to receive benefits such as paid family leave.

Washington State

In 2007 Washington became the second state to enact a paid family leave law. The state has a tradition of electing women; it has been in the top tier of states with the highest percentage of women in the legislature and has elected two women to the US Senate, Patty Murray and Maria Cantwell. The year the law was passed, Governor Christine Gregoire was at the helm and she had the support of key female legislative leaders. But because Washington does not have a funding mechanism in place, like California's temporary disability insurance program, and because of the state's severe economic downturn, Governor Gregoire was obliged to delay implementation until 2012 or beyond.

New Jersey

In 2009 New Jersey became the third state to adopt a paid family leave law. Unlike California, it took the state twelve years to pass the legislation, but proponents succeeded because the state had a funding mechanism: its long-established temporary disability insurance program, which partially compensates for lost wages due to "temporary nonoccupational disability or maternity." (Five other states have a temporary disability insurance law: California, New Jersey, Rhode Island, New York, and Hawaii, plus Puerto Rico.)

The cost of the New Jersey paid family leave law is paid by employees, who see about $33 a year deducted from their paychecks. The law allows six weeks of paid leave to care for a newborn, newly adopted child, or sick parent, spouse, or child. Employees can collect two-thirds of their pay, up to a maximum of $524 a week. Those who work for small businesses (under fifty employees) can take the leave but are not guaranteed their jobs back. "We found that to date, by far, the most usage is for bonding [with a new child] leave, but the next highest percentage is for taking care of an elderly family member," reports Eileen Appelbaum, former director of the Center for Women and Work at the Rutgers University School of Management and Labor Relations.

How did it happen in New Jersey? A strong coalition of New Jersey constituencies (disability groups, AARP, children's advocacy groups) built a grassroots organization. They had support from Democratic governor Jon Corzine, the unions, and the Democratic legislative leadership.

Cecilia Zalkind, executive director of Advocates for Children of New Jersey, gives much credit to Jon Shure, former president of a New Jersey Policy Perspective, who worked on media and messaging. "He took what was a disorganized campaign and put life into it," she says. Shure explains that the message had to be that working people are juggling work and family. "We had to counter the notion that [paid leave] was a perk, giving them something they didn't deserve. This isn't a government benefit. It's government playing the role of mediator to help them [employers and employees] resolve something they couldn't do on their own." He adds, "We didn't give up the economic argument to the business groups. We said this will make everybody more productive. It will help the economy."

One stumbling block is that claims like this are sometimes hard to prove. Shure acknowledges that "these are not data-driven arguments. They're emotional and value-driven arguments." Business groups were adamantly against the law, regardless of the compromises that were made. Shure decided: "We don't have to convince them, we have to beat them."

However, individual small business leaders did testify on the bill's behalf. They included Kelly Conklin, who runs a woodworking business, and Sheryl Magaziner, who owns an art gallery. "You don't need hundreds," Shure says, "just a few to counter the argument that businesses are against paid family leave." One piece of advice he gives to others going into battle: don't call the law "paid family leave." "We changed the name to 'family leave insurance.' It's hard to be against that. Everybody believes in insurance; not everybody believes you should be paid for not working," he says.

Loretta Weinberg, a former New Jersey state senator and an unsuccessful candidate for lieutenant governor in 2009, became a champion for the bill because of her own experience caring for her terminally ill husband. "The last couple of months of his life, I had control over my own destiny because I was a state legislator," she says. "I could be with him in the hospital, when he came home, and when he was in hospice. I thought about what it would mean if I had to worry about losing my job and my health benefits. That gave me insight about what it means to care for a loved one, whether it be at the beginning of life or the end of life."

Weinberg gives credit to Senate president Steve Sweeney, who led the charge. "He's with the ironworkers union, a big tough guy. He also has a couple of children," she notes. Senator Sweeney explains his passion for the bill this way: "I had a daughter who weighed two pounds and had Down syndrome. She was in the neonatal unit for seventy-five days. I saw families who worried about how much time they could take off from work and how much time they could give to their children and always worrying about how to pay their bills. I've lived it," he says. "I felt strongly about the legislation, but it was the toughest piece of legislation I ever dealt with in my life, [through] fourteen years as a county official and eight years in the senate." The bill passed the senate by one vote.

Weinberg agrees. "The business community fought us tooth and nail. They make it appear like the end of the world is coming. There is little that I have done that hasn't been fought, usually by the business groups." She recalls when she sponsored a bill that would allow new mothers to remain in the hospital for forty-eight hours. The business lobby, she says, "fought it down to the day we were on the floor and wanted to insert 'if medically necessary.' Those three words would have changed the whole law."

The debate in the legislature was emotional by all accounts. Robert Serrano, a thirty-nine-year-old grocery clerk, told lawmakers that "a leave option would have allowed him to spend more time with his wife,who died of leukemia about two years ago." Instead, Serrano recalled, he spent an exhausting year and a half trying to "balance a full-time job and trips to be with his wife in a Philadelphia hospital." He lamented, "I would come home after my night shift, I would take two- to three-hour naps and then I would head to Pennsylvania . . . and spend some time with her in the hospital, maybe two hours with her, and then I would have to leave again. I sacrificed a lot of time (working) that I could have been with her."[10] On the other side, Philip Kirschner, executive director of the New Jersey Business & Industry Association, said, "One would expect lawmakers to pursue policies to create jobs and strengthen the economy, not impose more obstacles on job growth."[11]

The backing of Governor Jon Corzine was crucial. He supported paid family leave as a senator and then became a personal lobbyist for it as governor, after he was severely injured in an automobile accident. "This family-leave insurance bill is personally significant to me. When I was in the hospital after my accident last spring, it was the strong support from my family that kept me going. I was fortunate my family members had the flexibility to be there for me, day in and day out. But not everyone has that luxury."[12]

Where to Go from Here

The world did not come to an end when New Jersey and California enacted these laws. Indeed, the law in both states has been underutilized, contrary to expectations. One legislator in New Jersey had expressed the fear that people would take advantage of it to go into the woods during deer season. Yet while underutilization is good for the health of the insurance fund, it is not so good for the families who could benefit from it. Possibly the poor economy has made workers reluctant to take the time off, even if the law gives them permission to do so. The state of the economy may make it hard to afford to settle for $524 dollars a week, even if that is better than no pay.

However, the big obstacle to Americans taking advantage of family leave insurance is that it's not yet part of our culture. Our typical answer to tough times is to work more, not less, which is what workers are doing. This trend is in sharp contrast to what is happening in the Netherlands, where both women and men have increasingly adopted a four-day work week to spend more time with their families. To galvanize grassroots support, Americans who can afford to do so will need to begin to make that trade-off between time and money. Which is more valuable?

Paid Sick Days

When it comes to guaranteeing paid sick days, the United States is, once more, the exception. We stand alone among twenty-one of the world's wealthiest nations by not providing our workforce with the legal right to take paid sick days either for themselves or for a sick family member. Forty percent of private-sector employees cannot take paid sick days. That includes 86 percent of hotel and food workers and 78 percent of low-wage workers.[13] Representative Rosa DeLauro (D-CT) has introduced the Healthy Families Act several years in a row. It would require employers with fifteen or more employees to provide up to seven days of paid sick leave a year. Despite strong support from labor and family advocacy groups, the legislation remains stalled in Congress. The bill got a spurt of steam behind it with the outbreak of the H1N1 virus in 2009 when, despite the risk of contagion, most workers did not stay home. The reason was simple: they feared they would be fired.

One state—Connecticut (limited to service workers)—and three cities—San Francisco, Washington, DC, and most recently Seattle—have passed paid sick leave laws. In Milwaukee, 70 percent of the city's voters had approved such a law in 2008, but in May, 2011 the law was repealed. Governor Scott Walker (R-WI) signed a bill that prevents any jurisdiction in the state from mandating legislation, such as paid sick leave, that exceeds state law.

The numbers are small, and they can be interpreted either as a glass half full or a glass half empty. Is this the beginning of a trend, or are these communities an aberration? There is no doubt that paid sick days have strong public support. Seventy-seven percent of Americans believe that paid sick days are "very important" for all workers. Americans of both major political parties support paid sick days as a "basic worker's right," with 96 percent of liberals and 68 percent of conservatives, a surprisingly high number.[14]

Connecticut

Connecticut became the first state to mandate paid sick days for service employees on June 12, 2011, after eleven hours of legislative debate. Democratic governor Dannel Malloy had campaigned on the issue in 2010 and came out a winner in both a tight primary and the general election. His approval rating, after having had to cut spending and raise taxes in his financially strapped state, is low at 38 percent, but 71 percent of the voters approve of the new sick days law, including 50 percent of Republicans.

Malloy championed the law as "good public health policy. My mother was a school nurse," he explains. The law is limited to service businesses that employ fifty or more people and covers some 600,000 workers in hospitals, hotels, retail establishments, and restaurants. They can take one hour of paid sick leave for every forty hours worked, without fear of losing their jobs.

"It's as much about public health as workers' benefits. Do you want people preparing your meal who are sneezing into your salad?" Malloy asks.

He observes that most people who voted against the bill already have paid sick time. "It's amazing that we did it in a terrible economy. We worked with industry to address their concerns and were able to carve out a more limited bill."

He had strong union support and the backing of Jon Green, director of the Working Families Party, dedicated to electing progressives and helping working-class families. As Green told *Daily Kos,* everybody benefits from the law because these are the jobs "where you would least want workers to feel compelled to come to work sick. When they do so, it puts us all at risk. This is particularly true for workers who care for vulnerable populations; according to one study, in nursing homes where workers lack paid sick days, patients get 60 percent more infections."[15]

The real story is that paid sick days was a winning issue for Governor Malloy. He had the political sense to recognize that and to frame the issue as a health benefit, rather than a union benefit. Why don't more politicians follow suit? Senators Ted Kennedy and Chris Dodd were key sponsors of legislation that benefited children and families and their popularity never suffered as a result. Can we move beyond that observation and conclude that a lawmaker's popularity would be enhanced if he or she took the lead on these issues?

Working at the Municipal Level

San Francisco adopted a paid leave ordinance in 2007. A recent report indicates that the business community's prediction of dire consequences for the city when the ordinance was adopted have not been realized.[16]

The greatest fear was that employees would take advantage of the law by not showing up for work whenever they felt like it, falsely claiming to be sick. But, the report notes,"despite the availability of either five or nine sick days under the PSLO (Paid Sick Leave Ordinance) the typical worker with access used only three paid sick days during the previous year, and one-quarter of employees with access used zero paid sick days. . . . This suggests that employees view paid sick days as a form of insurance—a valuable benefit when illness strikes, but saved until then and only used as needed."[17] As a result, "two-thirds of employers in the only city with experience with a paid sick days mandate for all workers are supportive of the policy."[18]

What is the best argument in support of the law? The US economy loses millions of dollars when employees come to work when they are sick and infect other workers. Their own productivity is also significantly reduced. One cost estimate is as high as $180 billion. Other studies maintain that the cost to employers of granting sick days is also high.[19] Precise costs in the United States will not be available until more municipalities and states adopt paid sick day laws. We do know that a majority of employers provide them and they do not appear to suffer economic harm as a result. They consider it the cost of doing business. It is largely low-wage workers who have no paid sick days; they are the group who need the power of the law to protect them.

The Take-Away Message

What have we learned from the states and municipalities that have succeeded in adopting family/work policies?

- **Counter the opposition of business organizations.** The challenge is to encourage those CEOs who implement these policies voluntarily to speak up publicly. Jon Shure recalls that Verizon New Jersey told him they already provided paid family leave and had no problem with the bill. When he asked if they would testify in favor of it, they said, "We have to check with headquarters." He never heard back. He found others who were willing to speak up.
- **Gain bipartisan support.** Experience tells us that Democratic governors and legislatures are more likely to support these bills. With the recent defeat of many Democratic governors and

legislatures, the task is more difficult, but not impossible. The National Governors Association has supported segments of the family/work agenda, such as early childhood education.

- **Form a broad coalition.** Families, the elderly, the disabled, unions, women's groups, religious groups, and child advocates. Then make sure everyone within the coalition speaks with one voice.
- **Be prepared,** even if the timing does not seem right. In California the paid family leave bill became law in one year. In New Jersey, it took twelve years. We cannot wait for ideal circumstances to lay the groundwork for legislation. The political environment can change unexpectedly, as we have recently witnessed, from one party to other, from one agenda to another.
- **Frame the question.** Changing the label from "paid family leave" to "family leave insurance" has succeeded in broadening the constituency and subduing the opposition. The concept of "fairness" was effective in Australia. Use it.
- **Tell personal stories.** Statistics are helpful, but personal experiences are powerful. In New Jersey, it was the governor's story and Loretta Weinberg's that humanized and personalized the issue. Almost every citizen has a similar story.
- **Do not accept the inevitable.** Most people believe that the way things are is the way they always will be, except for the privileged few. Our challenge is not to surrender to inevitability but rather to demonstrate that there is an alternative, a commonsense policy that enables working families to meet the most important needs in their lives: those of their job and their family.

When leaders of the women's suffrage movement debated the pros and cons of pursuing a state or federal strategy, they ended up pushing for both. That is what must be done for paid family leave and related family/work policies.

It would be easy to conclude that this is not the right time at either the state or federal level to push for these policies, when draconian spending cuts are being proposed for existing programs for children and families at both state and federal levels. Yet as I wrote this on Valentine's Day 2011, I received an e-mail from MomsRising, an Internet advocacy organization, titled, "Get ready, get set: Send your Valentine to Congress!"

"What? A valentine to a politician?" it read. "Yep, because when key programs for kids and families are at risk like child care, preschool, and Head Start, it's time to get a little crafty . . . let's break out the virtual glitter and stand up for kids today."[20]

At a time when we're hanging by our fingernails to hold on to what we have, how can we ask for more? When government intervention in our lives is being demonized, how can we demand greater government involvement?

The only way to answer these questions is to explain the high price we pay for maintaining the status quo and the long-term returns every working family in America would gain from greater investments in family/work policies.

CHAPTER 6

Win–Win: Workplace Flexibility

The benefits of paid family leave for moms, dads, and babies are well documented. We know that the first few months of a child's life are critical. Enabling parents to bond with and care for an infant results in improved brain development, better prenatal and postnatal care, a greater likelihood that children will be breast-fed and immunized, and lower accident and infant mortality rates.

The benefits for employers of paid family leave and other family/work policies are equally well documented: increased ability to attract and retain the most talented workforce, reduce turnover rates, and increase productivity.

If the benefits are clear, why can't we find common ground? First, the benefits are not widely known and understood by the business community. Their first reaction is, "This is another employee benefit; it will cost me money, which I can't afford."

Second, benefits are often difficult to quantify because they vary from company to company. Third, institutions have a built-in lethargy; they do not like change. Finally, business does not want government to tell it what to do.

Portia Wu, former vice president at the National Partnership for Women and Families, and now senior advisor for the White House Domestic Policy Council, observes "If the workplaces don't change, then we're not keeping up with reality. From what we've seen from the Chamber [of Commerce], they actually don't want a system. . . . I think it's easy to get businesses together to talk about worker flexibility, but again, they just don't want requirements from the federal or state governments. That's the rub." Some businesses may do a lot of these things voluntarily, Wu notes. "They just don't want to be required to do so."

Is voluntary action enough to make a difference for American working families? "I see that there are employers and employees doing all kinds of things that I never would have imagined. That's all on the voluntary side, things they are doing for their own self-interest. But there is still resistance, no question. Change is molasses-slow," says Ellen Galinsky of the Families and Work Institute.

How well is the private sector doing on its own? A 2008 report on paid family leave policies at Fortune 100 companies by Senator Charles Schumer (D-NY) and Representative Carolyn Maloney (D-NY) states that only 8 percent of private employers provide paid family leave, while 82 percent offer unpaid leave. Among the Fortune 100 sample (not all responded), nine out of ten firms "report offering some kind of paid leave—family leave, pregnancy-related disability leave, or allowed use of accrued paid sick days—for the birth of a child." The report notes that "the length remains far below the leave policies implemented in the European Union or nearly all other advanced countries."[1]

The report concludes: "Fortune 100 companies' policies should offer a model for implementing paid family leave as a basic employment standard for all workers in the United States, in addition to paid sick days. Paid parental leave is part of a broader set of new workplace policies that Americans need to meet the competing demands of work and family."[2] The policy goals in this report would satisfy the needs of millions of working families. There is only one catch: action on legislation to implement these goals is at a standstill.

In 2007, when *Working Mother* magazine issued its annual list of the one hundred best companies for working mothers, it was clear that even the best companies had much room for improvement. According to a report based on the magazine's findings, "Nearly one-quarter (24 percent) of the best employers for working mothers provide four or fewer weeks of paid maternity leave, and half (52 percent) provide six weeks or less."[3] There were some laggards: 7 percent provided no paid leave, and another 7 percent provided only one or two weeks. There were also some stars: Goldman, Sachs & Co. offered sixteen weeks paid maternity leave, plus four weeks for fathers and eight for adoptive parents.[4]

Is there enough evidence that employers will voluntarily adopt these policies because they know they're good for business? "I'm not very hopeful that work-friendly policies can be achieved through voluntary means by the employer. A lot of employers do provide [them], but the reality is that some workers are just left out in the cold," states work/family advocate Janet Gornick.

What are the alternatives? Do we fight the business community tooth and nail, as Jon Shure did in New Jersey? Or do we try to include the business community as a viable partner? Not an easy choice, because both will demand patience, and compared to the rest of the world, the United States has been patient too long.

Finding Common Ground

One territory where employers and employees are beginning to find common ground is workplace flexibility. When employees are asked what family/work policy they would put at the top of their list, the answer always is flexibility.

The Sloan Foundation's Kathleen Christensen is optimistic that business is moving toward greater flexibility because it makes good business sense. "We have reframed flexibility, which we see as a way of realigning the workplace with the needs of the workforce." Her organization's research has shown that flexibility is a strategic business tool, not just an accommodation. "It's also a nice benefit," Christensen tells me. She wants to make workplace flexibility a compelling national issue and a standard way of doing business. Several principles, she says, are absolutely critical for sound policy: flexibility has to be available at all stages of careers and lives and to all income groups, and both the benefits and the costs have to be "proportionately shared with both employers and employees."

Instituting flexibility would be a major cultural change that gets at the heart of how work is done. Flexibility means creating trust between employer and employee. It reduces the need for low-wage employees to punch a time clock to record their arrivals and departures and for higher-wage employees to put in extra hours of face time. All employees are entrusted to complete their tasks, regardless of what time or place they do it.

The Workplace Flexibility 2010 campaign defines "flexibility" similarly to its manifestation in the UK: "as any one of a spectrum of work structures that alters the time and/or place that work gets done on a regular basis.

A flexible work arrangement includes:

- flexibility in the *scheduling* of hours worked, such as alternative work schedules (e.g. flex time and compressed workweeks), and arrangements regarding shift and break schedules;
- flexibility in the *amount* of hours worked, such as part time work and job shares; and
- flexibility in the *place* of work, such as working at home or at a satellite location.[5]

Telecommuting enables parents with young children to join the work-force; it also makes it possible for retirees and people with disabilities to collect a paycheck. Environmentalists are enthusiastic endorsers of telecommuting because it reduces workers' carbon footprint. Employers calculate significant savings on office space and furniture. The federal government had 102,000 teleworkers as of 2009 and has a website (telework.gov) devoted to recruiting more. The *Washington Business Journal* reports that telecommuting increased 39 percent between 2006 and 2009.[6] According to a survey undertaken by the nonprofit WorldatWork, some 33.7 million Americans telecommuted as of 2009 (with a teleworker defined as anyone who works remotely at least once a month).[7] And according to Kate Lister and Tom Harnish, authors of *Undress for Success*, American companies could save $500 billion annually if they enabled more workers to telecommute.[8]

Researchers at Corporate Voices for Working Families analyzed data from twenty-nine of the largest US corporations and concluded that "there was a strong business case to be made for flexibility. It increased retention, reduced absenteeism and cost of turnover, recruitment and training." Christensen adds, "[Flexibility] also improves performance and productivity."

Pilot studies indicate that flexibility can also be negotiated on a team basis, rather than an individual basis. The team is committed to maintaining its productivity and decides where and how flexibility is possible for all the members of the team.

The old definition of where and when work is done is pretty obsolete, observed Lotte Bailyn, professor of management at MIT's Sloan School of Management. Nevertheless, "We find that men don't feel able to ask for [flexibility], particularly for family reasons. Women do feel legitimate in asking for it for family reasons, but there may be career consequences. So unless it's done collectively, it's not going to reach the goal of changing attitudes."

Has the economic downturn forced companies to pull back on flexibility? Some thought flexibility would take a big hit, but no, says Bailyn, "the majority of firms have kept flexibility in place, partially because you are talking about daily flexibility. It's low to no cost. It's a way to keep up employees' morale." Also, while the move by some companies to avoid layoffs by reducing hours has caused some employees financial hardship, others found relief in the transition to part-time. "Some people were afraid to ask for flexibility for fear of putting their job in jeopardy, so now they welcome it," Bailyn notes.

If flexible policies were the norm, instead of the exception, many women who leave their jobs after childbirth would return to work part-time. The primary reason they head for home today is the lack of flexibility, which forces them to choose between caring for a newborn or going back to work full-time.

Christensen believes that if flexibility does become accepted practice it would ultimately advance comprehensive federal "right to request" legislation, similar to what has been enacted in England and Australia. Such a law would legitimize the right to ask for flexibility. The law does not compel the employer to grant flexibility once it is requested, but it does require the employer to take the request seriously by stating a refusal in writing and/or proposing an alternative plan.

Building Coalitions

Christensen is working toward getting such a law passed in Washington, and building a coalition that reaches beyond the expected advocacy groups has been a key strategy. The coalition includes people in the disabilities community who, she says, "want to be vital members of the workforce but need some flexibility," and in the faith-based community, who "need time at some point to practice their faith." There are also environmentalists who support telecommuting as good for reducing fossil fuel use and improving air quality.

"I think the one that is most powerful, but not fully leveraged, is the aging workforce," Christensen says. "We have to build a coalition among working parents and older workers."

Older workers often need and want to work but require flexibility. Their contribution would be to ensure that "there is a proper transfer of institutional knowledge," and, I would add, experience.

Christensen notes, "As long as flexibility is seen only as a working woman's issue, as only a working mother's issue, then we've got the inevitable consequence of deviance. To the extent that we really open our eyes to the fact that flexibility is needed by workers across all lifestyles, ages, income, and faiths, then we begin to say this is what the American workforce needs, but it is also good for business."

According to Katie Corrigan of Workplace Flexibility 2010, the private sector needs to become more engaged in enacting work/family policies, and government needs to play a big role. She faults some Democrats for not engaging business to see what would work. The question is, how much common ground can be carved out for both Democrats and Republicans to stand on? Each group would have to take a step toward the center. More importantly, all groups affected by work/family policies (business, labor, the elderly, the disabled, and child advocates) would have to move these questions to a much higher position on their agendas. Flexibility would not be something "nice" to do, but something we "have" to do to be successful.

Building the Business Case

Professor Brad Harrington, executive director of the Boston College Center for Work & Family and a former Hewlett-Packard executive, believes voluntary action is working. He notes that work/family issues have always existed for lower-income working women but were not recognized until professional women raised these questions.

He tells me, "Work/family issues never really had much resonance with people until professional and managerial women brought them up. Blue-collar women, women in domestic service, and women of color—especially African-American women—responded to the whole work/family movement by pointing out that 'our mothers have always worked.' But when white, privileged women began to work, suddenly there was a problem."

The center opened twenty years ago to link academic research with decision makers in business. "Instead of businesses saying, 'All we care about is what you do at work, and what happens outside of work is not our issue,' they have to understand that the best way to keep talent is by seeing people from a whole-person perspective." That means, he explains, that businesses have to reconsider what they're asking a good employee to do. "If you work in retail, do you demand that they work until 1 a.m. and work on holidays? Or if you work for a global corporation, do you demand that they be able to travel at the drop of a hat? What we are trying to do is get organizations to understand that people have this dual agenda. [Because] businesses tend to become very organization-centric."

Harrington says that whenever he goes to work/family conferences, everybody knows his name. Why?

"It's probably similar [to] when you were one of the few women governors," he tells me. "Everybody probably knew who you were because you were the outlier. I'm one of five men at a conference with two hundred women, from both the corporate and academic side."

It's easy to understand why the field is now dominated by women. Women gravitate or are channeled into human resources positions more than men. Do they tend to work on family/work issues because they see this as their responsibility, or because of their personal experience combining work and family, or because they feel obliged to fill a vacuum?

Are there so few men in this field because the issue does not reach the CEO level, where men continue to outnumber women? As men increasingly experience the same conflicts as women between their family and work lives, and as their daughters struggle with the same conflicts, I expect they will become active and visible advocates for change, not only at conferences, but also in the corporate boardrooms where decisions about these issues are made.

Harrington's center frames the business case for work/life programs—which he defines as flextime, a compressed work week, part-time work, job sharing, on/off ramps (the ability to return to work after a prolonged absence), teleworking, child and elder care, and health and wellness—in terms of company benefits. He stresses that these programs improve financial performance and shareholder value, help attract and retain talent, improve productivity, and reduce costs.

Showing just how these programs aid the bottom line remains critical. Harrington says, "We see a lot of metrics and measures that show that talent retention, especially among women, is much greater in organizations that have more flexible work policies. The cost of employee turnover is another one of the fundamental measures." Since employees tend to favor flexibility over all other work/life programs, even on-site child care, it's a win–win situation for both employer and employee. "Child care is a cash outlay. My mantra is flexibility is free. There are some minor costs with increased benefits expenses, but by and large most of the benefits are pro-rated." Another popular flex benefit is telecommuting. "Companies that have gone in that direction have not only seen that it is cost neutral, but often they have cost savings because they have reduced their real estate footprint dramatically," Harrington notes.

Despite these clear advantages, there remains an implementation gap, the difference between what companies *say* they offer and what companies actually *do* offer. Some companies use these benefits only as a recruitment tool, with little or no intention of implementing them. As demographics change, though, Harrington remains optimistic that these benefits will become reality for the American worker. He notes that 57 percent of college degrees are going to women, and 60 percent of master's degrees. "Three out of five people who are [college] educated are women," he says. "The talent pool has clearly shifted. Companies are interested in getting the best talent. The companies we work with—Johnson & Johnson, IBM, Eli Lilly—want to see only the top 15 percent of students when they go to colleges to recruit. They perceive themselves as being in a war for talent." Add to that an increasing aging population and the younger millennium generation—all of whom believe that an employer should foster work/life balance—and you have a set of rising expectations that Harrington says "will put new pressure on employers to change old workplace patterns."

A Cultural Change

Flexibility is not just a program. "This is a cultural change," says Ellen Ernst

Kossek, professor at Michigan State University's School of Human Resources and Labor Relations.[9] She believes that we have "to move work/life issues from the margins to the mainstream. Companies think, oh, we can just adopt this flex-time program, but if you don't change your views on what it takes to be an ideal worker and think about how to adapt your culture, and how people of different views add value, including the aging, you don't change the culture. There are some broader social benefits—as people age they might want to be able to work from home; it would help low-income workers who don't have child care." She adds, "We need to help employers implement flexibility. There is a lot of innovation, but sometimes it doesn't trickle down. There is a lot of patchiness and unevenness. It is job-determined." Kossek suggests that government provide incentives to companies to implement family/work policies, rewarding those that make it easier for families to integrate their work and life.

Extending Flex Benefits to Low-Wage Workers

How job-determined is access to flexibility? Can low-wage workers at large companies like hotel chains participate? I talked with Donna Klein, a former executive at Marriott, and currently executive chair of Corporate Voices for Working Families, who reports that flexibility for low-wage workers is still in its infancy. "We've been working on flexibility for twenty years," she notes. "We encouraged companies to begin experimenting and implementing flexibility with their hourly workers. The findings, in terms of return on investments, are pretty identical to [those for] professional staff."

How does it work, I wondered, when low-wage shift employees have to work a specific number of hours each day? "The hours haven't changed; the number of hours is still driven by the workload," she explains. But companies are experimenting with creative strategies such as team scheduling, remote work, and job sharing. "But mostly it's flexibility around core hours of start and stop time." Klein says such changes are promoted not as a way to be nice to your employees, but rather as "a strategic way to more effectively manage the workforce."

Corporate Voices for Working Familes has developed two kinds of tool kits to teach implementation—one for employers and one for employees.

Both groups, Klein believes, need to be taught how to make flexibility work. Lowered turnover, she said, is only one of the benefits. Increased productivity and employee engagement are others. A growing concern for employers is the quality of the entry-level workforce. "It's decreased over the last twenty years," says Klein. "It's not just a numbers game; it's a quality of work game." Retraining capable employees is expensive; therefore it makes sense for companies to work to retain even their less-skilled hourly workers. It costs 100 to 300 percent of an annual salary to replace a trained worker.[10] Stated another way, the average turnover cost for an $8-an-hour employee, using low estimates, is $5,505. Some estimates are as high as $25,000 for employees in protective services, such as police officers and guards.[11]

Flexibility is about mutual respect between the employer and employees, but it is also about reciprocity, Klein explains. "It has to be a win for the company and the employee. It can't just be a win for the employee, that won't work long term. It's not about altruism, it's about a business solution to the way contemporary workers lead their lives." She adds that most small employers "have a knee-jerk reaction that it's too hard for them to have flexibility because they're too small, but then you have some small companies that have been very creative. We have a lot of educating to do of small employers and nonprofits on how to make this work. On the other hand, employers are recognizing the value of good hourly workers, so those good hourly workers do have power now because employers don't look at employees as widgets anymore."

The bottom-line questions remain: Does workplace flexibility mean an extra expense and an extra burden for employers? Does it work only for top management, or does it pay for employees at all levels? Jody Heymann, a professor of political science at McGill University, believes that flexibility works on every rung of the corporate ladder.[12] Few question that the perks, stock options, and bonuses for those at the top of the ladder are designed to attract and retain the best workers. The logic behind treating workers at the top better than those at the bottom has long been that top talent is scarce, so companies must compete for highly qualified professionals, whereas low-level workers are unskilled and readily replaceable, so there is no financial return in investing in them to keep them happy and on board. That sentiment may, thankfully, be changing. Heymann studied companies from several parts of the world: "We found privately owned and publicly traded companies—across wide-ranging sectors and of every size—that became more profitable as they improved the conditions faced by their lowest-level employees."[13]

Best Companies

There are seventy-five million hourly workers in this country, says Jennifer Owens, director of the Working Mother Research Institute, "and job satisfaction is dwindling. If they're not satisfied, they'll jump to another company." Just recently, *Working Mother* magazine began including hourly workers in its annual surveys of the best companies for working moms. The magazine has given high rankings to McDonald's, Marriott International, Sodexo food services, and two hospitals. Three out of five of the hourly employees at companies they surveyed were women, and they were paid a median wage of $11.49 an hour. One of the key benefits examined in the rating system was flexibility, including, among other factors, advance notice of monthly work hours, extended unpaid time off without penalty, and the ability to trade or share shifts.[14] Across all wage levels for the top one hundred companies listed, the magazine found that flexibility: child care and paid parental leave options were continuing to expand, and backup child care was becoming almost a norm. The magazine's surveys have also documented how much family/work policies have changed. In 1986, only two companies on the magazine's list (Control Data and IBM) allowed employees to work from home. In 2010, 100 percent of the companies offered telecommuting. Indeed, some of the fears businesses have expressed about giving workers flexibility are lifting. "People don't become bad employees because of flexibility," says Owens. "If you have a bad employee, get rid of them. Flexibility turns into productivity every time."

The key to implementing family/work policies rests with the CEO and with managers. Sometimes they lead by example. "Jim Turley [James S. Turley], the CEO of Ernst & Young, would take one afternoon a week off to be with his children. That sent a signal throughout the company that it was okay for everybody else to do the same thing. To implement flexibility as a company-wide policy, you have to train managers, alert them to how flexibility is a benefit, and then hold them accountable," Owens explains. "It's not enough to just have programs; you have to give women the power to get flexibility in different ways at different points of their lives."

Such policies make companies employers of choice. As the economy shows signs of improvement, the best people will be the first to leave companies that don't offer what they need. A full 70 percent of women with a child under eighteen are in the workforce, and companies offering them their top three criteria—fair compensation, meaningful work, and flexibility—will fare best.

"Flex Is the New Currency" headlines a 2010 blog post by *Working Mother*'s Helen Jonsen.[15] She notes that the financial industry in its heyday provided bonuses, wage increases, and other perks to keep top talent. "With the recession, those incentives were spooled back. So what's next? . . . Flex can be an umbrella under which employees understand they are valued. Flex is the new currency, bonus, trophy—if it is done correctly and evenly across a company."

Being valued matters. "If a company is there for you when you just had a baby or you have a crisis with an aging parent, you'll stay there forever," Jennifer Owens notes. It works two ways. Beth Sachs, founder of Vermont Energy Investment Corporation, is a strong believer in workplace flexibility (employees can even bring dogs to work). One benefit, she noted, was that her employees learn to be cross-trained. When people are skilled at more than one job, the company is the beneficiary.

How optimistic is Jennifer Owens that more companies are moving in this direction on family/work policies? She describes the situation as "stagnant." Flexibility may be catching on, but the number of companies nationwide that offer paid family leave is not growing.

Fixing the Leaky Pipeline at Deloitte

James Wall, now retired, had been at the forefront of flexibility at Deloitte, an audit, financial advisory, risk management, tax, and consulting firm with 170,000 employees in 140 countries. Wall, named Human Resources Executive of the Year by *Human Resources Executive* magazine in 2002, has spent the last fifteen years at Deloitte implementing family/work policies after he discovered the "leaky pipeline" in his own company.

For years he had been recruiting on college campuses, where the pool was 50 percent women. "The average length of time it takes from the point of entry off campus to a candidacy for partnership is eleven years. So I looked at the hundred candidates [for partnership] and there were seven women. That's when I went to the CEO's office and said we've got a problem here. If intellectual capital is our asset, then we're on a going-out-of-business trajectory because we're losing talent. The traditional response at the time was that women have other opportunities, and by the way, they have children."

Wall didn't think that was the right answer, though. So he decided to interview about two hundred women who had left the firm and ask what made them leave. The number one finding was that Deloitte was a hostile place for women to work. "Not in a sexual harassment way," says Wall. "It was just unfriendly, not a welcome place for women to be. This was evidenced by how we went after business, how we got assignments, how we conducted ourselves in the broader business community, and the clubs we belonged to." The second finding was that "the processes and systems, largely informal, that help you advance in your career in this firm work better for men than they do for women." The fact that it was difficult to have a career and raise a family came in third, much to the surprise of many who thought it would rank higher. "To say that the company wasn't supportive would be an understatement. The punch line was that Deloitte was kind of a crappy place to work," says Wall. The women's attitude was "It's hard as hell to get ahead, and, you know what, it's not worth it given everything else that I have to do to have a life and a family."

In response Deloitte created 50 to 60 programs offering flex time, child care, and other family aids to help address this issue—all of which benefited both women and men. "We tried to infuse a culture of responsiveness, support, and flexibility for all of our people, but especially for our women," stresses Wall. Yet he found that programs were not enough. "There were lots of neat programs but nobody used them. They believed if they had a reduced-hours career arrangement they might as well kiss their careers good-bye."

He realized Deloitte had to change its fundamental culture and initiated a multi-year training program, called "'Men and Women as Colleagues'" for all partners, senior managers, and managers, numbering eight thousand people. It dealt with a range of gender issues, including family/work culture.

"The second thing we did, which was very uncharacteristic of the company at the time, we announced what we were going to do, externally as well as internally. These accountability structures would not allow us to back away from our commitments. Our CEO was committed big-time to this. I found that one of the most effective levers to get some of our senior male executives engaged in this was to ask them whether they would want one of their daughters to work in a place like this, because they were very committed to their daughters. Comparatively 7 percent more women than men were leaving the firm when we started. That has disappeared to zero. Deloitte went up from 7 percent women out of one hundred candidates for partnership to 40 percent women."

The end result of more women in management, Wall says, is that "a diverse team, however you define it, is more effective at solving complex problems than a homogeneous team. When clients hire us they want to see something that vaguely resembles who they are."

So, Deloitte moved to fix its leaky pipeline not to be politically correct or to respond to a feminist demand for change, but because the status quo was bad for business? I ask. "That is exactly right," stresses Wall. "In fact we acknowledged early on that unless we had a fundamental business reason to do this, any other reason would not suffice. It was enlightened or not-so-enlightened self-interest. If we couldn't make a convincing argument to our partners, no matter what we called it, they wouldn't support it."

The company saved money in the process, too. "The cost of turnover in a knowledge-intensive business is somewhere between three and five times the salary of the person at the point they leave. Now, a 1 percent drop in turnover we could conservatively estimate would be a drop of over $1 million. So you could distribute to our partners a million more dollars just by dropping the percentage one [point]. If you dropped it 5 percent you were talking real money. We ran these calculations to our partners who were serious doubters and even they said, maybe I need to pay closer attention, there's something there."

Building Trust for Flex Time

Like Deloitte, Ernst & Young moved toward flexibility when it found women were leaving the company at a higher rate than men. It implemented a written policy guaranteeing that when an employee asked for flexibility, he or she would not be penalized, similar to England's right to request law. Maryella Gockel, Ernst & Young's flexibility strategy leader, reports that the company "just promoted our first partner who worked on a reduced schedule for many years," addressing the fear many employees have about requesting flexibility—will it hurt my career?

With CEO Jim Turley championing workplace flexibility, the company's only requirements are "that the work gets done and our clients are satisfied," says Gockel. "Then their teams can manage their own workload." She offers an example of an employee who wants to have a reduced schedule: "If she wants to work 75 percent, she asks the team who will pick up that other 25 percent of the workload. It's all about the conversation. It enables people to ask without fear of retribution."

How does that affect the bottom line? "There are pieces of the puzzle that cost money, like leaves and technology. But it can also actually save money, when you don't need office space and someone works on a 75 percent schedule."

Why aren't other companies doing it? If a culture of flexibility works so well for two of the world's major accounting firms, why isn't this a no-brainer for other companies who wish to attract and retain talent?

Gockel says, "It's a lack of trust; managers fear that the work won't get done. Managers who have children are the most supportive. My view is that as we globalize, our teams become more global, and flexibility has to be the way we work. We span different times zones," which means that the traditional nine-to-five schedule becomes irrelevant.

Gockel adds, "My passion around flexibility is about my own life experiences. The man I worked for had a traditional stay-at- home-wife, but his attitude was, 'You can take your brain wherever you go." One ancillary benefit of these policies, she says, is that the boss can say, "Don't bring your bad work/life problems to us."

One reason Deloitte and Ernst & Young are in the forefront of family/work policies is that they may be competing against one another for the best talent. Another reason may be that their employees' work does not have to be done in an office; it lends itself to telecommuting. I would like to believe that they are in the flexibility game because, as financial firms that know how to crunch the numbers, they can see that flexibility pays.

What both companies have learned is that their future success depends on enabling talented workers to remain in the workforce, both women and men. Companies that don't move in this direction are going to lose their best workers for the most highly skilled jobs, a situation that is *really* bad for business.

Companies Benefit Worldwide— But Not in the United States

Professor Linda Duxbury of the Sprott School of Business at Carleton University in Ottawa points out that when American global companies want to do business in Canada or Europe, "they can't opt out" of these generous family leave policies provided by every other developed country. "American companies provide benefits to non-American people that they don't provide to their own people. If I were American, I'd be ticked off. It's nonsense to say that it doesn't make business sense," she says.

Why can they do well with one set of rules in one part of the world, and say that they cannot do equally well if these same rules were applied in the United States?

The commonsense answer is, of course they can. When the CNNMoney website listed the fifteen best cities to find "smart new labor," they included Vancouver, in Canada, a country that has generous paid family leave laws. Clearly these policies have not reduced Vancouver's attractiveness as a good place for companies to locate.[16]

The Health Care Industry

The health care industry is one sector that is feeling the pressure to move toward greater flexibility.

"A lot of my workforce is female, 80 percent [15,000 employees]," explains Barbara Steele, regional President of ProMedica Health System in Toledo, Ohio. Asked about the importance of flexibility, she replies, "It's got to happen. Otherwise we won't have anybody to hire. We can't be working with rigid policies that don't allow people flexibility whether they have children or not. Our average nurse is fifty years old, and nursing is a heavy-duty job, and we're trying to see how we can keep people engaged in the workforce longer. We know that means that they might want to work four-hour days twice a week."

"More and more physicians are female and we see them struggling if they have small children," Steele adds. "A lot of our employees are single parents and they need flexibility.

Steele's passion for reforming workplace rules stems, in part, from her personal experience. "My son is grown and I have grandchildren now. When my son was young, I was working full-time and going to school full-time and I was responsible for everything in the household. Some of the time I was married and some of the time I wasn't. That is a handful and there's got to be more flexibility."

She began her career as a nurse and climbed the ladder to CEO. "As a staff nurse, I couldn't do it. I abandoned the bedside nursing piece and opted for a more flexible position in management. I had to go back and get two degrees. I went very fast on the nursing side of the ladder, from head nurse to supervisor, to manager, to director, to chief nursing officer. That all happened in four years. Then I decided I wanted to run the whole hospital." When she was promoted to president of the hospital, she became the first female in that position in its 125 year history.

"What was it about the nursing job that made it hard for you to continue?" I ask. Steele answers, "The hours were such that I had to work my share of all the holidays. I had to work my share of the shifts. . . . I had to work days one week and then afternoons the next week." She wanted to move up to management because she could have more predictable hours. "Having some predictability is the first step."

To make her company more attractive to her workforce, she says, "the number one item we're looking at is flexibility. We see that with our new workforce, the millennials coming out now. They have a different expectation about what the work/home life balance is going to be. We know we have to determine how we can build flexibility. We're looking at new ways to do work. How can we use technology to give workers the flexibility they need?"

The possibilities are great in finance and administration. "There's nothing that says the work has to be done between nine and five. At our company you can be considered full-time and work three twelve-hour shifts or five eight-hour shifts. We have changed the mind-set that people have to be in the office."

Steele's company's maternity leave and other family policies are part of written company policy. The key to her success is not found in any one policy; it is driven by her commitment to change the way work is being done. But when I ask her if she would support a federal law guaranteeing flexibility or paid family leave, she pauses. "I would have to think about that. It means I would have to cut out something else." Even stellar employers like Steele tend not to acknowledge that they are already doing what new laws may require.

The New Workplace

Joan Blades and Nanette Fondas describe the way in which work is changing in the title of their coauthored book: *The Custom-Fit Workplace*. According to Blades, "[There] are policies and practices, and organizational designs and job tracks, that allow people to seek—and hopefully achieve—a *custom fit* between their personal set of talents, responsibilities, and needs and the job's demands, constraints, and end products."

Blades is the cofounder of MoveOn.org and of the Internet advocacy group MomsRising. (Her first book, coauthored with Kristin Rowe-Finkbeiner, was *The Motherhood Manifesto*). Her goal continues to be to work "on economic security for families," she explains. Her new book "is a business book. It's about how businesses need to understand that it is good for their bottom line to honor their worker's responsibilities. The book is not about women. It's about work that includes men."

The authors made a not-so-surprising discovery: "More often than not, what is good for workers is good for the employer. We found that organizations that value the whole worker and accommodate the whole range of needs often benefit greatly. Happier, less stressed workers tend to do stronger work, even *more* work, than their beleaguered colleagues. Not only that, they are less likely to walk out the door and take their talent elsewhere."[17]

The old corporate-ladder, top-down, nine-to-five organization of work is being replaced by a new concept described in *The Corporate Lattice*, by

Cathleen Benko (vice chairman and chief talent officer for Deloitte) and Molly Anderson.

What is a lattice? "In mathematics, a lattice is a three-dimensional structure that extends infinitely in any direction. In the real world, lattices can be found everywhere from a garden's wooden trellis to the metalwork on the Eiffel Tower. . . . In the corporate world, the lattice model organizes and advances a company's existing incremental efforts into a comprehensive, strategic response to the altered corporate landscape. It recognizes that career and life are no longer separate spheres but are now interdependent."[18]

How does the "lattice" change the bottom line? The answer, according to Benko and Anderson, is "engagement," defined as "the extent to which employees go the extra mile to deliver extraordinary results for the company internally and to serve as brand ambassadors externally. Research has substantiated the connection between engaged employees and improved corporate operating results. One survey of thirteen thousand US workers across major industrial sectors compared highly engaged employees to employees with moderate to low engagement and found that companies with highly engaged employees enjoy 13 percent higher total returns to shareholders and 26 percent higher revenues per employee."[19]

When requesting flexibility, the authors offer the following tips:

- Plan how you will be able to get the work done.
- Put it in writing.
- Keep the request professional, not personal—that is, focus on the benefits that accrue to the business.
- Suggest a trial period.
- Set an end date for evaluation.[20]

The list compares favorably with the parameters laid out in the right to request laws in England and Australia.

The bottom-line question remains: does workplace flexibility mean an extra expense for employers, or does it pay unexpected dividends?

It is counterintuitive to believe that giving workers more benefits, like paid family leave and the right to request flexibility, will not impose new costs. Yes, there will be some costs, depending on how the policies are framed, but they will be offset by lower turnover and improved productivity. Some argue that these policies should not be called "benefits" at all; they should be the normal way of conducting business. What is clear is that laws that apply equally to every employer create a level playing field. If all employers play by the same rules, increased productivity and profitability are likely to be enjoyed all around.

Yet unhappy employees cost money, too. As Teresa Amabile and Steven Kramer, authors of *The Progress Principle*, wrote for the *New York Times*, "the Gallup-Healthways Well-Being Index. . . shows that Americans now feel worse about their jobs—and their work environments—than ever before. People of all ages, and across income levels, are unhappy with their supervisors, apathetic about their organizations and detached from what they do. . . Gallup estimates the cost of America's disengagement crisis at a staggering $300 billion in lost productivity annually. When people don't care about their jobs or their employers, they don't show up consistently, they produce less, or their work quality suffers."[21]

When workers are concerned about a sick child, or being late for pickup at a child care center, they cannot avoid bringing their problems to work. The boss who recognizes the connection between work life and family life, and takes steps to accommodate it, will be rewarded by not only a happier workforce, but a more productive one.

When flexibility means working part-time, many employees discover that they cannot afford to do so, not only because of a smaller paycheck, but also because they may lose their benefits. The National Labor Relations Act does not cover part-time employees, defined as those working from one to thirty-four hours weekly. Access to pro-rated benefits varies widely in the United States, from company to company. European Union countries are covered by an EU directive that forbids discrimination against part-timers and requires most benefits to be pro-rated. One result is that the rate of female part-time workers is higher than in the United States. For example, the figure is 60 percent in the Netherlands. In contrast, slightly less than 20 percent of the female workforce in the United States is employed part-time, according to the US Department of Labor.[22]

One way to make part-time work possible for more workers is to amend the Labor Relations Act to enable part-time workers to receive benefits according to their hours worked. As I write this, such legislation is pending in Congress, sponsored by Congresswoman Lynn Woolsey, (D-CA), as part of a "Balancing Act" bill that includes more generous family leave policies. However, prospects for passage, at this point, remain dim. The best employers do provide benefits for part-timers because they have learned that part-time workers often return to full-time work when they grow out of the child-rearing age. The custom-fit workplace concept has it right: one size does not fit every stage of life.

CHAPTER 7

The Early Years: Child Care and Early Education

The first step that children take away from their homes and into the world of child care and early childhood education is the most important step they will ever take. The quality and quantity of their care and learning will have an impact on how well they will do in their school years and throughout their adult lives. Yet in the hierarchy of education, early childhood education is on the bottom rung. It has the lowest-paid and least-educated teachers. Quality varies widely. The best is reserved for the most affluent; middle-income and low-income families—who stand to benefit greatly from quality care—are often left to settle for low-cost, low-quality care wherever they can find it.

New studies in brain science verify that the years from birth to age five are the most important years for children's development, affecting both cognitive skills like reading, math, and science and noncognitive skills like the ability to focus, complete a task, and work with others. Later remedial work is both more expensive and less effective.

New economic analysis tells us that the payback for early childhood investments is huge; seven dollars or more are returned for every one dollar invested, according to James Heckman, a Nobel Prize–winning professor of economics at the University of Chicago.

Why are the early years so neglected and the college years so prized? The main reason is that until the recent massive entrance of women into the workforce, child care—here meaning care given to children from birth to age three—was believed to be the parents' responsibility alone and early child hood education—for preschoolers aged three to five—was little known. Neither were the benefits. The tension inherent to the choice between children staying with their mothers in the early years or being cared for by others has threaded through the child care debates for decades and prevented the early years from being taken seriously as a legitimate and respected field worthy of private advocacy and public funding.

Higher education is aptly named: it has the best teachers, the best salaries, and the highest respect. Our expectations of higher education are clear—college graduates are our future professionals; they are expected to create prosperity for themselves and for their country. The spirit of the GI Bill continues to encourage investment in higher education; it remains the portal to the American Dream. The constituency for higher education is unified and powerful, evidenced by dramatic growth from year to year in the number of students enrolled and the number of dollars spent, both public and private. The difference in earnings and unemployment rates between high school and college graduates has become ever greater. In 2011 college graduates had half the unemployment rate as high school graduates and earned $2.1 million in a lifetime compared to $1.2 million for high school graduates.[1] The 2008 median annual earnings for full-time, year-round workers, ages twenty-five and older, were $24,000 for those with no high school diploma; $33,800 with a high school diploma; $39,700 with some college but no degree; $42,00 with an associate's degree; $55,700 with a bachelor's degree; $67,300 with a master's degree; $91,900 with a doctoral degree; and $100,000 with a professional degree.[2] Of women aged twenty-five to thirty-four, those with college degrees earn 79 percent more than those with a high school diploma. Men in the same category earn 74 percent more. A college degree is becoming a prerequisite for jobs that can adequately support a family. The rate of return is clear. Even though the annual cost of a four-year college rose from $8,672 in 1980–81 to $21,189 in 2009–10,[3] the cost of private colleges rose to $32,790 on average. The enrollment increased 15.6 percent between 1973 and 2008.[4]

Quality child care and early education often determine whether a person completes high school or graduates from college. The direct correlation between education and earnings argues for greater investment in the early years. Armed with that knowledge, can we as a nation raise the bottom rung of early childhood up to the top of the education ladder, where it belongs? If the purpose of education is to create self-supporting, healthy, and productive citizens, access to quality child care and early education is as important as access to higher education, and far less costly. A comprehensive child care and early education policy similar in scope to the GI Bill will be required to achieve that goal. Without such an ambitious approach, millions of young children will continue to fall behind their classmates almost from the moment of birth, without the likelihood of ever catching up. This trend represents an unacceptable loss of talent or "human capital" that we can no longer afford.

Creating a Continuum, and Cost Savings

Child care and early childhood education are really just two elements of what should be a broad continuum of programs that support the developing child. Each part of this continuum would produce cost savings:

- **Home visits** for prenatal and postnatal care by nurses and other professionals would result in more healthy mothers and fewer low weight babies, resulting in lower infant mortality rates and lower health care costs.
- **Paid parental leave** would enable one or both parents to be the primary caregivers in the first three to six months of an infant's life, thereby saving health care and child care costs for both families and taxpayers.
- **Quality affordable child care** would foster critical brain development and the mastery of noncognitive social skills.
- **Early education** would enable children to come to school ready to learn, reducing the need for special education.
- **After-school care** would provide children of working parents with a safe and stimulating environment.

How do we create such a cohesive and inclusive system for the care and education of young children? The United States, unlike many other countries, has never developed a cohesive child care system—though the US Department of Defense has done so for military families, as we'll see later in this chapter.

Child Care: Good or Bad?

The simple question of whether child care is good or bad for children has impeded the conversation. The answer is not either-or, the answer is, "It depends." High-quality child care is "good"; poor-quality child care may do more harm than good.

Many parents are in the unfortunate situation of being unable to make a choice between the two, either because of prohibitive costs, lack of access, or evaluating is difficult. The advance toward creating a child care system has been further stalled by the lack of consensus on the purpose of child care. In *The Tragedy of Childcare in America*, Edward Zigler, founder and director emeritus of Yale's Edward Zigler Center in Child Development and Social Policy, with coauthors Katherine Marsland and Heather Lord, pose this question.[5] Is child care simply a storage facility intended to keep young children safe and clean? Is it a social service that allows parents to work and not be dependent on welfare? Is it to reduce poverty? Is it a developmental tool to get children ready for school? Is it to prepare the next generation of workers? Different rationales create different constituencies. It is one thing to provide child care for Rosie the Riveter but another to provide it for Mary the welfare recipient. "Depending on the rationale," says Sonya Michel, author of *Children's Interests/Mothers' Rights*, people "will subscribe to it nor not, or find it favorable or not."

Quality Care for All

Neither have we decided whether child care subsidies should be available only for the poor or whether we should have a high-quality system available to all, as in France and Sweden (Sweden, which has the most generous system in Europe, subsidizes 85 percent of child care costs for all of its citizens).[6] Current US policy dictates that child care subsidies are intended to enable poor mothers to leave the Temporary Assistance for Needy Families (TANF) program. The key word is "temporary," which distinguishes this welfare program from the earlier version, Aid to Families with Dependent Children (AFDC), which had no lifetime restrictions. TANF is designed to encourage poor mothers to enter the labor force as soon as possible; the system worked fairly well in good economic times but when their eligibility for TANF expired, many families were pushed into poverty during the recent recession, because in addition to losing this vital source of income, many lost their homes, or their jobs, or both. Again, the recession has forced many states to severely cut childcare subsidies, at a time when poor families need them most to remain in the workforce.

Our views on whether child care is good or bad for children seem to differ according to class. It's fine for poor mothers, but debatable for other income groups. Do we oppose poor mothers staying home to care for their children because we consider them to be bad or lazy mothers? "Some people believe that welfare only rewards their laziness," decries Anita Hill. Ironically, it is poor mothers, who can least afford it, who are most in need of quality child care because it helps create a level playing field for their children when they start school. Higher-income families have more quality care options than poor families, including the ability to provide one-on-one care by hiring a nanny. Middle-income families are feeling the pinch as well, as an increasing percentage of their earnings are devoted to child care. Quality child care that would attract and welcome all income groups, like the French *écoles maternelles*, would be the ideal.

"Child care in this country has never been presented as a service for women to help them enter the labor force," Sonya Michel explains. "It is just a patchwork of private for-profit and . . . some public services, not like the public school system. . . . If child care is just seen as something for poor kids, then you're going to have poor service. Whereas if middle-class families are involved, they're going to demand good services and they're going to get them."

She criticizes the women's movement for never adopting child care as an issue. Also, she observes, "it's a momentary life cycle thing. When you have little kids the most important thing to you is child care. The minute they're in school, you're worried about after-school care. Then you're worried about getting them into college. It's hard to get the general public on board for the long haul."

Should the Government Share Responsibility for Raising Young Children?

The question that hovers over child care as a system is: should the government share responsibility for the care and education of young children? For some that would represent an invasion of the sanctity of the family. Gøsta Esping-Andersen, author of *The Incomplete Revolution*, finds evidence to the contrary: "There is a widespread belief that externalizing family responsibilities will jeopardize the quality of family life and underlying family solidarities. All available evidence points towards the exact opposite conclusion. We have seen that inter-generational ties seem stronger and more frequent if the potential caring obligation is manageable and the same goes for fathers' participation in child care."[7]

Perceptions, however, are hard to change. One can readily predict Sarah Palin's response to a comprehensive child care system: "Here we go, another step in the creation of the nanny state."

Sonya Michel, in writing about the history of child care in America, traces the ongoing debate over whether mothers should stay home with their children or go to work. She documents the first Boston Infant School, founded in 1828 to relieve "mothers of a part of their domestic cares" so that they could seek employment.[8] In the late nineteenth and early twentieth centuries, philanthropists supported the creation of day nurseries, which rose up in several cities, but the movement soon lost steam when advocates of protective labor legislation concluded that "family life is sapped in its foundations when the mothers of young children work for wages."[9] Mothers working were thought to cause delinquency, and one study concluded that maternal employment could create sexual promiscuity in daughters.[10]

Michel presents the dominant view of the era through the words of Lee R. Frankel of United Hebrew Charities, speaking in 1905: "Why is it necessary for mothers to work? It is a very unfortunate thing that under modern industrial and economic conditions it may be impossible for a man to earn enough to properly support his family, and it is most deplorable that as a result it becomes necessary for the mother to go out into the world and work for those lives entrusted to her care." His alternative was "a system of pensions that shall give a widow the chance to rear her own children."[11]

The federal government became directly involved in child care during periods of national emergency. The first was during the Great Depression when so-called emergency nursery schools were created through the Works Progress Administration (WPA) in 1935.[12] During World War II, the government established child care centers to accommodate "Rosie the Riveter" factory-working mothers, who were applauded for their patriotism. A documentary of that time portrayed happy mothers at work in an armaments factory, and smiling children playing in a day care center. This was the ideal. Immediately after the war, when the soldiers came home and needed the jobs the women had held, another part of the documentary showed a child being hit by a bicycle while the mother was at work. The implication was clear—the mother should have been at home. The swings of the pendulum suggest that the debate about whether or not women should work outside the home is based on economic expediency rather than on a particular theory of child rearing. The divisions over child care infiltrated the US government as late as 1959 when the US Women's Bureau was pitted against the US Children's Bureau over the question of whether working mothers were neglecting their children, or whether mothers worked out of necessity.[13]

The debate continues in new and more subtle forms. When I was tying my sneakers in my gym's locker room one morning, I overheard a young woman, who was dressing her two toddlers, say to an older woman, "I'm sorry that I haven't gotten to the meetings. I've been too busy." The older woman replied in an approving tone, "Don't worry. You've got your priorities right, you have two beautiful boys." The message was that she was devoting her time to her children and properly so.

Many parents continue to share that view. Edward Zigler writes, "Research finds that parents strongly endorse the notion that they alone bear responsibility for the care of their children. This belief appears to have been internalized even by low-income working mothers," who said in focus groups, "Nobody asked us to have those kids."[14] "Right on" is what Palin and her supporters would say, missing the point that these "kids" are not just "their" kids, they are "our" children to the degree that they will become our future doctors, engineers, nurses, technology experts, caregivers, teachers, and taxpayers, or our future unemployed, juvenile delinquents, prisoners, and welfare recipients, depending to some extent on the quality of their early childhood development.

The Wide Scope of Child Care

The wide scope of definitions of child care presents another obstacle to creating a system. The most common form of care, aside from babysitting, is not in regulated centers but is kith and kin or informal care, defined as "provided by grandparents, aunts or uncles, and other relatives of the child, as well as by friends and neighbors."[15] While this is less expensive care, the quality is variable and the care less reliable. Another option is family care, which is care offered in a home setting with a limited number of children—usually four to six. While much family care is good, occasionally it is outright dangerous. Parents can have nightmares after reading about a fire in Texas in March 2011 that killed four children because the family caregiver had gone out shopping while leaving a pan burning on the stove. In testimony before a congressional committee, Zigler described the various qualities and kinds of family care as a "cosmic crapshoot."[16]

Greater—if uneven—quality control is found in center-based care, usually for children aged three to five. Center directors are more likely to be well trained and the children divided into groups by age.

Zigler agrees that a variety of child care options may be a necessity in America, but the result is that it tends to be "low-quality, expensive, and difficult to access." He estimates that 12 percent of child care is so poor that it is indeed "bad" for children.[17]

Child care regulation in America is a state responsibility and it varies widely. It is based almost exclusively on structural inspections and not on programs. Forty-one states require criminal background checks for caregivers, but only twenty-four states require child abuse and neglect registry checks.[18]

The major reason for wide variations in the quality of child care is that the pay is poor and there is almost no opportunity for advancement. In 2004, caregivers earned an average of $8.37 per hour. Twenty-five percent of center-based caregivers and 35 percent of home-based providers have incomes below 200 percent of the poverty line.[19] No wonder morale is low and turnover is high.

Knowing that the quality of care varies dramatically, what should parents do? The decision of whether to send a child to care depends on the quality of care and the needs of an individual child. Unfortunately, it also depends on what parents can afford. The best long-term answer is quality care for all children, no matter what their family's income. As might be expected, the percentage of earnings spent on child care goes up as income goes down. Middle- and upper-income families spend 6.3 percent of their income on child care; families between 100 and 125 percent of poverty level spend 16.3 percent.[20] That expenditure alone pushes them deeper into poverty.

Lost Opportunities

In 1935, when the Aid to Families with Dependent Children (AFDC) program provided grants intended to permit poor mothers to stay home (but not enough to keep families out of poverty), the support was much maligned as a handout to the undeserving poor. When I attended a governors' meeting in the East Room of the White House in the 1980s, President Ronald Reagan told one of his favorite stories about the "welfare queen" who bought cigarettes and gin with her welfare check and then took off in her new white Cadillac.

Attitudes like these have led to America's long and disappointing history in work/family policy, but no chapter is filled with more regrets than the demise of the Comprehensive Child Development Act of 1971. Before it was pushed into the grave by a veto from President Richard Nixon, the act was regarded as the launching pad for a more inclusive child care policy because its provisions were not tied just to welfare. Rather, the act would have allowed low-income families to qualify for free care, and others to pay according to a sliding scale.[21]

The debate over the act started out well, with a loose coalition of twenty-one advocates from the labor, education, welfare, women's rights, civil rights, and children's advocacy movements, headed by Marian Wright Edelman, director and founder of the Children's Defense Fund.[22] The bill proposing the act had the support of the Nixon administration and Congress. The House bill had 120 sponsors, one-third of whom were Republicans.[23] But support began to erode when conservatives rose to attack what they called "the invasion of the family by the federal government" and referred to the bill as the "child control act." The John Birch Society swung into action with thousands of opposing letters. The once friendly coalition began to fall apart as factions from the right and the left could not reach agreement. Nixon's veto message, written by Pat Buchanan, who later became a candidate for the Republican presidential nomination, declared in part: "For the Federal Government to plunge headlong financially into supporting child development would commit the vast moral authority of the National Government to the side of communal approaches to child rearing over the family-centered approach."[24]

What would the bill have achieved? The original legislation called for $700 million for welfare recipients and $50 million for new child care centers. It would have put us on the path to creating a widely accessible child care system. No bill of equal dimensions has been seriously considered since. "Senator Alan Cranston introduced a child care bill every year, [but] it just sat there. It was really symbolic," Ann Rosewater, who worked on the original bill representing the Children's Defense Fund, recalls.

What are the lessons learned from this "we almost got it" story? The right wing will likely once again launch a powerful campaign against any national child care policy. They will appeal not only to conservative groups, but to others who remain conflicted about whether or not their children should be cared for by others while they are at work. Not only will this concern arise for very young children in child care; it may also be raised about preschool education. In my first term as governor of Vermont in 1985 my priority was to establish public kindergarten in all schools. Opponents included those who complained about cost, but they were joined by groups who testified that parents should be the sole educators of kindergarten-age children. The good news is that soon after, kindergarten was widely accepted and the conversation had turned to the importance of "school readiness." The following year, I established a grant program for early childhood programs. Progress is possible.

Child Care: Welfare or Education?

One question that has plagued advocates of child care / early education is: is it a social welfare program or an education program? When I was deputy secretary of the US Department of Education (1993–96), I discovered that Head Start was not lodged in the Department of Education. It was housed in the Department of Health and Human Services. When I inquired whether it could be moved into the Department of Education, I was bluntly told no. No one, it seems, wanted to make a determination. We know that Head Start, the subject of many and sometimes contradictory evaluations, has been effective for low-income children and their parents. But it serves only 50 to 60 percent of eligible families, and as of this writing, Head Start is not designed to help working parents with child care because the program's hours are limited and do not coincide with normal working hours.[25] That is true for many child care programs, which is the main reason parents resort to kith and kin care as the only solution for long and unpredictable working hours.

Other government steps taken to support child care and early childhood education include:

- A Child Care Bureau established in 1995 to help low-income families (it's now called the Office of Child Care)
- The Child Care and Development Block Grant enacted in 1990, the primary source of federal child care funding
- The Child and Dependent Care Credit, a tax credit enacted in 1976 that is the second largest source of child care assistance,which is based on a sliding scale to target the most assistance to low-income families (but in reality it is ineffective for low-income families, as they have limited or no tax liabilities)
- The Temporary Assistance to Needy Families (TANF) program, established to help women reenter the workforce
- The Earned Income Tax Credit, while not targeted at child care, provides low income families additional income to help pay for it.

These unrelated pieces do not create a comprehensive child care policy that would embrace children from birth to age five. But the argument in favor of such a system has new ammunition: the capacity to do brain imaging, which shows early brain development; and the ability to do economic analysis, which demonstrates the high rate of return on early childhood investments.

This information has created a new constituency for change, which includes scientists, economists, and business leaders. These new members of the coalition have the potential to exercise great power. They speak a different language than the child advocates, who have valiantly been trying to make their voices heard year after year. The new constituencies speak with one voice on the purpose of early childhood education: school readiness leading to lifelong success. Their concern is clear: without attention to the early years, we will not have an educated, skilled workforce when we need it. Despite its broad appeal, not all child advocates agree this is the right focus. One longtime child advocate told me, "We don't want to just educate little workers."

The good news is that these new constituencies are shining the spotlight on our youngest citizens, whose needs have long been ignored. With the help of the scientific, economic, and business community, child advocates have a new opportunity to be heard.

Long-Term Benefits: Making the Business Case

Two long-term studies of innovative and comprehensive child care programs have been recently completed, revealing the impact of high-quality preschool for adults who are now forty years old. The studies show significant differences between these adults and a control group who did not attend the schools. The Carolina Abecedarian Project, conducted by the Child Development Institute of the University of North Carolina at Chapel Hill, studied low-income children born between 1972 and 1977, randomly assigning them to either a control group or a group placed in full-time child care. The child care activities focused on social, emotional, and cognitive development, with an emphasis on language. As adults, those children who had attended child care were more likely than those in the control group to delay the birth of their first child, and they were more likely to attend college. Long-term effects were also found in the HighScope Perry Preschool Study in Ypsilanti, Michigan, which started in 1962 and followed 123 African-American children who were born into poverty and stood at high risk of failing in school. The study randomly assigned the children, at ages three and four, into two groups: a control group and a program group. Children in the program group were enrolled in a high-quality preschool for two years and then entered the public schools. The follow-up study "found that adults at age 40 who had the preschool program had higher earnings, were more likely to hold a job, had committed fewer crimes, and were more likely to have graduated from high school than adults who did not have preschool."[26]

Prior testing of early education programs had focused exclusively on cognitive skills, by measuring math and English test scores. The most common finding was that children had improved scores when they left the program, but soon after they entered public school, there was a "fade out" and their test scores became no different from those of control groups. The conclusion was that these programs had no long-term impact. The new assessment of noncognitive skills, such as the ability to focus, complete a task, and work with others, tells a different story. There *is* a long-term impact that enables these children as adults to cope better with the vicissitudes of life and become more productive citizens.

The results of these studies inspired businessman Rob Dugger to become a passionate proponent of investing in early childhood. He is comfortable wearing multiple hats, as cofounder of the Partnership for America's Economic Success and chairman of the Partnership's Invest in Kids Working Group (which works with economist Heckman) and founder and managing partner of Hanover Investment Group, among other things.

He explains his interest in early education this way: "The essential facts are that the economy is like a jet plane. It consists of metal and engineering and technology and land and capital and people. The real source of power for the American economy is human capital." According to Dugger, the best information on the future quality of American capital was provided by the US Department of Defense in 2008. "They did a study of seventeen- to twenty-four-year-olds [in Mississippi] and they found that 75 percent of them could not qualify to be a US army private." (The three most common reasons for their unfitness were failure to graduate high school, criminal record, or physical unfitness, including obesity.)[27]

That information prompted Dugger to create the Partnership for America's Economic Success. "It's focused on solving the country's 'jet fuel' problem," he says. "In order for us to solve our economic and fiscal challenges we have to get off this runway and out of the storm clouds and into the clear sunlight. We've got to have people who are able and ready and educated to work."

Where do you begin? "You begin as a country and stop the 'gotcha' politics on the right and on the left and focus on what this country needs," Dugger stresses. "It needs a competitive workforce. You learn that you only have $10 when you thought you had $100. That is what our fiscal situation is teaching us. So where do you invest your $10? Where the return is the highest. [It's] highest in the first five years of life."

Societies that put kids first survive, says Dugger. "The fact is when a ship is in trouble, it's women and children in the lifeboats and the rest of us are going to the highest part of the boat to sing." But we haven't invested in our children and that is dramatically affecting the American workforce, Dugger says. "I give speeches all around the country to business groups saying, you know what I know. Your business doesn't run without people. Thirty percent of your workforce is going to retire within the next 30 years. We have three million jobs that people can't take because people are not qualified. Businesses should look at their own self-interest, building the strongest, most family supporting, most intelligent, and smartest workforce the world has ever seen."

I talked to Dugger just after he had heard Florida's Republican senator Marco Rubio say, in a speech, that the United States is the greatest country that ever existed. "I asked myself, what part of this Exceptionalism are you talking about?" he recalls. "What part of it is focused on every kid, not just rich kids? What part of it is focused on having older, richer people bear their fair share of the deficits they are creating? My feeling is that this idea of American Exceptionalism is delusional."

Dugger believes that families will move to countries and cities that support children. To me, he says, "If you want talented, family-oriented, smart people to live in Vermont, you had better provide them with a place that is absolutely committed to support the lifetime of those kids." Without that support, he says, "talented people won't move to Vermont. Vermont will not be able to take advantage because technology will allow smart people to work anywhere they want to in the world. The only thing Vermont offers that can't be gotten via the Internet is its wonderful environment. There are many places in the world that have wonderful environments that are economic dead zones because they don't support quality family life."

Dugger believes solving our problems begins with prenatal care, at the state level. "A lot of disadvantaged women and middle-class moms just got out of high school and college and they don't know how to deal with pregnancy and their mothers are living halfway across the United States in a retirement home in Arizona. Who is going to show these gals how to take care of themselves? Every one of them should be wrapped in the arms of the community and state and we should say, 'You are carrying one of the most valuable resources our state has. The society is aging. The economic value of what you are carrying in your womb is going up by the minute. It is like an Internet stock that is going straight up. We need you to eat right. We need you to sleep right. We need you not to smoke or drink. That child has to be born healthy.'"

He doesn't let fathers get away without instructions either: "You are the genetic father of that child and right now from this day forth are committed to making sure that child does absolutely great. We may not all be loving couples, but you're going to be a great dad."

That's a tough message, but at its core is a fundamental belief that the nation and its business community need to get used to responsibility and take the steps necessary to make this nation work well. "By the way," Dugger reminds us, "you don't get away with your wallets."

Does he represent the thinking of other businessmen? The Committee for Economic Development, a nonpartisan research organization comprised of business and academic leaders, has been a strong proponent of early education: "Children age three and up whose parents want them to enroll should have access to preschool programs that meet recognized standards for fostering education and school readiness along with social and physical development. . . . While states should be responsible for ensuring universal access to prekindergarten, the federal and state governments should share responsibility for financing it."[28]

In my own state, the Vermont Business Roundtable has a reputation for being more progressive and less partisan than the US Chamber of Commerce. Perhaps that is why it has been engaged in promoting early childhood education for twenty-five years. Its director, Lisa Ventriss, agrees with Dugger's perspective: "If children don't get the right start in their prenatal life, they're going to be handicapped from the day they're born," she says. To bring the business community on board, Ventriss recognizes that investment in child care and early childhood education is "not just about warm and fuzzy motivations. Business is all about outcomes, and the question is, are we getting a return on our investment in the education dollar? If a child enters kindergarten not ready to learn, as half of Vermont's kindergartners do today, then they already have a terrible handicap and they never catch up. "

The business community, she says, understands this when it's framed in a way they can relate to: "If 50 percent of your product fails, [if] it is rejected and you have to recall it and get remedial training or repairs, nobody in their right mind would tolerate that quality. So businesses understand that 100 percent of kids need to be ready to learn." She references the same report Dugger mentioned earlier, which shows that 75 percent of seventeen- to twenty-four-year-olds are unfit for military service. That report recommends that state and federal policy makers move to ensure that all of Mississippi's at-risk children have access to high-quality prekindergarten, noting that research shows the correlation between preschool education and capacity for future learning.[29] Ventriss says studies like this one have messages that resonate with the business community.

The Vermont Business Roundtable supports legislation to expand access to early childhood education for two different models, one school based and the other private, because "we also recognize that child care is an industry in Vermont," she explains. Navigating those waters between public and private care is tricky, but the goal is clear: to provide every three- and four-year-old access to a high-quality preschool should their parents want to send them to one. "Our goal is to simply expand the base of business support for public investment in early childhood. We've moved away from the 'why?' People understand. Now it's about implementation," she notes.

Implementation will require new money. Ventriss acknowledges that while business leaders have become converted to the belief that early childhood education is important, they are still reluctant to open their wallets. The call to shrink the size of the federal government and many state governments does not bode well for immediate investments in early childhood education. Most lawmakers would see these initiatives as an increase that we cannot afford, unable to see the long-term savings that will accrue.

The first step to create change is to articulate the problem. Business leaders like Bill Stritzler, chair of the Vermont Business Roundtable and managing director of the ski resort Smugglers' Notch, are firm believers that there is "a direct relationship between early childhood education and economic development." Stritzler sees the connection despite the fact that as a ski resort manager he is not dependent on highly skilled workers. "There's a lot of technology today in our industry. A lot of management skills are required. You'll find that the better educated your housekeepers are, the better job they do. Well-educated high school graduates have developed reasoning skills and organizational skills and those skills are helpful in housekeeping."

"We believe that we can't raise taxes in Vermont today, so the only way we'll be able to generate enough revenue for the state is to take care of the citizens," Stritzler continues. "If we can have a better-educated workforce we'll generate higher incomes and we'll be able to invest those revenues in the citizens who need it. I know it's a difficult sell because you have to invest today for ten or twelve years from now. When they drill for oil they don't expect to get a return on investment the year after they drill. It takes time. That's the same thing that is true for early childhood education."

The legislature, he complains, also has trouble thinking long term as well as figuring out who is in charge. "I testified before the House Commerce Committee and they told me I should be testifying before Education. When I went before Education they told me this is really an issue for Commerce. How do I figure out where I'm supposed to take this issue?" We have to find an answer to Stritzler's question if we are to succeed in making the business community an active part of the child care coalition.

Rick Davis, a Vermont developer with a passion for early childhood education, told me about a woman who was being recruited for an executive position in Middlebury, Vermont, but almost declined the job because she couldn't find child care. "She was finally able to get some child care and move to Vermont. It's a little different angle. Child care is an economic development issue. An employer can say, 'I want to bring my business to Vermont because it's the best place for kids.' What a selling point! What a marketing tool! Instead of come to Vermont because we have the best tax rate or because we have the lowest energy costs, come to Vermont because it's the best place to raise your child. It's very powerful."

Signs of Hope from the US Chamber of Commerce and Governors

The US Chamber of Commerce is on board about the relationship between early childhood education and a skilled workforce. The Institute for a Competitive Workforce, an affiliate of the US Chamber, published a report that concludes, "Early Childhood Education is not only a smart investment with positive returns, but it is the right thing to do. Our nation cannot afford the cost of inaction. In decades past, the United States proudly claimed premier international status as home of the best and brightest. Today's US rankings, however, prove that we have a long way to go to reach the top of the list again. With current early childhood education resource levels, too many kindergarteners will continue to begin school ill-prepared . . . the research is clear. Early learning opportunities for children from birth to age five have great impact on a child's development and build a strong foundation for learning and success later in life."[30]

The Chamber's report acknowledges that we're falling behind. "Other countries know what we are just figuring out. High-quality pre-K programs can have a significant short- and long-term impact on children and society."[31]

Does that mean we are building, brick by brick, a new and formidable bipartisan constituency for children from birth to age five? We can't come to that conclusion yet, because the Chamber also has supported Tea Party and other candidates who want to cut the programs that would create these "early learning opportunities." But they are talking the talk, and that is a step in the right direction of walking the walk.

The early learning message is being heard by the nation's governors. The National Governors Association has published two booklets on the subject, *Building the Foundation for Bright Futures* (2005) and, more recently, *Building Ready States*. The executive summary of *Building Ready States* begins: "With more than 60 percent of all children from birth to age five spending time in the care of someone other than their parents, publicly supported early childhood programs must provide safe, nurturing, and developmentally appropriate experiences that foster healthy growth and learning. Yet the current configuration of early childhood care and education programs and services is failing to provide too many young children with the positive early experiences needed to prepare them for success in school and life. Moreover, the children who would benefit the most from high-quality programs are the least likely to be enrolled in them."[32]

These words could have come from any early childhood education advocate. It is significant that they now issue from the National Governors Association, an organization not known to be partisan or on the cutting edge. All of its policy statements are the result of bipartisan consensus. The report lists a variety of state actions, from the formation of an early childhood cabinet in Ohio to an early learning quality initiative in Pennsylvania.

Powerful spokespersons for the business community are both sending and receiving the message: early education matters. It is the key to the recruitment of qualified young men and women to the workforce, and to the military. Our economic and national security are at stake. The research is persuasive. How do we move forward from understanding the message to translating that message into action?

Winning Bipartisan Support: Oklahoma

The most encouraging trend is that in some parts of the country, early education is being supported by conservatives, moderates, and liberals, by Democrats and Republicans. Oklahoma, a conservative state with a large Evangelical population, has had a pre-K program since 1998. It is funded by the public schools and open to all four-year-olds, not just poor children. Eighty percent of the school districts are covered. Quality is maintained because all lead teachers have a bachelor's degree and must be certified in early education. Wages are at the same level as those of public school teachers.

In Tulsa, Oklahoma, a study of the effects of a pre-K program on school readiness by Georgetown University reported significant results. "Gains for Hispanic students are especially impressive," a report on the study notes. "Specifically, Hispanic students experience a 79 percent gain in Letter-Word Identification, a 39 percent gain in Spelling, and a 54 percent gain in Applied Problems."[33]

Since 1992, some two thousand Oklahoma children, from six weeks through age four, got an early start on education through the Community Action Project of Tulsa County. Director Steven Dow tells me, "If you look at the body of literature about how you narrow the achievement gap and give people the best opportunity to improve their economic livelihoods, education is the most promising strategy." A Yale law school graduate, he acknowledges that "early education is not enough. It has to be high-quality education, and maintaining that principle of high quality is a lot of work. When we think what our customer base is, it's very young kids from at-risk environments."

I ask him how he gained support for early education from a population with conservative values. He answers, "When I first started many years ago there was the threat of the 'nanny' state, that it's not the government's job to work with young kids. I think as a result of the very compelling science that's out now, and the better recognition by policy makers of the value of early childhood education, I am less concerned. We get support from churches. We've seen support from faith-based communities in our work. The Evangelical movement has a philosophy that says it's our duty that people are given 'their God-given potential,'" he explains. He stresses that it's not effective to spend more money later to address gaps caused by the lack of child-development programs. "We make sure the gaps don't develop in the first place."

The Tulsa program was designed as a model that could scale up nationally. At present, it is high on quality but low on enabling parents to work. "The reality is that it is difficult to do both simultaneously," notes Dow. "Low-wage workers have work schedules that differ dramatically from our schedules and from day to day. This week you work seven to two, then tomorrow from six to midnight. We're less a work support system and much more of an intervention that's important for children."

Could we have good child care that also meets the needs of working parents? The Nordic countries provide quality child care that is available for parents with fluctuating work hours. Dow acknowledges that this could happen here, too, if we were willing to fund it. "I frankly am not convinced that we have the public will," he says. "It doesn't feel like we're in a place in this country's history where we think that all of the kids in the community are deserving and where we think the playing field should be level." That's the sad part. A few childcare centers have begun to provide longer hours to meet the fluctuating schedules of working parents. It is too early to know whether this pattern will remain the exception or become the rule, but the need for longer hours is clear. Fortunately, some foundations have the vision to pave the way, but it is only a beginning.

Funding from Philanthropies

The Tulsa project relies heavily on a major philanthropist, George Kaiser, who made his fortune in oil, gas, and banking and is a devotee of early education. The program does not receive state funding, but legislators from both sides of the aisle have steadily increased the budget for pre-K education.

Policy makers, despite hard economic times, are increasingly convinced that these early investments pay off. According to the Pew Center on the States, Pennsylvania's pre-K programs have decreased the rate of special education by nearly 50 percent through second grade, reduced grade repetition by 33 percent through eighth grade, and lowered the incidence of juvenile arrests by 32 percent.[34]

Even if these figures turn out to be overly optimistic, these programs meet their expected goal of enabling children to be ready for kindergarten and first grade. States are beginning to see this as a good investment. Governor Chris Christie of New Jersey, who first described early childhood education as babysitting, has become a convert to the cause, exempting some, but not all, programs from severe budget cuts. The state legislature had voted that all at-risk children are entitled to preschool. "This was not funded," laments Deborah Howlett, president of the New Jersey Policy Perspective, a nonpartisan think tank.

New Jersey's education funding system, mandated by a court decision, gives more funding to poor districts than others to enroll four-year-olds in preschool. Under pressure from the budget crisis, legislation is pending to transfer some of these funds to the suburban districts, which resent that they do not not receive an equal share. This tension provides a hint that the long-term view that pre-school, particularly for poor children, will benefit everyone is not yet fully accepted. Even governors who have accepted the importance of early education are having a hard time finding the money.

In Illinois, the down payment has been made by philanthropic foundations, including the Ounce of Prevention Fund, the First Five Years Fund, and Illinois Action for Children, which have funded several child advocacy associations. State senator Jeff Schoenberg is an advisor to the J. B. and M. K. Pritzker Family Foundation. He explains: "Our task was to create a small cadre of champions on both sides of the aisle in the Illinois legislature. One of the lawmakers asked to be a champion was Barack Obama. The group succeeded in setting aside a fixed percentage of the budget for early childhood education. We could provide lawmakers with proof about how these programs make a difference. Research has to be readily available to influence the public policy debate."

Harriet Dichter, national director of the First Five Years Fund, notes that "some of our greatest supporters are Republicans. The science has become so compelling that it creates the public will," she says. Schoenberg makes the same point: "The argument that investing in early learning provides a greater return is irrefutable. Foundations play a unique role in funding innovation, but ultimately the public sector is the only one that brings things to scale," he acknowledges.

Foundation-sponsored programs provide the evidence that early childhood is the best time in a child's life not only to close the achievement gap but to prevent the gap from occurring in the first place. Only federal and state governments have the ability to create a child care and early education system that will not be limited to the lucky few, but will be available for all. New findings in science and economics are buttressing the argument to build a strong case for public investment.

What Has Changed?
Our Understanding of Neurology and Economics

Recent scientific studies are summed up in a report by the National Scientific Council on the Developing Child: "When we fail to provide children with what they need to build a strong foundation for healthy and productive lives, we put our future prosperity and security at risk. Two recent developments have stimulated growing public discussion about the right balance between individual and shared responsibility for that strong foundation. The first is the explosion of research in neurobiology that clarifies the extent to which the interaction between genetics and early experience literally shapes brain architecture. The second is the increasingly recognized need for a highly skilled workforce . . ."[35]

Economic analysis by James Heckman has changed the way we measure our investment in early childhood. In an article in *The American*, he reports: "Investing in the youngest among us yields rates of return that are comparable to the high return on stocks over the long run."[36] When I ask Heckman what got him interested in this subject, he simply replies: "I am an economist," without acknowledging that he was the first economist to look at the rate of return for early education investments. He became concerned when he saw that we were not developing the right skills for the labor force. Proportionately, more youth are graduating from college than ever before, but they are graduating from high school at a lower rate than forty years ago. "Compared to 50 years ago," he writes, "relatively more American children are being born into disadvantaged families where investments in children are smaller than in advantaged families."[37] Heckman came to believe in early education after he had looked at job training and literacy programs for adults and found that the results were not as good as those of investments in early childhood. He compares education to a tree, discovering that "rapid growth is in the early years. That leads to the question, 'when is the optimal time of investment?' So the logic of economics leads to the technology of skill formation. It's a logic that shows how one stage of life feeds into another and feeds into the next and the next. If children develop a strong base early in life, you increase the ability of children to grow up on their own and benefit from school and from American society. The benefit is much higher for somebody who gets a very strong base," he explains.

Simply put, when you have the ability to learn, you just keep on learning. Children engaged early on are also less likely to require special education. But how exactly do you determine a rate of return? "We've done some very careful cost-benefit studies. For instance there are different ways to calculate the benefit of reduced crime," he explains. "Crime costs taxpayers $1 trillion a year, so any savings would be significant. We come up with rates of return [in early education] in the order of 6 to 10 percent a year, depending on the assumptions."

One of the major contributions of Heckman's research was quantifying what have come to be known as soft or noncognitive skills. He cites one study that tracked children through adulthood. "Children . . . in the control group were more or less the same at age ten. There was a big difference at the age of five or six, but it died out. So they were not smarter by IQ levels but they were achieving more. They're doing a lot more through life," he told me.

This startling difference had not shown up in earlier studies, which didn't track adult outcomes. The ability to complete a task and to master social skills could be considered more important than test scores. Not only do they determine a child's life course, but they are harder to learn after a certain point. It goes back to the old adage: prevention is more effective and less costly than remediation, every time.

Doug Staiger, the John French Professor of Economics at Dartmouth College, agrees with Heckman's conclusions. "There are two sets of skills that children are learning. Interventions affect both, but we measure only one, which is the academic side. But in fact a good teacher is affecting the noncognitive skills such as being on time, learning to work with others, and learning to concentrate and delay gratification. What's being tested is a narrow slice of knowledge. If we gave you a broader test that covered what you would need to know to be successful in life, you would be ahead."

Heckman illustrates the importance of noncognitive skills by describing his research on the GED (General Educational Development) tests, which may be taken by those who have not received a high school diploma to earn a certificate equivalent to a diploma. He found that the GED students did just as well as ordinary high school graduates on academic tests. "What's happening is that they're just as smart but what they are missing is these noncognitive skills. You have a whole group of people (one in seven high school students) who start out as normal high school [students] but are not able to do anything. They drop out of school, they drop out of the military, so virtually everything they attempt, whether it's marriage, or the military, or school, or staying on a job, they almost always quit. They lack a lot of these noncognitive social and emotional skills," he says.

He does not close the door on later intervention but believes that if you wait until young people "are fifteen, sixteen, or seventeen, the strategy you want to target is much more on noncognitive motivational systems than trying to raise IQ."

I ask him, knowing all this, what would you recommend for a state or national policy? "I think of it as a private and public effort. There really is a strong case that the private sector can support this," Heckman answers. He expresses some caution about the role of government. "There is a fear that many have about intruding into the lives of children. I think what's important is that the program be culturally sensitive and adaptive." He notes that groups like the Mormons and Hasidic Jews have very strong feelings about raising their children; the government has to work with these groups.

The economic case for early childhood education may overcome some of the concerns of parents who fear the hand of government intruding in their lives. One of the main speakers at the Vermont Business Roundtable summit in 2010, headlined "Early Childhood Investments," was Rob Grunewald, associate economist at the Federal Reserve Bank of Minneapolis. His talk was replete with slides explaining brain development and the effects of the Perry Preschool. This is news, I said to myself, when an economist from the Federal Reserve Bank promotes early childhood education with the zeal of a kindergarten teacher.

The Heckman Equation

How do we spread the net of knowledge wider and motivate policy makers to make substantial investments in early childhood education? That is the job undertaken by Rich Neimand and Peggy Allen (recently replaced by Sarah Hobgood), who are being funded by a group of philanthropists to translate Heckman's work into messages that can be understood by a variety of audiences. Neimand points to a website called the Heckman Equation, which makes the economic theory simple:

+ **INVEST:** Invest in educational and developmental resources for disadvantaged families to provide equal access to successful early human development.

+ **DEVELOP:** Nurture early development of cognitive and social skills in children from birth to age five.

+ **SUSTAIN:** Sustain early development with effective education through to adulthood.

= **GAIN:** Gain a more capable, productive and valuable workforce that pays dividends to America for generations to come.[38]

"We don't deal directly with the elected officials. We speak to the policy makers, who speak to the elected officials," Neimand explains. Their most persuasive argument? "We find that everyone believes a child deserves early childhood education, but as soon as you ask them to take out their wallet, they balk." People generally understand the rate-of-return argument, but that doesn't override other cultural attitudes. "People feel the best kind of early childhood education is for one of the parents to stay home with the child, which we know in this day and age is not feasible for most families. On top of that, they ask why [they] should give more money to disadvantaged families to have more children when [those families] can't really take care of them."

Neimand answers that question this way: "By advantaging the disadvantaged you advantage everyone. The best economic argument is that if you maximize your tax dollars that go into early education, you'll be paying a lot less for the cost of remediation down the line. We frame it as an opportunity. The end is really a more productive and sociable adult. That starts to make sense to people. When you talk about the disadvantaged child, that's a real turn-off to middle-class voters. When you focus on the benefits to the wider society—health, education, and prosperity—these are the issues voters care about."

Neimand is not an economist or an educator. He's a social marketer: "I don't care how I sell something as long as it gets sold." He maintains a passion for social justice but believes people no longer have an understanding of the social contract. "People ask, what's in it for me? How much does it cost? The answer better be that there's a lot in it for you, and it doesn't cost as much as you get in return."

"What's in it for me?" is a question often asked by funders, both public and private. In my first term as governor of Vermont in 1985 I was determined to make a good case for on-site child care centers in the workplace. The benefits would be clear: lower turnover rates, less absenteeism, and greater productivity. I invited fifty employers to hear Arnold Hiatt, CEO of the Stride Rite shoe company, explain the business case for his child care center at the Lexington, Massachusetts, headquarters. The center was open to both his workers and members of the community. Many CEOs at the conference expressed interest. I believed this would be the beginning of a growing national trend. Years later, I discovered that the movement toward on-site child care turned out to be a blip on the screen rather than a trend line. There were exceptions, like the Hewlett-Packard factory I visited in California when I was deputy secretary of the US Department of Education. I had a chance to chat with mothers and fathers there, who used their lunch hour to play with their children in the on-site child care center. Management was enthusiastic and the employees were delighted that they could drop in on their kids during the workday. But in the mid 90's this happy arrangement was an anomaly, not the norm.

More recently I spoke with Eliza Cain, the young co-owner of the Red Hen Baking Company in Vermont, who was eager to provide child care benefits for her employees but found that financially she couldn't make it work. The investment was too high and the answer to "what's in it for me?" was too unclear. She is now exploring easier alternatives, such as providing child care benefits in a cafeteria-style benefit program, and a child care referral system. An increasing number of employers are following that pattern. On-site child care works well for those who use it, but it requires an initial and ongoing financial outlay and the benefits accrue only to a small number of employees for a limited time period, which makes the program more difficult to justify.

"What's in it for me?" is not necessarily a selfish question. Any family/work program initiated by business leaders has to be a win–win situation, whether it's early childhood education investment, workplace flexibility, paid sick days, or paid family leave. The challenge is to make the benefits to both parties explicit and measurable.

An Unexpected Leader: The Department of Defense

There is one employer who could be a model for the country: he runs the largest and most comprehensive child care program in the United States, serving 300,000 children from six weeks to the age of twelve. He is the secretary of the US Department of Defense. How did the military get into the child care business? Because it had to, in the interest of national security. The Military Child Care Act of 1989 was adopted after the country repealed the draft and opted for a volunteer army in the late 1970s. "The military was forced to deal with how are we going to recruit people and make our work in the military attractive," explains Linda Smith, formerly in charge of family policy with the Defense Department and now executive director of the National Association of Child Care Resource and Referral Agencies. With that transition from the draft to a volunteer military, the Defense Department was forced to work to attract people to serve in the armed forces—and these new recruits were more likely to be married, to have children, and to have spouses who worked. The same trend of a growing female workforce affected the military. Suddenly child care was an issue.

"Essentially child care became not just a program for people who might want to go shopping or attend an Officer's Club meeting, but for women who are . . . on active duty [or] who are pregnant and who, after their pregnancy, have to go back to work. So child care became more of a workforce support than a social support program," Smith explains.

When the bill was being considered, an Army official testified before Congress: "Like our counterparts in the corporate world, we have found that child care is a major force issue. Lack of availability of quality child care impacts on productivity and is an increasing factor in work absenteeism and tardiness."[39]

A report from the House Armed Services Committee stated, "Child care is an important readiness and retention issue for military families: readiness because single parents and dual service couples must have access to affordable and quality child care if they are to perform their jobs . . . ; retention because family dissatisfaction with military life—and particularly the inability of many spouses to establish careers or obtain suitable employment—is a primary reason trained military personnel leave the service."[40]

The result is that the military child care system—and it is a *system*—is the gold standard of quality child care in America.[41]

That was not the case in 1982, when a GAO report found that 70 percent of the military's child care centers did not meet fire and safety codes. "At one installation, a child care center housed in old barracks adjacent to stables suffered from pest control problems and a sinking kitchen floor."[42] At the Presidio Army base in San Francisco, allegations of workers sexually abusing children alerted then Congresswoman Barbara Boxer to demand hearings.

How did the military raise the quality of child care to such a high level?

At present 98 percent of their centers are nationally accredited, compared to 8 percent on the civilian side. The focus is on unannounced inspections four times a year. To put that in perspective, Smith explains, in California "they require inspections for child care centers once every five years and homes every seven years. That's not good enough."

The Department of Defense developed a set of standards that govern staff/child ratios, staff training and qualifications, child abuse prevention procedures, background checks, funding, parent participation, and health and sanitation. Its program holds that the most important key to high-quality child care rests with the wages, benefits, and training of the staff. Wages are $12 an hour, compared to the minimum wage offered in many nonmilitary child care venues, and staff has the full range of benefits of other military personnel. The management staff is required to have a bachelor's degree or equivalent.

This solves a problem that plagues civilian centers: staff turnover, which can run as high as 300 percent annually. That lack of continuity for young children almost certainly dictates that the quality of care will be bad. In the military system, child care providers have the opportunity to build a career based on a ladder that coincides with their training and education. Child care is available to active-duty and reserve military personnel, DOD civilian personnel, injured service members, surviving spouses, those acting *in loco parentis* for military personnel, and DOD contractors. The average weekly fee paid by parents in a military center in 2010 was $102 per child per week. Fees range from $44 per week for low-income families to $137, significantly lower than in civilian centers.[43]

The military has solved the quality problem. Unlike funding for subsidized child care in the domestic budget, the military budget continues to include strong, adequate funding for quality, affordable, and accessible child care. It's not hard to see why. "DOD considers child care a workforce issue, as it impacts the effectiveness and readiness of the force," says Barbara Thompson, director of the Office of Family Policy/Children and Youth in the Office of the Secretary of Defense.

The purpose of investing tax dollars in an excellent child care system is clear to the Defense Department. Child care is not a "feel good" issue. It's a tough national security issue. If men and women cannot find child care options in the military, they cannot enlist, or, once enlisted, they will not stay. But the motivation for the military's investment goes deeper than attracting and retaining parents. When we recall that today 75 percent of young people are considered unfit for military service, we can understand why DOD took notice. While not every potential recruit's rejection from the military may be attributed to a poor education, no doubt a high percentage of those "failures" began before the age of six, when they entered school unready to learn. The lack of a child care system for the civilian population is as great a threat to our national security as it is to our economic prosperity. In the civilian population the problem is more diffuse; it is not possible to issue commands about salaries, training, and standards. Adequate funding is much harder to obtain. A call to action to the civilian population is not the same as a call to arms in the name of national defense.

Our challenge is to issue that same clarion call for the education of young children everywhere, whether their parents wear a uniform or not. How do we achieve that? In *Be All We Can Be*, a report from the National Women's Law Center on the military's child care system and lessons that can be drawn from it, we find three lessons highlighted:

> Lesson #1: Do not be daunted by the task: it is possible to take a woefully inadequate child care system and dramatically improve it.
>
> Lesson #2: Recognize and acknowledge the seriousness of the child care problem and the consequences of inaction.
>
> Lesson #3: Improve quality by establishing and enforcing comprehensive standards, assisting providers in becoming accredited, and enhancing provider compensation and training.[44]

The military, which accredits private child care programs before it provides referrals to them, has leverage to improve quality in the private sector. "Military families cannot get assistance [for child care] without [the program] passing an inspection. In California," Linda Smith explains, "I wrote to every single legislator and the governor and said, 'Look, military families in your state are not going to get any help with child care because we're not getting these programs to pass inspection.' Unlike in the days of Vietnam, people today want to support military families."

The most difficult part of the list of lessons learned is that high quality requires additional funding. Inspections conducted four times a year cost more than one inspection every five years. Paying caregivers according to an ascending wage scale that parallels their education is more expensive than paying the minimum wage. And adequately subsidizing parents to a degree that will make child care affordable requires a greater outlay of tax dollars. The federal government and state governments provide some funding now, through various grants and programs, in a scattershot way. The problem is twofold: there is no continuum of services, and only a fraction of the families who could benefit from quality child care are able to find and pay for it. Those problems have become severely aggravated during the ongoing recession.

Assuming that there is agreement on improving quality, affordability, and accessibility, how could we achieve consensus on investing a greater percentage of our tax dollars into child care and early childhood education? In the 2011 budget battle, which threatened a government shutdown, large budget cuts were proposed (and to a lesser degree enacted) to programs like Head Start, Women, Infants, and Children (WIC) nutrition programs, TANF, and Community Development Block Grants. Why are programs for children still the most vulnerable part of the budget? The easy answer is that children don't vote. Neither do they contribute to political campaigns. The more complex answer goes back to the question of whether the government should be involved in child care and early childhood education in the first place.

Fear of a growing and dangerous federal deficit and concern about state deficits is fueling dramatic domestic budget cuts. That's the bad news for American families. There is a small glimmer of good news. Policy makers are beginning to question budget priorities. Could we get more in return for our tax dollar if we invested more heavily in early education? Unexpected allies sometimes show up in strange places. I watched a segment of *PBS NewsHour* the evening of April 7, 2011, and saw two men who are not in the habit of sitting side by side: Benjamin Todd Jealous, president and CEO of the NAACP, and Grover Norquist, head of Americans for Tax Reform and and author of *Leave Us Alone: Getting the Government's Hands Off Our Money,*

Our Guns, Our Lives. They concurred with a report that had been recently published by the NAACP, *Misplaced Priorities: Over Incarcerate, Under Educate*. The report tracks the steady shift of state funds away from education and toward the criminal justice system. The report offers recommendations that will help policy makers in the states downsize prison populations and shift the savings to education budgets.

When a bona fide tax-cutting conservative like Grover Norquist finds himself on the same side as the NAACP, it is a sure sign that a new conversation has begun. Unfortunately this story does not have a happy ending. The same Grover Norquist exacted a no-new-taxes pledge from 270 members of Congress that contributed to the failure to reach an agreement by the so-called Super Committee (Joint Congressional Committee on Deficit Reduction), charged with finding a long-term solution to balance the budget. All but one of the candidates for the Republican nomination for President have signed on as well.

Despite the grim mood of the country in the winter of 2011–2012, we cannot be daunted by setbacks. Success today is defined by avoiding budget cuts, not by establishing new programs even if they would have a proven high rate of return. Our charge is to continue to develop a child care system that is as good as that provided to military families. All Americans deserve to have access to affordable, accessible, quality care for their children. What the military invests for national security, the nation must invest for economic security.

CHAPTER 8

New Family Portraits

The 1950s portrait of the ideal family has almost become a museum piece: Mom standing by the kitchen counter wearing an apron; Dad sitting in an easy chair, wearing a shirt and tie; their two children—the boy always somewhat older and taller than the girl—playing quietly on the rug in front of the fireplace. Why, I wonder, is Dad always reading the newspaper and Mom incessantly stirring batter in a bowl?

That's the way it *was*, and that's the way it *is* for 21 percent of American families today, only Mom is more likely to be dressed for yoga than for the kitchen and Dad is no longer wearing a tie.[1] However, in 79 percent of American families, both Mom and Dad are getting the children off to school before each rushes off to work.[2] Surprisingly, working families today—despite their guilt feelings about not spending enough time with their children—actually spend more time with them than their parents did. Two economists from the University of California, San Diego, reported that child care time by parents was about 12 hours a week before 1995. "By 2007, that number had risen to 21.2 hours a week for college-educated women and 15.9 hours for those with less education."[3]

All parents, regardless of income, want the best for their children. Most parents question, from time to time, whether they are good parents, and both Mom and Dad are likely to be stressed, depressed, or both. Many families swing back and forth between the two models, depending on the time in their lives, whether they have an opportunity to work full- or part-time, their financial resources, their personal preferences, and cultural expectations.

How Did My Family Manage?

When I am asked how I managed to have a political career and raise four children with my then husband, I don't have a clear answer. The most accurate reply is that I muddled my way through, but since I tell women not to berate themselves, I will answer that I did it in stages. When I got married at the age of twenty-five, considered "old" in 1959, I believed I could easily have a career in journalism and have a family. Marriage would be no substitute for my ambition. My goals were influenced by witnessing my mother's life. She became a widow when I was two and a half and my brother was seven. She brought us to the United States from Switzerland at the onset of World War II because she feared that, as a Jewish family, our lives were in danger. It seemed likely that Hitler, who had occupied the countries surrounding Switzerland, would march over the Alps and take our country over too. We arrived at the port of New York City on June 15, 1940, met by my father's German cousins who had preceded us, and we found our first apartment in Forest Hills, New York. Our family of three never experienced poverty, but neither was income security guaranteed. I felt my mother's anxiety when I saw her struggle with different odd jobs. A lack of formal education had not prepared her for widowhood.

When I was ten I was asked to give up my room so we could take in a boarder; my mother babysat briefly for a psychiatrist's twins who were never allowed to cry; she spent evenings sewing sequins on hat pins, paid by the piece; and later she had more success as an Avon lady—all to make ends meet. No wonder that I wanted to prepare for self-sufficiency. I also wanted to become a wife and mother. Later I attributed my maternal yearnings to the many moving medieval Madonna and Child masterpieces I had lingered over in museums and cathedrals while traveling in Europe. Baby Jesus was irresistible.

When I met my first husband, I was a newspaper reporter in Burlington, Vermont, my first job after having graduated from the Columbia School of Journalism in 1957. Arthur had just started his position as an instructor and physician at the University of Vermont Medical School. We never discussed how we would manage our careers and raise a family. We assumed that he would be the breadwinner and my journalism career would fit into the side pockets of his life. I believed it would work out, but I had no role models to guide me. I had known of one physician's wife who was also a doctor and who continued to work after the birth of her two sons. I was eager to learn how she had done it.

I knew from the start what I did *not* want, and that was to be like a typical 1960s doctor's wife I had met at teas for the Woman's Auxiliary to the American Medical Association, who had sacrificed her career to "put her husband through medical school" and then, for her reward, settled into full-time motherhood. A woman's identity was closely tied to her husband's in those days. Protocol demanded that every envelope be properly addressed to Dr. and Mrs. Arthur Kunin. I, like most of the women of my generation, had no first name. When my daughter Julia was born in 1961 I dropped all ambivalence about family and work and reveled in the miracle of motherhood. I saw myself as the original earth mother when she nursed at my breast; I was now part of the Great Chain of Being. I was happy and determined to take total responsibility for her care.

When did my attention wander off from motherhood and back to thoughts of a career? On my thirtieth birthday, my friend Terry and I were sitting at an outdoor café in Cambridge, Massachusetts, rocking our navy blue English baby carriages back and forth in rhythm. We lived in Cambridge, where my husband was pursuing post-doctoral research at Harvard and I had recently given birth to our second child, Peter. I said to Terry, "My God, I'm thirty. What's going to become of my life?" (This was the hippy era, when the mantra was "Don't trust anyone over thirty.") If I could have foreseen that one day I would become governor of Vermont, I would have enjoyed my cappuccino considerably more. Instead I decided to take an art history course at Radcliffe College and become an art historian. But before I could pursue that route, we moved back to Vermont for my husband's job. That made it impossible to get a graduate degree in art history. My choices were limited by my husband's decisions, a situation shared by many women.

What Did You Do Before? "Nothing."

When I spoke at an annual lunch of the League of Women Voters of Palm Beach County in 2011, I was impressed by the competence of their president, who appeared to be of retirement age. She had successfully increased League membership, which was a contrast to the declining membership in most of the country.

I asked out of curiosity, "What did you do before?"

She immediately responded, "Nothing."

When she saw my amazed look, she explained. Her husband's job had forced the family to move every two years. She raised two children but could not develop her career; instead, she used her skills to become a conscientious volunteer and contributed greatly to whatever community she found herself in. Nothing?

"Nothing" was how I had felt on my thirtieth birthday. I had tried to find part-time work. For a short time I covered the Boston Common Garage trials (concerning larceny and conspiracy in the construction of a parking garage under Boston Common) for the Associated Press, but one day when I came home and changed Peter's diaper, I discovered safety-pin pricks on his buttocks. I glared accusingly at the babysitter, fired her, and quit my job. When we moved back to Vermont, I became pregnant with our third child, Adam, and enrolled in a master's degree program in English literature with the intent to teach. Three months after the birth of our fourth child, I accepted my first job offer and became a part-time instructor in freshman English at Trinity College, in Burlington, Vermont. My schedule was three classes of freshman English, with fifty students in each class. I stayed up past midnight to correct papers and rushed home between classes to nurse the baby, who refused to take a bottle. (This was before nursing mothers had breast pumps that actually worked.) It was the most exhausting job I ever had. Still, as a mother reentering the world of work, I was grateful that someone would hire me.

Gradually, my husband took on more responsibility for the children and became adept at preparing his favorite meal: stay-a-bed stew. It could be placed in the oven in the morning, left to sit there all day at a low temperature, and be ready to eat at night. It was clear to both of us, however, that my work life was secondary to his. How would I categorize our work/life arrangement? We started out as a traditional 1960s family, if we don't count the subversive career thoughts I harbored. I suspect that my husband had some sense of guilt, knowing that his career had sidetracked mine. That is one reason why, when I first got involved in running for office, he was highly supportive. In retrospect, I do not blame him for my delayed development because I was usually a willing accomplice. I came of age as a mother and a politician in a transitional time, when the women's movement was beginning to illuminate a new world in front of our eyes. Some women my age looked the other way. I was transfixed. The women's movement gave me permission to change my timetable for reentry into the adult world. The usual schedule for mothers was that they would wait until their children were fully grown and safely ensconced in college. The environmental movement and the women's movement had both drawn me in with a passion and given me a cause. Instead of waiting, I ran for a seat in the Vermont legislature when my children were three, six, eight, and ten years old and served for three terms, before being elected lieutenant governor and then governor.

My husband and I eased our way into becoming a two-wage-earner family as our children grew older and more independent. My six years as a state legislator were the equivalent of a part-time job. Vermont has a citizen legislature, which means it is in session four days a week, about five or six months a year. I often cooked dinner the night before, but I could usually eat it with my family the next night, possible only because of the forty-five-minute commute from the capitol to my home. When I was elected lieutenant governor my schedule became more crowded but was still flexible. The position is considered to be part-time. The only constitutional requirement is to preside over the senate and become acting governor when the governor left the state, or succeed him if he died. I used the time to respond to most speaking invitations around the state and prepare for the next step. The leap from lieutenant governor to governor was high. Being governor is a 24/7 job, no matter how big or small the state. By then our family had changed: three of our children were in college and one was in high school. Still, I experienced conflicts between my official role as governor and my other role as mother and wife.

In the early 1990s, when I was writing my first book, *Living a Political Life*, a memoir, the first draft had so many passages about guilt that my editor took large chunks out. Most distressing to me is that my children have almost no memory of the chocolate chip cookies I baked, the macaroni and cheese I cooked, or the hours on the playground I spent shoveling sand—for eleven years between 1961 and 1972.

The answer to the question of "How did you do it?" is that there is no simple single answer. Each person walks through the labyrinth at a different pace, and even in a different direction, before she or he comes out the other side. I know that if my husband had not been the primary wage earner and supported my ambitions I would not have had the flexibility or finances to launch and sustain a sixteen-year political career. I had one other advantage not often discussed: a high-quality nursery school (what would now be called a preschool), called Jill's School, that my youngest son Daniel loved to attend. Then there was Mabel Fisher who babysat, and later Shirley Labelle whose specialties were apple pie and baked potatoes. Her real talent was that she greeted my children when they came home from school. Without the help of these women, I would have been still standing by the stove stirring batter.

Fitting the Pieces Together: A Personal Process

What's the conclusion? Fitting the puzzle pieces of work and family together into a neat picture was and continues to be a personal process that changes over time and depends on a supportive infrastructure. Policies like paid family leave, quality child care, and workplace flexibility are the support beams for families who must or want to have time for both their work and their families. Others choose not to combine work and family because they prefer to be the sole caregivers for their children for a certain number of years, or they are forced into the stay-at-home mom role because they can't find a job with flexibility or are unable to find affordable child care. Many families move back and forth between three family photographs: the Mom and Dad two wage earner family frame, the Mom single wage earner family frame, and the Dad single wage earner family frame. Some families live together. Some, through divorce or separation, live apart, needing to spread incomes across two households. Still others have formed a far different family portrait, with two moms or two dads. We have begun to understand that what matters most is not the configuration; it is the amount of love and support that each family can give to everyone in the photograph.

Equally Shared Parenting

There is an alternative for two-parent families. It is one that does not force parents to choose between home and work. It is less dependent on policies set by others and more reliant on what parents decide to do for themselves. This configuration is both old and new. Some call it shared-care parenting; others call it fifty/fifty parenting. It's old because it's what farm families used to do; it's what small shopkeepers did when both husband and wife minded the store and the children played in the back. I have a memory of walking into a shoe repair shop in Switzerland, when my husband had a sabbatical year in Bern. The shoemakers, husband and wife, worked cheerfully side by side. It seemed ideal.

In the new version of this old model, Mom and Dad share equal responsibility for both caregiving and wage earning. They want, above all, an egalitarian marriage. Marc and Amy Vachon, authors of *Equally Shared Parenting*, live by the philosophy "that gender should not determine the division of labor at home," they explained to journalist Lisa Belkin, who profiled them for *New York Times Magazine*.[4] A similar trend is described by Kristin Maschka in *This Is Not How I Thought It Would Be*. She describes a journey that started out with the good intention of achieving equal work and caring responsibilities with her husband but collapsed after they had a child and finally was successfully retrieved when Kristin started her own business.

Is equally shared parenting a trend or an aberration? Jessica DeGroot, founder of the Third Path Institute, calls these couples "shared-care families." She believes couples can negotiate a path somewhere in between the single-wage-earner family and the dual-wage-earning family. She describes the Third Path dream: "that men and women, from all different walks of life, and for reasons that span the life cycle, will be able to succeed at work while also creating significant time for their lives outside of work." She moved into this new terrain because "we felt strongly that we didn't want to use a lot of outside child care, but we also both liked working, so we really organized our lives around those values. We both redesigned our work so that we would have time for the kids."

Many, but not all, shared-care families are self-employed, Jessica says, which gives them control over their own schedules. And after ten years of promoting her Third Path, DeGroot believes progress has been made. "Even five years ago, fathers were bumbling fools or distant and uninvolved. You now see competent men doing things with their kids."

The primary benefit of this arrangement is parents who are "thoughtful to keep the time and energy for the needs of the family," DeGroot says. "We do need to create families that have a resiliency around money, and that comes from having both people capable of earning money. Resiliency comes because shared-care families are thoughtful about spending. They see that time is as valuable as money."

The main motivation for equally shared parenting or fifty/fifty couples is that they have made the personal choice "not to do day care," explains Martine Gulick, my grandson's French teacher. "We always have been able to work it out, me working two or three days a week, and my husband being home the other days." Her husband is an airline pilot with flexible hours. "He has no problem staying home with the kids while I go to work. I am fortunate that he has a job that affords flexibility. I was able to stay home with the kids when they were very little. I think we also made a conscious decision to go for quality of life over maximizing our earning potential."

Another difference, usually less talked about, is that in many households mothers *have* to do everything because they are single parents. There's been a dramatic increase in the number of single parents; it has more than doubled since 1975, rising from 16 percent to 41 percent.[5] The trend for African-American families is more acute; 67 percent of African-American babies were born to single mothers in 2009.[6] (Though many of these mothers may have live-in boyfriends, there are no available studies about how much these men contribute to caregiving and housekeeping.)

I ask DeGroot whether the recession has forced families to work longer hours, not less, depriving them even more of family time. She responds that the next ten years isn't about changing the naysayers, but about being a resource for those who want to share work and parenting life. This is not, she says, a "win–lose situation. It's the future and the answer."

Feminists and Gender Equality

Feminists were the first to call for equality between the sexes, so that *she* does not always change diapers, cook dinner, and do the dishes while *he* reads the newspaper. It was a battle between the sexes, not a truce. In *Gender Equality*, authors Janet Gornick and Marcia Meyers note, "Feminists argue that women will not and cannot achieve parity with men as long as they shoulder unequal responsibilities for unpaid care work. . . . They suggest that the interests of men, women and children are essentially in conflict: children can have more time with their parents only if women reduce their employment commitments and career prospects; women and men can achieve greater equality in their employment only by reducing their time spent caring for their children."[7]

Equally shared parenting relies on a joint recognition that gender roles for women and men must change to achieve equality. It is not a harangue by either party "to do more." It goes one step further: both parents make a commitment to a new arrangement, not only because one party does not want to have total responsibility for caregiving or supporting the family, but because each wants to share the joys and rewards of both roles.

Gornick and Meyers examine the gender question through a different lens: "The most pressing conflicts of interest arise not between men and women, nor between parents and children, but between the needs of contemporary and current divisions of labor, workplace practices, and social policies. To resolve these conflicts we do not need to choose sides, but rather to focus our attention on an end vision of what an earning, caring, egalitarian society that promotes the well-being of children might look like."[8] Women's equality is a means to an end, not an end in itself. "Two devoted parents who value their work, who are equally engaged in family life, who nurture and inspire their children to do the same is what getting to 50/50 is all about," write Sharon Meers and Joanna Strober in *Getting to 50/50*, a book whose subtitle says it all: *How Working Couples Can Have It All by Sharing It All, and Why It's Great for Your Marriage, Your Career, Your Kids . . . and You.*

Division of Labor

Shared-care parenting advocates Marc and Amy Vachon see themselves as "equals and peers," writes Lisa Belkin. "They would work equal hours, spend equal time with their children, take equal responsibility for their home. Neither would be the keeper of the mental to-do lists; neither of their careers would take precedence. Both would be equally likely to plan a birthday party or know that the car needs oil or miss work for a sick child or remember (without prompting) to stop at the store for diapers or milk."[9]

How do their divisions of labor differ from today's practices? The average stay-at-home wife does thirty-eight hours of housework a week, while the average husband does twelve. When both are working, she does twenty-eight hours of housework and he puts in sixteen. Clearly, far from equal.[10]

Lesbian couples are more successful at sharing. While "straight parents get into the blame game about who is shirking responsibility, lesbian moms bicker about not getting enough time with the kids," psychologist Nanette Gartrell explained to Belkin.[11]

There are no traditional roles for lesbian and gay couples, so they start with a blank slate. Most heterosexual couples have to keep an eraser in hand to rub away stereotypes. Often it's simply less exhausting to stop arguing and revert to tradition. Traditional roles aside, if one person stays home to care for the child, it often is the mother simply because the father usually earns a higher salary. Women pay a career price for this decision, but men may pay a psychological and emotional price. The pressure on a sole wage earner is enormous; the stress of singlehandedly supporting his family may give many a father sleepless nights.

The encouraging news is that the wage imbalance is beginning to shift. During the latest recession, when we saw wholesale layoffs from industrial jobs, women's earnings held steadier than men's because they were more likely to be employed in health care and education—two fields with fewer layoffs. Often it was the wife's paycheck that kept the family afloat.

Statistics show that women are increasingly becoming equal breadwinners. The typical working wife today brings home 42.2 percent of a family's earnings. In 1975 that figure was 31 percent.[12] And in the highest-earning 20 percent of families, almost 30 percent of working wives today, compared to 12.6 percent in 1967, make as much as or more than their husbands.[13] These numbers were not imaginable by the previous generation and have not been fully digested by this one.

Why do we tend to adhere to the traditional gender role portrait? Is it because we're sentimental about the good old days, even when we know that they weren't that good? We tend to forget that some of those ideal portraits developed deep cracks over time that caused many couples to split. Or do we continue to feel the social pressure that tells us that the old model is still the best; children should be raised by their mothers? Regardless, the lingering attachment to the old model has not impeded the development of new models. That is where we are today: new family configurations that give parents options about how to care for and support their offspring.

Job Sharing

The key barriers to shared care, Marc and Amy Vachon believe, are "financial considerations and cultural expectations."[14] The typical first reaction to the idea of shared care is "we can't afford it." But sometimes two part-time jobs, or reduced-hour jobs, add up to a better income than that of a single earner. Savings can be significant. For example, child care costs average $28,000 a year for one family of four. The Vachons reduced their own child care costs by 40 percent when they cut back on their work hours.[15]

The money question, difficult as it is, may be more easily resolved than the question of cultural expectations. To what extent can we revise our gender-stereotyped norms of who does what, when, and how? Vermonters Sarah and Jason Bertucci are finding out as they chart a new course: they not only want to share their work and family life with each other, they want to share the same job. Both are teachers. I spoke to them when their daughter, Mica, was twenty-two months old. They started job sharing when Sarah became pregnant. "I would go [to Middlebury High School] on Monday and Tuesday and Jason would go on Thursday and Friday and we alternated every other Wednesday," Sarah explains. "Both the students and the staff would say how uncanny this was." Jason adds, "It was neat for our high school students to see mom and dad passing off the baby and to ask us questions about why we did it."

It worked "because we were just so aligned in how we ran the classroom and what we expected of students. I think it helps that we are married and that we work so well together," Sarah explains. She has not met another married couple like themselves. "Most people, [if they] have heard of job sharing at all, have heard about it with two women job sharing." Most job sharing between teachers is done in elementary school, but Jason believes it makes more sense in high school because the day breaks up into classes.

Why don't more couples job-share? Jason and Sarah admit that such an arrangement can be a difficult sell. When their job share in Middlebury ended, they looked for a similar arrangement but found no employer willing to try it out. Jason recalls one high school principal's response: "It's too weird for us." Jason notes that managing two people "sounds different and strange. People feel that they're taxed enough as it is." Then there is the question of providing benefits for both employees. He believes job sharing would become more common if there were a network of job-share employers as well as job-share seekers. The most compelling reason for employers to do so, he said, "is that they pay for one person and they get two. Yes, there are going to be some places where they have spent a little more time communicating, but you get two people's thoughts on things, you get more hours."

The Bertuccis now teach full-time in different schools and the grandparents are taking care of Mica. They hope to make a job-sharing arrangement at another school, one that will not consider it "weird." For other couples who want to try this family/work arrangement, Sarah has advice: "I would say plan to do a lot of checking in and processing with your partner. Being able to communicate well is really important and you have to have a lot of patience."

What would it take for the public to become more accepting of job sharing?

"It would take the white male leadership of this country to value parenting more. When we come in contact with other couples they ask us, 'Which one of you is working and which one of you is off?' So it's like one person is working and the other is on vacation. When you think about the long-term benefit to society, I think raising a child is more important," Sarah says.

Stay-at-Home Dads

A work/family arrangement that is less unusual, but still not common, is the stay-at-home dad. Derek Burkins is the primary caregiver for his two sons, but one name he does does not want to be called is "Mr. Mom." "I'm a father," he says, "a stay-at-home dad." He has cared for his sons Riley, now seven, and Porter, now five, since birth.

Why are fathers in nurturing roles so easy to tease, or even mock? At a gathering of women attending a workshop on politics, one of the speakers described the early days of her political career when her husband became a stay-at-home dad. "He had never done laundry. He didn't know how to separate whites from colored. So everything came out pink." (Laughter.) "He let the kids dress themselves, so my son went to school in tights and a tutu." (More laughter.)

Is it just that gender role reversal is funny, like men dressed in drag often are? Do women get a special kick out of seeing men's ineptness as homemakers because it makes them look that much better? Do they not want to recognize that their spouse can be as good a parent as they are because they want to retain control as "gatekeepers," not allowing any man to step on their turf?

Men laugh at "Mr. Mom" for other reasons: the guy who wears an apron, changes a diaper, or vacuums the rug is seen as lacking masculinity. "Why don't you get a real job?" declared the father of a male friend who intends to become a stay-at-home dad while he continues to work at home and his pregnant wife completes her medical internship. Other men feel threatened themselves, reluctant to reveal their feminine side, fearful of being called hen-pecked, a wimp, queer, a loser, or all of the above. Both men and women express some discomfort when sex roles are confused, and laughter is the easiest, and sometimes the most cruel, response. Today, when we are more accepting of gays and lesbians—including in the military—does that mean we are more accepting of gender roles that do not conform to stereotypes? Both women and men have to surrender some of their old assumptions if the stay-at-home dad is not going to be an object of ridicule and the off-to-work mom is not going to be tagged as a bad mother. We're moving in that direction, but we're not there yet, observes Burkins.

"Mr. Mom is a sitcom. When Dad is home, everything goes wrong," Burkins says. "Women will say, 'I have to get home because my husband is taking care of the children. When I get home there will be chaos.'" He suggests that women give their husbands more time alone with the children. "Let him have them for a weekend. It will be an eye-opener."

Burkins often gets praise from skeptical sources. Once when he was grocery shopping with one child on his back and the other seated in the shopping cart, a woman remarked: "That's wonderful that you're doing the shopping. When my husband shops I give him one list and he comes home with another." He also gets extra scrutiny. As the primary caregiver, he says,

"I feel I have to do everything at a higher level." "You know your baby is spitting up," a woman once said to him disapprovingly at the supermarket.

Men continue to have to explain themselves to an untutored public. Mitch Fleishman was at the pool with his two children on a weekday while his wife Natalie was at work as a vice president for development at a Vermont hospital. A woman said to him, "You have a wonderful life." He retorted proudly, "No, I have a wonderful wife."

When Derek Burkins and his wife, Melody, decided he would be the stay-at-home dad, it was because they wanted one of them to stay home with the children. He knew "it was something I wanted to do. I really looked forward to the opportunity, as terrifying as it was."

"What was terrifying?" I ask.

"I don't think anyone is ever really prepared for a baby for the first time unless you've grown up with a large family. In more modern families, where you only have one or two children, you don't necessarily have that experience of taking care of children twenty-four hours a day. It was a steep learning curve. You come home from the hospital and okay, here we go! I had never changed a diaper; I don't think I had ever given a baby a bottle. I don't think I had even held a baby at that point," he recalls.

What did their families think?

"My parents were very careful what they said to me. They knew it was our thought-out choice and it was something I really wanted to do, but they asked, 'Are you sure you want to do this?' What if it does not work out, they feared, where does that leave your career?" he explains.

He had no problem with maintaining his masculine identity. "I was never one who had to get his identity from taking care of the family. My philosophy has always been that it's give and take," something the couple agreed on when they were students at Dartmouth College.

"Being a parent changes your life completely," Burkins acknowledges. It has also changed his sons' perception of what mommies and daddies do. "When I asked my six-year-old son what he wanted to be, he said, 'I want to be a stay-at-home dad.' In addition of course he wants to be a race car driver and an astronaut. I was surprised that both of my boys love babies; they tickle their cheeks and are very gentle with them."

The hardest part for stay-at-home dads is similar to what stay-at-home moms experience: isolation and loneliness. To counter those feelings, Burkins does what mothers do: he participates in play groups and community activities. He was elected to his town's board of selectmen, sits on the preschool board, and serves on the town's conservation commission. Once in a while, like a harried mom, he finds "I need time alone, so I take an hour-and-a-half bike ride. One weekend I just went to a cabin by myself to think."

There are rewards. The best part of being a stay-at-home dad, Burkins says, is that "I have a close relationship with my sons; we're the best of friends."

Melody Burkins, senior director for strategic initiatives at the University of Vermont, says the arrangement works well from her perspective, too. "It's actually better than we thought it would be. He's a very social person; he has a lot of play dates with a lot of women. He mostly deals with women all day, now that he's been accepted into the club. At first, when they had toddler play dates, they were like, 'We'll see how long he lasts. He's just filling in.' Then they saw that he was there every week, every day. He said this is what I'm going to do. It was very important to him because his father wasn't around much."

The effect on the kids, she says, has been "amazing. We're both geologists. He's passionate about getting outside and hiking. He's out with them constantly and that's what they do. There's a whole new level of how far he lets them go."

The hardest part for her was having to let go. "I like control, I like to manage. When you are at work you don't know what they do all day. I feel like every father has felt, not knowing the schedule. I learn about it at the dinner table. I had to learn that Derek is in charge of that. What I gained from giving that up was the freedom to focus on my work." The couple keeps communications open, she says, but Derek runs the house. "He does all of our expenses. He won't let me do the laundry. He loves to cook. He calls me an impatient sous chef. I've gained the ability to do what I need to do and I know things are being taken care of. They may not be exactly the way I would do them. We've carved out what we each do."

When I ask how we could enable more dads to be primary caregivers, she responds, "I think we need to educate women. It comes back to our preconceptions that men will be all fingers when it comes to kids. Some women are afraid something will go wrong. I say let them make a mess. It's not exactly how you would do it. I think a lot of women are used to the home being their space. They have to learn that it may be a little different."

Recent scientific research made a new discovery that strengthens the argument for dads as caregivers. Testosterone levels drop when men get involved with their children in activities such as playing with their babies and changing diapers. The greater the child-dad involvement, the lower the testosterone level. Some men may be threatened by that observation, but it seems that Mother Nature looks at it differently. By reducing hormone levels, men are able to be more care giving dads.[16]

How fast are we moving in this direction? Fast enough to have an article in the *New York Times* Styles section: "Why Dad's Résumé Lists 'Car Pool,'" by Lisa Belkin.[17] She writes, "The résumé gap isn't just for mothers anymore. . . . The good news seems to be that gaps on résumés are now so common as to be the norm, recruiters and consultants say. The bad news? That's true, unless you're a man." The article advises men to follow the same strategies as women who wish to increase their chances of returning to the workplace after taking time out to raise children: volunteer, work at home, work part-time, and get an MBA.

Belkin goes on to quote Brian Reid, thirty-three, who in 2002 founded RebelDad.com. Reid notes that acceptance of returning fathers "seems to be generational. It makes dads nervous knowing that they are not likely to be interviewed by a peer, who gets this, but by a 55-year-old middle manager, who might have a wife or a daughter who has left the workplace and come back, but who doesn't understand it in a man."[18]

The *Stay-at-Home Dad Handbook*, written in 2004 by Peter Baylies with Jessica Toonkel, provides useful pointers for stay-at-home dads whether they are home by necessity or by choice. Baylies concludes that the main reason dads stay home is to keep their kids out of day care. Unlike Derek Burkins, Baylies believes that the hardest part for many men is "losing your status as a breadwinner."[19]

For support and advice, he suggests finding other like-minded dads in the neighborhood. Men are also communicating online at at-home-dad networking sites like Baylies's AtHomeDad.org. Jeremy Adam Smith, author of *The Daddy Shift* and a more recent convert to the at-home-dad scene, recommends

Kansas City At-Home Dads, one of the largest networks in the nation. He writes, "Young twenty-first-century couples share a fundamentally different set of expectations about their roles and goals than our twentieth-century parents and grandparents did. Mine is the first generation of men to date a cohort of women who were born into feminist consciousness and who expect to have careers, financial self-sufficiency, reproductive freedom—and a man who is willing to share (not *help with*) domestic labor."[20] He quotes a 1990 *Time* magazine poll that states that 48 percent of men between the ages of eighteen and twenty-four would consider staying home with their children. The figure today would be higher. He reports that stay-at-home dads come from all walks of life and often don't think of themselves as stay-at-home dads, and many work part-time.[21] They "have a range of motivations for taking care of kids. . . . Like many other people who should know better, I reflexively assumed that stay-at-home parenthood is a luxury of the affluent. I was wrong," he observes.

Smith also asks, "Why should poor, working, and lower-middle-class parents be more likely to stay home with children (or split the care) if they are less able to afford it? Part of the answer lies in the cost of child care. . . . In short, poor, working-class, and even many middle-class parents can't afford for one parent *not* to stay home or for both of them not to split shifts and share care."[22]

Smith quotes research that concludes that working-class men are beginning to define fathering as a "worthy masculine endeavor."[23] Fathers who label themselves as stay-at-home dads remain few but are growing in numbers and diversity. According to the US Census Bureau, less than 2 percent (165,000) of fathers fit in this category, but the census does not include in this figure unmarried fathers, fathers who make any money while at home, or fathers who work nontraditional hours so they can be home with their children. If we apply a broader definition, some two million dads would fit the category in 2010, that is, one in fifteen fathers. As a result of the recent recession, more unemployed fathers are spending time taking care of their children. One-third of fathers with working wives now are either part-time or full-time caregivers.

The model of the stay-at-home dad, whether he does paid work or not, is providing a fresh example for all dads, encouraging them to engage more closely with the upbringing of their children and the management of their households. The lesson for moms is to give dad a chance to flex his caregiving muscles. It is possible to share the domestic territory and continue to be a good mother. If the laundry isn't folded just right, let it go. The most important thing is that it's clean.

I confess, there were times when I didn't easily cede my mother turf to my husband, to babysitters, or to my teenage children. My biggest fear was that something would happen to one of my children when I was not there: they would get into an accident, be picked up for smoking marijuana, or do badly in school. It would be *my* fault, the *bad* mother. I knew that as a politician living in the public eye, every misstep would grow into a news story that would magnify their misbehavior or my neglect tenfold. I wanted to do everything possible to spare them and me that ignominious publicity. I was lucky. Only once did a reporter call me to inquire whether it was true that my youngest son Daniel had passed a fake ID at a downtown bar. Daniel denied it. I believed him. The story was dropped.

Different Choices at Different Times

Families make different choices at different times in their lives. Monica Ormsby, whose husband was a writer, became the breadwinner when she held a high-power job in New York City and her husband became the caregiver for their first child. It worked for them, but still, she felt conflicted.

"There still is this professional mother guilt. There is social pressure to be the nurturer," she says. "I made enough money to pay the nanny, and my husband was at home," but she remained stressed. "I didn't know what the baby's schedule was; I didn't know what foods he was eating." The couple moved to Vermont, where the roles reversed and she became the stay-at-home parent. "I shifted my energy and delved into my kids' lives. I went to every field trip they had, I got involved in local politics."

Now, with her children aged four, nine, and eleven, Ormsby is in a third stage, having started her own online business sending out party invitations. "I would not have realized the need for this, had I not been an at-home mom. Dealing with all of these birthday parties, PTO fund-raisers, and bake sales, I have become a domestic CEO."

Her conclusion is that you don't have to do it all at once. "Women can't do it all, and it's okay not to. You don't have to be focused on climbing the ladder. That's not what it's all about. For me balance is most important. You don't have to be perfect."

Some Unexpected Benefits

Not every family can afford to make such a decision because they may need both incomes to pay the bills, or because their jobs do not provide flexibility. All families, however, have the possibility of moving toward more equally shared parenting.

Men's share of domestic work has increased steadily over the last thirty years. One unexpected bonus of this trend is that women are more attracted to men who share household and caregiving responsibilities. Their sex life is better.[24] "There is nothing sexier than a guy who has just capably cooked dinner and then washed and put away your clean laundry," notes Amy Vachon.[25]

The chief causes of marital strife, according to various studies, are arguments over money and who should do what in the household. Small wonder that a man who shows his appreciation for his wife's domestic responsibilities by making dinner and lighting the candles is more lovable than the guy who grabs a beer and stretches back in the Barcalounger to watch TV, while she's nursing the baby in one arm and wiping spilled milk off the kitchen counter with the other. "You just don't understand" can be transformed into "Thanks, honey, you do understand!" and a hug.

"DADS HAPPIER WHEN THEY SPLIT DOMESTIC DUTIES"

Here's a new stress-reliever for overloaded dads: Go home tonight and fold the laundry!

In a finding that bodes well for de-stressing moms, a new British study reports that men are happier when they split the domestic duties with their partners and spend more time with their kids.

> The survey, which interviewed more than 1,000 fathers over two years, reports that 82 per cent of men said they'd like more time with their family, and agreed that it was not a "a woman's job" to look after children.
>
> In fact, the happier dads had partners who worked full-time and roughly the same hours that they did. [26]

Money or Time?

Many people believe that time is more important to them than money. We all say it. We tend to believe it. But do we actually make our work/life choices based on that set of values? We know that we can't ever have enough of either time or money. That is why if we want to move from wishful thinking into action, we are forced to create our own boundaries—to discipline ourselves to reduce work hours and expand free time.

Can families make time as important as money? I received a homemade Valentine last year, a single sheet of white paper covered with little red hearts and stamped with five words: "Give the Gift of Time." It's what all families would wish to give and receive, but many are living too close to the economic edge to survive on less income. Other families have a comfortable lifestyle that they do not wish (or do not know how) to modify. In the quest for time, all families have become "jugglers."Much negotiating over who picks up a toddler from day care, who takes a child to the soccer game, who picks up another child from dance lessons, and who picks up milk and orange juice for breakfast occupies their day. The difference between the current generation and that of their parents is that both husband and wife do the juggling.

John de Graaf, head of an organization called Take Back Your Time, believes that we have to make time more important than money. "My view is that the time pressure in our society, in an overworked society, [is] exacerbating virtually every problem that we face. I'm not against work and believe in the importance of a job well done. But we've made work everything and we've gotten completely out of touch and forgotten other values that we hold dear like our family and our community and our health," he tells me.

Take Back Your Time celebrates "Take Back Your Time Day" on October

24. The date marks "the difference between how much Americans work in a year and how much Europeans work. The Europeans are done work by October 24," de Graaf says. He continues, "We looked at things like family leave, maternity leave, sick time, vacation days, and flexibility and it became clear that the United States was in the eighteenth century. Every wealthy country and even poorer countries gave people more time to have time. It was shocking for us."

"When I was a college student," he recalls, "one of the problems we were going to face in the twentieth century was too much leisure time, and of course it didn't happen at all." I myself recall the fashion statement of the '60s was men's leisure suits in pastel colors made of light synthetic materials. Where are they now? They can no longer even be found in thrift shops.

"The stress from time pressure is the number two issue that Americans feel, next to financial stress," says de Graaf. "Conservatives say that Americans have such long hours because they love to work, [and] if you give them vacation time you'll only make them miserable. That just isn't true."

He quotes a Gallup poll that finds that Americans are 20 percent happier on weekends than on work days and 30 to 40 percent happier on holidays, and that people who don't get vacation times are twice as likely to get heart attacks. The problem, he says, is that people "don't take this issue seriously. They see it as 'just a lark.'" When de Graaf promoted legislation that would give workers one or two weeks of paid vacation and paid sick days, "people were acting if it was going to be the end of civilization."

What Makes People Happy

"Having stuff doesn't make people happy," de Graaf says. "We have to learn to take satisfaction from non-market activities."

Derek Bok, a former president of Harvard, agrees. He writes:

> A number of studies have found that average levels of satisfaction with life have not risen appreciably in the United States over the last 50 years, even though real per capita incomes have grown a great deal during this period. . . .

> Observing these trends, analysts have described the pursuit of financial goals as a treadmill in which people's aspirations are forever beyond their reach, leaving them perpetually unsatisfied. . . .
>
> Even those who succeed may become so preoccupied with money that they neglect the human relationships that affect their happiness. In fact, researchers have found that the more people care about becoming rich, the less satisfaction they tend to derive from their family life. Finally, those who do achieve some financial success are likely to find much of their added happiness short-lived. . . . People grow used to the extra possessions that higher incomes allow; luxuries turn into necessities and aspirations rise, leaving them no more satisfied with life than before.[27]

Bok's research indicates that senior citizens are happier than younger Americans. He suggests this "may help policy-makers decide to give a higher priority to improving the lot of younger Americans through measures such as more affordable child care or higher-quality preschool education than to raising Social Security benefits."[28] A good point, except that older Americans have AARP, a highly organized lobbying group to represent their demands, and younger Americans, particularly children, have no such political clout.

Bok sums it up: "The vast majority of Americans appear to be happy most of the time. Even in the lowest income quartile of the population, more than 80 percent profess to be more happy than not. Moreover, the happiness they feel does not seem to come primarily from mere pleasure-seeking or from selfishly looking out for number one. Rather, apart from such basic conditions as how well people feel, how much freedom they enjoy, and whether they possess the necessities and comforts of life, the most important sources of happiness seem to include having close relationships with family and friends, helping others, and being active in community, charitable, and political activities."[29]

The Founding Fathers believed that the pursuit of happiness was an inalienable right. Thomas Jefferson wrote in the Declaration of Independence, "We hold these truths to be self-evident, that all men are created equal, that they are endowed by their Creator with certain unalienable Rights, that among these are Life, Liberty and the Pursuit of Happiness."

Much has been debated about the meaning of these words. What is indisputable is that the pursuit of happiness is considered as great a right as life and liberty. Two hundred and thirty-five years later, we are still trying to define happiness, whether it is money or time. Most of us would argue we need both—a sufficient amount of money to assure economic security, and enough time to enjoy it with our families and friends. How to strike that balance between two often competing desires remains our challenge.

It is good to remind ourselves, as we adjust caregiving and breadwinner roles, not solely on the basis of gender, but on individual ability and preference, that letting go of the old stereotypes may be a creative, satisfying, and positive development not just for gender equity. Men and their offspring would be equal beneficiaries. Families that feel less beleaguered and happier can give the greatest gift to their children—loving care.

Norman Rockwell would have difficulty finding one model of the typical American family for the next cover of the now defunct *Saturday Evening Post*. Neither can we agree with the observation Leo Tolstoy made in the opening sentence of *Anna Karenina*: "Happy families are all alike; each unhappy family is unhappy in its own way." Happy families, too, are happy in their own way. There is no single formula for the distribution of time and money that guarantees greater happiness for any type of family. Consider this old adage: "No man lying on his deathbed says, 'I wish I had spent more time at the office.'" I was reminded of it when I attended a memorial service for the husband of a good friend. His wife said, with a hint of surprise in her voice, "All he talked about at the end was how much he loved his family. And Blair didn't usually talk that way."

CHAPTER 9

How Women Leaders Make a Difference

"I have three children and always worked. I know how difficult it is to balance work and family," explains Representative Carolyn Maloney (D-NY). She recalls when, pregnant with her first child, she asked her employer about the company's family leave policy. "They said there was no leave policy; women just left. I said, 'Well, I don't intend to leave. I intend to come back.'"

Maloney is one of a small group of women in the US House of Representatives, including Rep. Rosa DeLauro (D-CT) and Rep. Lynn Woolsey (D-CA), who sponsor most of the legislation that helps families mesh their work and family lives. Many women in leadership positions who have struggled with family/work conflicts in their own lives are inspired to change policies for others. Speaking from personal experience adds credibility and passion to their cause. "I think we know the problem," Rep. Maloney explains.

As the first female governor of Vermont (the fourth elected in her own right in the nation), I was conscious of gender at one level or another, much of the time. It influenced how I decided to dress, how I chose my hairstyle, how often I smiled, how tough or conciliatory I was, and, sometimes, the issues that I put at the top of my agenda. Still, approximately 90 to 95 percent of the time I governed like the somber male governors whose portraits stared down at me from the walls of my executive office. They were the only role models available to me. Like them, I had to produce a budget, make sure roads were in good repair and the state economy was strong, and tend to the daily management of the government. My best estimate is that about 5 to 10 percent of the time I veered off the usual male course. How? My life experience as a woman and as a mother influenced some of my priorities.

For example, when I was a legislator, I attended a public hearing on domestic violence. There, for the first time, I heard in person the stories of women who had been repeatedly kicked, beaten, and demeaned by their husbands or partners. "Finally," one woman, with tears moistening her cheeks, said "I had the strength to get out." She went to a shelter; it changed her life. When I was elected governor, I asked the legislature to fund domestic violence and rape crisis centers throughout the state. How much was that decision influenced by my gender? I can only conjecture that I was drawn to attend the hearing in the first place because I could empathize with the issue and then felt compelled to address it. Many men would support these issues as well, but I do not recall seeing a man in the church basement where the hearing was held.

In my second term as governor, I focused my state-of-the-state speech entirely on education. I had reached the conclusion that I could have the greatest impact on the largest number of Vermonters by investing in quality education. I had visited hundreds of schools and observed the difference between "poor" sparsely funded schools and "good" well-funded schools. I had only to look at how many books were in the library to tell the difference. I was determined to equalize learning opportunities because as a mother I wanted my children to have the best teachers in the best schools, starting with kindergarten. I understood that other parents felt the same way.

Other initiatives come to mind: doubling and tripling funding for child care and creating Dr. Dynasaur, the first state program to provide health insurance for children and pregnant women. I was not unusual. Studies have shown that women tend to fight more strongly than men for programs that affect families and children. But not *all* women respond according to gender. Political party affiliation often matters more; sometimes Republican women are torn between loyalty to their party or to family and women's issues. Other women, regardless of party, know the problem well but "do not want to be pigeon-holed into these issues," explains Portia Wu, senior advisor for the White House Domestic Policy Council.

When I ask Rep. DeLauro if she would have a better chance of passing the Paycheck Fairness Act if there were more women in Congress, her quick answer is, "No." That legislation would strengthen two other acts—the Equal Pay Act and the Fair Labor Standards Act—in an attempt to eliminate the nation's lingering disparity between what women and men earn for the same jobs. It passed the house in 2009, when Nancy Pelosi was Speaker, but failed to make it through the Senate the following year. DeLauro recalls that Senate vote as a major disappointment. Despite the lobbying efforts of more than two hundred organizations, including the American Association of University Women and the National Women's Law Center, equal-pay advocates were two votes short of passage. Says DeLauro, "We didn't get Olympia Snowe and Susan Collins"—both Republican senators from Maine. "It was really shocking to me because both of these women are really committed to women's equality." Senator Snowe's vote to be loyal to her party might have been explained by fact that she expected a Tea Party candidate to make a bid for her seat in an upcoming election. But even in the House, reports DeLauro, "we've never been able to engage the Republican women. As a matter of fact, they're the people who get up on the floor and speak against [the act]. I want to see more progressive women and more progressive men. Based on my experience, just because you're an elected official and a woman, that doesn't mean you're going to vote for [women's issues]."

The fierce party polarization that has overtaken Congress has made it difficult for women from either side of the aisle to become sisters. The bitter and prolonged battle over raising the debt ceiling may eventually cause a backlash against politicians who refused to compromise. There is hardly a law inscribed in the nation's law books that has not been a product of compromise. It is the keystone of the democratic process. There was some speculation that if there had been more estrogen and less testosterone in Congress during the debt ceiling crisis, the standoff would have been resolved much sooner. I surmise that the result would also have been fairer, with equal attention paid to cuts and taxes, because most women are more interested in getting a question resolved than in who wields the upper hand and claims victory.

Republican women in the Senate did acknowledge gender when they supported some parts of the health care law, such as the cost of mammograms and Pap smears and eliminating the disparity between men and women's health insurance premiums, but no Republican woman or man voted for the final bill. Neither did they join the battle to maintain funding for Planned Parenthood, which had been slated for elimination in the 2011 budget passed by the House. While there is no evidence that a few women in Congress can make a big difference on family/work legislation, there is evidence that adding a significant number of women to a legislative body would make a real difference.

Loretta Weinberg, former New Jersey state senator, believes that the answer to the passage of a federal paid family leave law is to "get all the congresswomen together." The problem is that even if all the congresswomen supported paid family leave, they would not prevail because they comprise barely 17 percent of the lawmakers. That percentage ranks the United States in sixty-ninth place (in descending order from best to worst) in a ranking of 178 countries. Comparatively, Rwanda ranks first, at 56 percent, and Sweden at 45 percent. Afghanistan and Iraq are at 27.7 percent and 25.2 percent, respectively.[1]

Rosabeth Moss Kanter, former editor of the *Harvard Business Review* and author of *A Tale of O,* which looks at the role of outsiders in organizations, did early studies on diversity and examined how many "others" were required to influence a homogeneous organization. Her conclusion was 30 percent. So, how many women would it take in Congress to change the outcome of hotly divided legislation such as paid family leave? Let's increase Kanter's figures to 40 percent to create a hypothetical situation. If 40 of the 100 US senators were female, we should not expect them to vote in unison. Men rarely do. Let's assume that 10 women voted against paid family leave and 30 women voted for it; that places 30 votes in the "Yes" column. If half of the 60 men voted for paid family leave and 30 voted against it, that would add another 30 votes to the "Yes" column. Now the bill has 60 votes, enough for passage and enough to overcome a filibuster. The conclusion is that not every woman has to be supportive of a bill in order to declare victory. But when a significant number of women are in elective office, they can provide the tipping point, especially on controversial legislation that is often decided by one or two votes.

Working at Both Levels: State and Federal

Governor Chris Gregoire of Washington State has been forced to conclude that, because of a large state deficit, the state will not be able to provide paid family leave without help from the federal government. That help is unlikely to appear anytime in the near future because the federal government is moving in the opposite direction, struggling with a deficit of its own and cutting domestic programs that help families and children. It is hard to know which way to turn to get traction on these issues: toward state governments or the federal government. Neither, during this period of high deficits, appears to be capable of funding a new program like paid family leave, which would have a price tag for the short term but would translate into cost savings and a prudent investment over the long term. That long-term argument is always a difficult sell to cash-strapped lawmakers, but the arguments are economically powerful. Paid family leave will enable more new parents to care for and bond with their babies, which will give infants a healthier start and reduce health care costs. Studies have shown that women are more likely to return to their jobs if they can take paid family leave, thus increasing family incomes and tax revenues. Savings will also accrue if more family members can care for their elderly parents and avoid requiring Medicaid to subsidize the cost of nursing homes. Why can't we be patient and wait for employers to implement these policies on their own? Because progress has been slow, and some employers have even pulled back on such policies.

The importance of working at both the state and federal levels simultaneously for family/work legislation was exemplified by the passage of the Family and Medical Leave Act in 1993. "By the time he [President Bill Clinton] signed it, half the states already had laws," explains Ellen Galinsky, head of the Families and Work Institute. The state versus federal argument is not a new one. Action at both levels heightens awareness for change and builds widespread political support. When the battle for women's suffrage took place in the nineteenth and twentieth centuries, women's organizations were divided over whether to work for suffrage state by state, the strategy of the American Woman Suffrage Association, or to fight for an amendment to the US Constitution, the strategy of the National Woman Suffrage Association. Embattled for many years, the two organizations eventually merged and won passage of the Nineteenth Amendment.

Women have not always stood alone in battling for these policies: Senator Edward "Ted" Kennedy, who died in 2009, and Senator Christopher Dodd, who retired in 2010, had been staunch allies on issues relating to women and children. Representative DeLauro stresses the importance of male supporters of paid family leave, because while Democratic women have been visible proponents of the legislation, they are also the expected supporters, making their voices less likely to be heard.

Leaders like DeLauro point out that the family/work policies they push for end up being seen as what DeLauro describes as "feel good" issues, rather than the tough economic issues that they are. Take the case of Head Start. "The data is all there," she says. "It reduces the taxpayers' expense." Yet when she brings these issues up, she is branded as a liberal spendthrift.

It is disconcerting that family issues like child care and Head Start should be so vulnerable to budget cuts in Washington. President Barack Obama put it best when he said in his budget address in 2011, "There is nothing courageous about asking for sacrifice from those who can least afford it and don't have any clout on Capitol Hill. And this is not a vision of the America I know."

DeLauro believes that the reason for neglect is that the work that women do is undervalued, despite the fact that they are the most economically challenged group—particularly unmarried, widowed, and divorced women. "That's why when we talk about them we talk about economic issues," she says. "The economic security of women is about the economic security of families. The public policy to date has not dealt with the kinds of lives that families are living today."

Not all women support family/work issues, but women like Governor Gregoire have usually started the conversation and been the first to sponsor legislation. As another example, Senator Patricia Schroeder introduced the first family leave bill to Congress in 1985. She had been just thirty-one when she was elected and became a role model for a new kind of congresswoman; she proved that a mother of young children could hold elective office. When she brought her children into the House Chamber, the press noted that she was the first person to bring diapers into that sacrosanct male space. The unpaid Family and Medical Leave Act (FMLA) was not passed until eight years later. The only Republican woman in the Senate at the time, Nancy Kassebaum (R-KS), did not support the bill, but all four of the Democratic women senators did. It was a different time. Six Republican women joined their Democratic sisters on the House side, including Olympia Snowe, who then represented Maine in the House. By the time the bill passed by a healthy margin, (71–27 in the Senate; 265–163 in the House), it was laden with compromises that sprang from strong business opposition, limiting its beneficiaries to 50 percent of the workforce. Still, it remains a landmark. The bill had been previously vetoed twice by President George Bush, but it was one of the first bills to be signed into law when Bill Clinton took office.

The Bully Pulpit

Support by a chief executive makes a difference. When Republican presidential candidate Senator Bob Dole ran against Clinton when he seeking a second presidential term, Dole proposed the repeal of the Family and Medical Leave Act. "Every day Bob Dole said he was repealing the Family and Medical Leave Act Bill Clinton was getting more and more votes," recalls Judy Lichtman, senior advisor and past president of the National Partnership for Women and Families. Once the law had been put in place, it became nearly impossible to repeal because so many people had enjoyed the benefits.

The bully pulpit of the presidential spouse has been put to good use by both recent First Ladies: Hillary Clinton and Michelle Obama. They understand, sometimes through firsthand experience, what is at stake for today's American families. Hillary Clinton, as First Lady and then as a senator from New York, took the lead on several pieces of family/work legislation. Her book, *It Takes a Village to Raise a Child*, describes how important the support of family, friends, and communities is to the well-being of children. When Barack and Michelle Obama arrived in the White House, they put a spotlight on such policies, raising them higher on the national agenda. Not only did they convene the White House Forum on Workplace Flexibility and create the White House Council on Women and Girls, the president also appointed Vice President Joe Biden to chair the Middle Class Task Force, which held a conference on "finding solutions for families balancing the dual demands of work and caring for family." They decided that the federal government could do more to crack down on violations of the Equal Pay Act and created the National Equal Pay Task Force. Despite being constricted by the deficit, the Obamas have made an effort to put the family/work debate on the national agenda.

Female Leadership in the Private Sphere

What about the private sector? Are women CEOs, corporate board members, and human resources directors more receptive than men to workplace flexibility and paid family leave?

Ellen Galinsky explains, "When we look at the predictors of which companies provide the most work-life assistance, we find that having a person of color or a woman in charge is often predictive."

Agreement comes from Marsha Firestone, president and founder of the Women Presidents' Organization (a membership organization for women presidents of multimillion dollar companies). An overview of the WPO's annual survey of its members by *Knowledge@Wharton*, the online business journal of the Wharton School at the University of Pennsylvania, reveals that:

> 100% of the 50 fastest growing women-led companies provide health insurance, 88% provide 401ks, 80% provide life insurance and 66% offer telecommuting. Nationwide, 62% of private companies offer health insurance and 47% offer retirement benefits, according to the Bureau of Labor Statistics; 59% of private company employees have access to life insurance and just 5% have access to flexible workplace policies.

"So what I have come to believe is that it's not just anecdotal that women tend to be more nurturing," Firestone says. "I think they are, and I think these statistics verify that."

An office built on women's norms would be more innovative around policy issues that relate to family, suggests Monica McGrath, a human resources consultant, executive coach and adjunct professor of management at the Wharton School. That doesn't just mean offering flextime—it means helping women manage their child care responsibilities and family roles while also helping grow their careers.[2]

"There [has been] a shift in the last twenty years. Human resource officers are looked at as strategic business partners," explains Shirley Davis, head of the Society for Human Resource Management. "We have a seat at the table. Globalization has changed the way HR operates; it has changed the way we recruit. We are on the cutting edge of the way business is changing.

Competitors can steal your best employees away."

From a human resources perspective, Davis says, flexible schedules should not be the exception but the rule. "We have to have managers who understand that everyone works differently, people with disabilities, for example, and more men have family responsibilities. Then there is the sandwich generation [caught between child care and elder care]. This is not just an issue for those who have children. We used to think that visibility [in the office] creates value; that is not the case at all."

She notes that not all managers are quick to adapt to a flexible workplace. "Some employers have a poverty of imagination [and are] not sure how to do it. We help them . . . do it, with a resource guide and a tool kit. We have to demystify [flexibility]. We still have a long way to go," she concedes.

Her constituency includes 250,000 resource professionals in 140 countries. The organization has been in existence for sixty years. She sees how the workplace has changed: more working women have children; more women are responsible for caring for children with disabilities. High on everyone's list is flexibility. "That is a demand that is going to continue to increase," she observes.

Top management is still male dominated, she says, "but when we get to 2020 we will listen to what women want, and the tables will turn more and more."

Women human resources managers may respond more readily to the changing needs of the workforce than men, but they cannot implement new policies without a supportive constituency—both at the top, from the CEO and her or his board of directors, and below, from their workforce. Globalization has had a huge impact on how they do their work. "In complying with international law we are on the cutting edge of how business is changing," Davis says.

Complying with international law means those American companies that work in countries that have paid family leave policies, paid sick days, and flexible work policies have to comply with those established policies. Globalization may turn out to be the American family's best friend. If American companies can be successful abroad under these policies, why couldn't they be equally successful at home? Thus far, American corporations have not been under the same pressure as overseas corporations, from either governments or grassroots constituencies, to implement supportive family/work policies. And the argument that adopting them would reduce US competitiveness and the number of jobs has gone largely unchallenged in state legislatures and Congress, where business lobbyists hold sway. The counter argument is that those few American corporations who have established family/work policies are now at an economic disadvantage compared to those who don't. "When a country guarantees paid leave, all firms must follow the same laws, but when a company unilaterally improves working conditions, its employee compensation expenses may be higher than those of its closest competitor down the street," explains Jody Heymann, a professor of political science at McGill University.[3] The advantage of federal law is that it provides, in one sense, what businesses want: a level playing field.

Would the work/family standards that are becoming the global norm be adopted sooner in the United States if more women achieved the rank of CEO and served as directors on corporate boards? The answer cannot be definitive, because the number of women on corporate boards, like the number of women in Congress, is too small to provide a complete picture. It remains at 16 percent where it has hovered for the last six years,[4] a figure far below the 30 percent Rosabeth Moss Kanter believes necessary to have an impact on an otherwise homogenous organization.

Ilene Lang, president and CEO of Catalyst, an organization founded in 1962 to promote women's leadership in business, has no doubt that if "more women were on boards, they would make these [family/work] decisions. If you look at the leadership of a company today and it's all white men, there's something wrong with this picture," she tells me.

Why Aren't Women Making It to the Top?

Promoting better family/work policies is not the only reason to have more female CEOs and corporate board members. One need not be a feminist or even an advocate for better family/work policies to recognize the obvious: diversity pays. It raises the bottom line. So it is puzzling that the trend is going the other way. According to a census conducted by the Alliance for Board Diversity, "Collectively, women and minorities lost ground in America's corporate boardrooms between 2004 and 2010. White men still overwhelmingly dominate corporate boards with few overall gains for minorities since 2004 and a significant loss of seats for African-American men. . . . Women—particularly minority women—did not see an appreciable increase in their share of board seats."[5]

Catalyst analyzed why women had not moved into corporate leadership positions, as had been expected. Popular wisdom had been: "Just give it time. Not yet, but soon. When women get the right education, the right training, the right work experience, and the right aspirations—to succeed at the highest levels of business—then we'll see parity."[6] It hasn't happened. Why?

In a study that surveyed almost ten thousand alumni who graduated between 1996 and 2007 from twenty-six business schools in Asia, Canada, Europe, and the United States, it found that less than half were working full-time.[7]

The survey showed that female MBAs earn less from the start. Gender earning gaps appear at the entry level, after women receive an MBA and take their first job. Women on average were paid $4,600 less than men. The wage gap—which prevents women from ever catching up—is not a matter of different aspirations or even, as is commonly thought, a matter of parenthood; the findings hold for men and women without children, too.[8] One would expect that women eventually catch up, but the answer is no. Men were twice as likely as women to have reached the CEO/senior executive level, and to have had higher salary growth.[9] The study concluded that women were poised to make it to the top, but very few did.

We have to dig deeper to ascertain why. One possibility is that high-earning women are already thinking ahead to how they will combine caregiving and work and don't want to aim for a position that requires their presence 24/7. It is ironic that until more women reach the top, where they will be able to change policies and practices, the status quo will prevail and more women will tend to hold themselves back from the top, because there haven't been changes to those policies and practices.

Another answer may be that they are aware of the trade-off between work and family and consider the trade-off worthwhile only if the job provides as much gratification as being home with the family. "If women do opt out, it's not because they can't handle their families," Wharton's Monica McGrath notes. "It's because they feel they really can't advance."

> Stereotypes and biases that keep women from advancing are "more subtle" than in the past and "possibly unintentional," but they still exist," McGrath says. She recalls an executive management meeting she once witnessed as a consultant, in which a woman was being considered for an overseas post. Although she was clearly the most qualified for the position, one manager remarked that the woman probably would not want the job because she had two small children. "'They actually thought that this was a sensitive remark," McGrath points out. In the end, the company did offer the position to the woman, who happily accepted. "They were not planning to be discriminatory. A company based on women's norms would be more sensitive to these issues."[10]

Another reason that women may trip on the ladder to the top is that they are not included in the informal networks built up at places where men typically meet, such as the golf course and the men's room. "If you're in the network, you know what those next steps will be to take advantage of the opportunity, and if you're out of the informal network, you may just not know," says Nadya A. Fouad, coauthor of *Stemming the Tide: Why Women Leave Engineering*.[11] Women are skilled at learning the rules, and from grade school on, they were told that if they studied hard, showed up in class every day, and got good grades, they would succeed. If they played by the rules and believed in merit, though, they were undercut by internal politics. The transfer of power from one person to another, in any venue, is rarely based on merit alone. It is governed by a complex set of informal rules that are not written down—that is why Machiavelli's *The Prince* is still in print. These rules are transmitted verbally at almost any time, in any place. To understand them, women have to be in the room. (The ladies room is beginning to be as important as the men's room. I have gleaned important information from my colleagues in the legislature while adjusting my lipstick and combing my hair. The only word of caution had become: make sure you know who is in the stalls before you start talking.)

One theory to explain the continued meager presence of women in corporate leadership is that women do not negotiate as aggressively as their male counterparts. Politeness has been ingrained; fear of rejection is high.

Some women may be grateful to be chosen for the job in the first place and dare not ask for more. They are more likely than men to assume that the offer was fair and equitable because they are unaware of the salary landscape. They simply do not know how much to ask for.

A former college president, who would prefer not to be named, told me about a woman he had recommended for the presidency of another college. She told him the salary she had been offered and asked for his advice. He told her that the salary was far below the norm of college presidents. He suggested she ask the trustees, "You wouldn't want to pay the first female president of your university less than a man, would you?" She got what she asked for, and more.

Women make up 46.7 percent of the Fortune 500 labor force and more than 50 percent of management, Catalyst's Ilene Lang told the Joint Economic Committee of Congress. "But despite their sustained participation and economic influence, women have experienced a shockingly slow rate of progress advancing into business leadership—regardless of industry. According to Catalyst research, the percentage of women Executive Officers and board directors in *Fortune* 500 companies stuck at 15.2 percent and a staggering 97.4 percent of *Fortune* 500 CEOs are men."[12]

That translates into thirteen female CEOs for every five hundred males, making them a rare species indeed. What is lost is not only talent, but the advantages of diversity.

More Diversity = More Profit

Lang makes a powerful economic case for diversity: "On average, companies with more women board directors significantly outperform those with fewer women by 53 percent on Return on Equity, 42 percent on Return on Sales, and a whopping 66 percent on Return on Invested Capital. What's good for women is good for American business."[13]

She is not alone. McKinsey & Company, a large international management consulting firm, concurs. In a report titled *Women Matter*, McKinsey concluded that "the companies where women are most strongly represented at board or top-management level are also the companies that perform best. . . . We analyzed the answers of 58,240 respondents to our survey, and then compared the results for these companies, depending on the proportion of women on their governing bodies: it emerged that companies with three or more women in senior management functions score more highly, on average, for each organizational criterion than companies with no women at the top."[14]

This conclusion has been confirmed again and again. The executive summary of *Groundbreakers*, a report by Ernest & Young, states: "Several studies from a broad spectrum of organizations—including Catalyst, Columbia University, McKinsey, Goldman Sachs and the Conference Board of Canada—have examined the relationship between corporate financial performance and women in leadership roles. Their undisputed conclusion is that having more women at the top improves financial performance."[15]

Kristen Svensson, who runs a mentoring program in Brussels for would-be corporate directors, explains the advantage of diversity: "If you have 12 gray-haired men, average age 65, on a board, they tend to think about business prospects and strategy from the same perspective. But if you put a 45-year-old from a hot company and a woman and an international representative on the board, the quality of the debate will deepen."[16]

It will also be different. A survey that found that 65 percent of women directors believe that "increased diversity would be needed to rebuild the public's trust in corporate governance. Only 35 percent of men agreed."[17]

Women had both the disadvantage and the advantage of having seen Wall Street from the outside, unlike most of their male colleagues who have long been comfortable insiders. Insiders tend to be enamored of tradition; this is the way it has always been done. I experienced the same phenomenon in politics. As a newcomer to the political wheeling and dealing that went on to pass legislation, I was inclined to ask, "Why?" Not having been beholden to tradition, I was in a better position to question it. Having just moved from the outside world of being a citizen to the inside world of being a politician, public opinion was still fresh in my mind.

For example, one of my early bills concerned lobbyists. It would have required lobbyists to register and declare how much money they spent on contributions to legislators, including wining and dining. For me this would have been a positive step toward clean politics. For them it was an outrage; how could I question their integrity? I served in the legislature long enough to see a weaker version of my bill adopted.

I have learned that a mix of both insiders and outsiders is healthy for any institution. Not to be forgotten is the citizen, client, or customer who—when leadership is not relegated to sixty-five-year-old white men—can recognize himself or herself in the corporate board group photograph.

Why isn't this information about the positive impact of women persuasive enough to encourage corporations to seek out women to serve on their boards or to promote them to top positions? There is much speculation about the answer. Some blame women themselves.

Instead of attributing the miniscule number of female corporate leaders to women's behavior, family/work conflicts, and lack of ambition, why not look at who sits on boards today? Most corporate board members are comprised of former or present CEOs. They appoint one another to sit on one another's boards. The system is somewhat incestuous. "Power seeks people that are like them. It's more comfortable," explains Christina Shea, now retired executive vice president for external relations and president of the General Mills Foundation.

That observation rang true when I served on the board of the John Hancock. I had joined a tight-knit white boys club that perpetuated itself. Most board members had one thing in common: they served on one another's boards. To their credit, they went beyond tokenism; In 1991 I became the second woman to join the board after I had finished my third term as governor.

What Are the Young Men Thinking?

The typical corporate board member who sits at the glossy long table in the expensive wood-paneled boardroom remains, in my mind, that stereotypical sixty-five-year-old man. I am inclined to excuse him because he may be a product of his generation—not that far removed from the TV series *Mad Men*. I had believed that when the next generation took over, the picture would quickly change. These are the younger men whose wives are likely to have jobs of their own and whose daughters have ambitions. I was wrong.

Writing in "Annals of Communication," for *The New Yorker*, Ken Auletta notes:

> Among the hottest new companies—Facebook, Twitter, Zynga, Groupon, Foursquare—none, as Kara Swisher reported in the

> blog All Things Digital, has a female director on its board. PayPal has no women on its five-member board; Apple has one of seven; Amazon one of eight; Google two of nine. When I asked Mark Zuckerberg why his five-member board has no women, his voice, which is normally loud, lowered to a whisper: "We have a very small board." He went on, "I'm going to find people who are helpful, and I don't particularly care what gender they are or what company they are. I'm not filling the board with check boxes." (He recently added a sixth member: another man.) The venture-capital firms that support new companies have even sharper imbalances; Sequoia Partners lists eighteen partners on its Web site, none of them women.[18]

What are these young men thinking? Despite being on the cutting edge of modern technology, they are in a time warp when it comes to women in leadership, not unlike their fathers and grandfathers. It would be a healthy exercise for them to begin "checking boxes" and filling them with "helpful," talented women who would boost their bottom line.

Who Is Qualified?

When a woman *is* given a board-membership business card by one company, she is considered a safe appointment by others, because she has been vetted. Suddenly, her board dance card is full. That was the case for former secretary of commerce Juanita Kreps, who served on many boards, including the New York Stock Exchange in the 1980s. The same parameters hold true for African-Americans, such as Vernon Jordan, a close friend of President Clinton, who sits on numerous boards.

President Carter noted that he had difficulty filling cabinet posts with qualified women on the day he appointed Kreps to the post of secretary of commerce in 1977. Kreps took a different position: "I think it would be hard to defend the proposition that there are not a great many qualified women," she said. "I do think we have to do a better job of looking in the case of both women and minorities."[19]

Does that mean we have to look harder, or should we change the definition of "qualified"? I argue for both. If the requirement is that the person be a former CEO, it will be difficult for a woman to "qualify" because so few women are CEOs. As long as "qualified" is measured by "who has held the job before," progress is unlikely. The challenge is to redefine "qualified," which is what I was able to do when I made cabinet appointments as governor. Many of the women (approximately half of my cabinet and subcabinet appointees were women) had so-called gaps in their résumés, and others had no obvious management experience, but, reading between the lines on those résumés, I saw strong leadership qualities. Few had resumes that were like those of the commissioners who had preceded them, not only because of gender, but also because of experience. I took some risks. None, it turned out, led to regrets. Whenever I was given a list of all-male candidates to choose from, I sent it back with the instruction, "Find me some women."

Betsy Costle showed me her résumé when she applied for the position of counsel for the Vermont Department of Banking and Insurance (since given the additional responsibility of Securities, and Health Care Administration). I discovered a ten-year gap. That was when she was home raising her children. She had gone to law school several years later. She questioned her own qualifications, telling me, "I have some experience, but not precisely for this job," unlike the young man I had interviewed who was competing for the same job. He was super-confident that he could transfer his skills to this position, even though he had worked in a completely different department. It's not hard to guess who got the job. She did, because I could see reflections of myself in her résumé. I, too, had taken ten years off when my children were young. I understood the value of those "at-home and volunteer" years. If I had been a male governor, I surmise that I would have chosen the male candidate, not because of sex discrimination, but because *his* résumé would have looked more like *mine*. Betsy Costle turned out to be highly qualified and subsequently became commissioner of the department.

Among my other appointments was that of a Republican state representative, Gretchen Morse, to the post of secretary of the Agency of Human Services, after I had observed her skills as she shepherded a complex new funding formula through the legislature to revise how state dollars were sent to local schools. I was criticized for the appointment by the highly partisan Democratic Speaker of the House, who was quick to pronounce: "Why the hell did you appoint a Republican?" Others questioned her management credentials, which were indeed sparse. After I left the governorship, Morse became director of the Chittenden County United Way. Twenty years later, I attended her retirement party, and the accolades from the community were overwhelming.

I had the opportunity to appoint Molly Beattie as the first woman to be commissioner of the Department of Forest, Parks, and Recreation. She had just received her master's degree in forestry but had never been a supervisor. I took a chance. It was well worth it, because when Bill Clinton was elected he chose her to head the US Fish and Wildlife Service, the first woman to hold that post.

The lesson learned is that determining who is "qualified" is a more subjective assessment than most people acknowledge. Moving beyond the parameters of precedent leads to a new definition of "qualified." Demanding a new, more diverse list proves Juanita Kreps right; there are qualified women out there—we just have to look. Sometimes, however, it is women themselves who do not believe they are qualified. Claire Cain Miller, writing for the *New York Times*, tells the story of Virginia Rometty, the first female CEO of IBM:

> Early in her career, Virginia M. Rometty . . . was offered a big job, but she felt she did not have enough experience. So she told the recruiter she needed time to think about it.
>
> That night, her husband asked her, "Do you think a man would have ever answered that question that way?"
>
> "What it taught me was you have to be very confident, even though you're so self-critical inside about what it is you may or may not know," she said at Fortune's Most Powerful Women Summit. . . . "And that, to me, leads to taking risks."[20]

Failure to take risks, or continuing to appoint people who look exactly like the people who preceded them, perpetuates the status quo of male leadership; it also deprives an institution of fresh energy and ideas and, quite likely, a more successful organization.

European Corporate Boards

European countries have had a lower percentage of women on their corporate boards than the United States. About 68 percent of companies in Europe have no women in executive leadership, compared to 11 percent in the United States.[21] But they are taking aggressive steps to remedy that imbalance.

The arguments for parity in corporate leadership were sufficiently powerful to convince Norway to enact legislation in 2002 requiring 40 percent female membership on many corporate boards by 2008. The four hundred companies affected by the law met the target. Early results have been mixed. A University of Michigan study concluded that the new female corporate directors had less experience and did not improve the quality of board performance or the firms' bottom line. Still, the Nordic countries are leading the way, with female corporate board membership in Norway at 40.2 percent, in Sweden at 26.9 percent, in Finland at 25.7 percent, and in Denmark at 18.1 percent.[22] And France recently passed a law with a 20 percent gender diversity quota for board membership by 2016. Spain and the Netherlands are on a similar trajectory.

Quotas speed up the process. In 1993 Norwegian women held 3 percent of corporate board seats; in 2002, that figure was 6 percent. "If organic growth is 3 percent every ten years," says Elin Hurvenes, founder of Norway's Professional Boards Forum, "it would have taken 100 years to get to 40 percent."[23] Instead the quotas were enacted, threatening to shut down companies if they did not comply with the diversity minimums. Not inconsequential is the fact that women represent 70 percent of all purchasing decisions, according to one study, 80, 85, or 90 percent according to others. These figures argue for more female board members who would have more direct knowledge of women's buying habits.

Quotas have had another global impact—they significantly increased the percentage of women in Parliaments at a much faster rate than in the United States. Quotas, however, are not well received in English-speaking countries. Great Britain became concerned about its 12.5 percent female representation on corporate boards and considered quotas, but concluded that "prescriptive alternatives of the recommended business led approach do not achieve significant change."[24] The British commission charged with evaluating the issue recommended that the country's top one hundred companies "should aim for a minimum of 25 percent female representation by 2015."[25]

An alternative to quotas was proposed by Helena Morrissey, a money manager who set up a program, backed by the chairman of Lloyds Banking Group, to elevate more women to corporate boards. She called it the 30% Club. "We want to get there with momentum instead of regulation," she says.[26]

The former minister for women and equality in England, Harriet Harman, attributed the 2008 financial meltdown to the lack of women in leadership: as reported in the *New York Times*, "she partly blamed the lack of women in senior roles in the financial industry for the crisis, saying if it had been 'Lehman Sisters' rather than Lehman Brothers, the company might have survived."[27]

Jacki Zehner, retired from a career as a partner at Goldman Sachs, has a variation on that theme. In an interview she explains, "I think we [women] think about risk differently." She notes that hedge funds on average had an annual return of almost 6 percent, but hedge funds run by women did better, with a return of 9 percent. During the downturn in 2009, when funds as a whole dropped 19 percent, funds run by women went down just less than 10 percent.[28]

"What If Women Ran Wall Street?" asks a 2010 headline in *New York Magazine*. The article quotes hedge fund manager Henry Lee: "The notion of taking chances is definitely more male. Look, men are much more willing to take a shot at something with incomplete knowledge." Having women around, he says, "prevents extreme behavior—or irrational exuberance."[29]

Exercising Investor Power

Where will the momentum for change come from in the United States? The answer is investors, according to PAX World president and CEO Joseph F. Keefe. He has launched a "Say No to All Male Boards Campaign" by sending letters to 165 institutional investors, investment advisers, and individuals asking them to oppose all slates of director nominees with fewer than two women. He cites the "nexus between greater board and management diversity, on one hand, and improved corporate governance and financial performance on the other."[30] When I spoke with him last, he had received only three responses, but undaunted, he plans to send out 150 more letters. When I ask him why the response was so meager, he replies, "They told me, this is politics, we care about the bottom line. My response is this is about the bottom line. They're not going to change because they want to make the world a better place. They'll change because they will be better off financially."

Instead of mandating diversity from above, let's start from below. If 3 or 4 percent of shareholders spoke up, Keefe believes they would have the same impact as shareholders had on investment in South African companies during apartheid, when the public boycotted some American companies who had offices located in that country.

In his letter, Keefe writes, "*Investors* are not raising their voices and insisting that companies do better. . . . It is time for investors to weigh in and make a difference." He suggests that investors demand that proxy voting guidelines include gender diversity policies, because "advocating for board diversity is the right thing for us to do, as fiduciaries, on behalf of those who entrust us with their investments."[31]

Could his ideas catch on? A Swiss company, Naissance Capital, based in Zurich, announced in 2009 that it would be starting the Women's Leadership Fund in 2010. According to co-founder R. James Breiding, the fund was created after several studies showed a correlation between the number of female directors and a company's performance. The fund's board includes Kim Campbell, former prime minister of Canada, and Cherie Blair, wife of Tony Blair, former British prime minister. "The evidence shows that companies who give women an equal chance to shine and equal responsibility are also likely to be more profitable companies. . . . We simply can't go on making the most of the talents and potential of half the population. . . . For a revolution is happening. And those firms and countries which don't understand this are going to be left behind. In developed and developing nations, women have become the drivers of economic growth," Blair stated on the fund's website.[32]

The organization 85 Broads was founded in 1999 by women who worked for Goldman Sachs (at 85 Broad Street) to encourage networking among women in business. Today, there are thirty-four regional chapters worldwide. The need for women to network and share information and contacts among themselves is one indicator that women still have to create formal organizations to be in the loop, while men do it more naturally.

The far-reaching progress that women have made in the last thirty to forty years, in entering the labor force, enrolling in institutions of higher education, and fighting blatant sex discrimination, obscures the more slender barriers that hold women in check at some point in their lives. Many women themselves see no cause for alarm, until they get their first job, have their first baby, and discover that they are making less money than the man sitting in the next cubicle. Once we begin to dig into the question of why so few women are in corporate leadership positions, we find that the issue is complex. If public perception is that the playing field is already level, why try to change it? If the few women who make it to the top continue to enter a predominantly male power structure, how do they leave their imprint? One strategy that has proven to work for men who strive to work their way to the top—in both the public and private spheres—also works for women. It's called mentoring.

CHAPTER 10

What Women Need to Create Equal Opportunities in the Workplace

For women who want to break through what's typically been called the glass ceiling, a good mentor can be critical to success. Men are less in need of formal mentors because mentoring is in the air they breathe from the moment they step through the corporate door. They see themselves reflected everywhere. Past CEOs sit in their gold-framed portraits on the walls. Together they form a welcoming committee. A man can scan the corner office and see another man, who looks rather like him, through the plate glass window. While waiting for a meeting, he sits comfortably on the black leather sofa and overhears familiar chatter around the water cooler about which sports team won or lost the night before. For reinforcement he has only to turn the pages of the *Wall Street Journal* lying on the coffee table to know that this is where he belongs. Testosterone is everywhere. Women tend to sense it in the air. They can either accustom themselves to it with a shrug, or try to change it.

One of the first things I did when I stepped into the governor's office after I was elected was get rid of the black Naugahyde sofa and matching chairs and replace them with cheerful, dark red tweed. That was after I had put the toilet seat down in the executive bathroom.

Claiming a spot in a typically male environment can be everything from humorous to harrowing for women. Yet most women who do it have had, like I did, the benefit of a mentor. For many women, that mentor will be male. When *USA Today* asked female CEOs to identify one mentor who had influenced their careers, thirty-three of the thirty-four who responded said their mentors were men.[1] The conclusion is not surprising, because there are fewer female CEOs to fill that role.

Mentoring for women has to be more intentional—men have to seek women out, and likewise, women have to seek male or female mentors who see their potential in ways that they themselves can't envision. My most effective mentor was unexpected—Emory A. Hebard, a conservative Republican who chaired the Vermont House Appropriations Committee when I served in the Vermont House.. Hebard championed me as the key Democrat on the committee and gave me the responsibility of reporting bills and serving on conference committees. Four years later, he left the legislature to run for state treasurer and he promoted my candidacy to become the next chair of the committee, despite hesitation from my own Democratic leadership. Neither of us ever used the word "mentor." We just had an understanding; I would be loyal to him, and he would support me. Mentoring can be as simple as a show of confidence.

It is no accident that a total of five university and college presidents claim former Princeton University president Harold T. Shapiro as their mentor: President Shirley Tilghman of Princeton, President Ruth Simmons of Brown, President Amy Gutmann of the University of Pennsylvania, Chancellor Nancy Cantor of Syracuse, and President S. Georgia Nugent of Kenyon College. I asked Shapiro how this happened. What did he do? He answers, "I consider this one of the satisfactions of my career. There's a lot of talk about mentoring—the most important thing to do is give people the opportunity, the chance to demonstrate their leadership, and then provide strong support."

I wondered whether being the father of four daughters had influenced Shapiro. A Catalyst study had shown that 83 percent of men mentoring women had daughters.[2] Yet when I ask if this was the case, he demurs and points out that his wife also had a professional full-time career, at a time when most women did not. More importantly, though, he had always been sensitive to issues facing women in the workplace.

As a mentor, Shapiro didn't offer day-to-day hand holding. Rather, he would take a bigger step; he would recommend women for new positions. "Someone would call me and say, we have an opening for a president; do you know anyone at Princeton? And I would mention two or three people. I would bring people to other people's attention. You'd be surprised how effective that is. You have to go out of your way to create opportunities."

He would tell the women, "There's a great job here, you might want to apply." Some of the women, he says, "self-mobilized"; others had to be encouraged.

How did he select them? "It was different in different cases. I spotted women who were distinguished members of our faculty who also showed an interest in the institution. I looked for people who showed they really cared about the institution's welfare, as well as their own work. Sometimes I had to sell the idea; they had no concept that that's what they wanted to do."

Some men shy away from lending a woman a helping hand in the workplace for fear of being accused of having romantic interests. Shapiro never let that get in the way, but he did take steps to thwart any such impressions. "The truth is in the last twenty or thirty years, I never met with a woman in my office unless someone else was there, or the door was open. I just thought it was good practice, overall."

He continues to stay in touch with his mentees several times a year; either they call him or he calls them. He downplays his influence. "These people don't need advice. They're pretty darn intelligent."

The five presidents who call Shapiro a mentor have had different family responsibilities. "One was not married and had no partner or children. One had a partner but a commuting relationship with no children. One was married to a professor here and had a single, very accomplished child. One had a single child that had serious development problems. One was divorced and had two children to care for. In short, the competing family activities were very different in these different cases," he recalls.

What they had in common was Harold Shapiro, a man who is modest about his success in mentoring women leaders. He acknowledges that promoting more female college and university presidents has two major benefits: "it increases the talent pool and it is good for the students."

Christina L. Shea also credits a boss who gave her a chance—as well as being in the right place at the right time—for her success as the first female president of an operating division at General Mills: the $2 billion Betty Crocker division. Now the mother of four adult children, she built her career over thirty-five years. "Fortunately," she says, "every time I got to a critical point, when I wanted to work part-time or take a leave, I found people—generally men—who agreed."

When Shea's second child was born with growth and development problems, she decided she needed to take some time off. When she requested a part-time schedule followed by a year of leave, her boss said he'd find a way to make it work. "He told me, 'I'd rather have you part-time than some of the men around here who work full-time.' He confessed to me that he wished he had spent more time with his kids when they were young. He took a lot of hits for this from other managers. I had four years of flexibility and came back as a vice president."

Not all women receive recognition for their ability, like Shea did, either because they are on the low end of the pay scale or because their ability is not recognized. Qualities like aggressiveness that are commendable in a man may be questionable in a woman. Women sometimes are caught in a double bind, charged with being too tough or too soft, or never getting it just right. Shea agrees that "there always has been a tighter bandwidth that women have to operate in. You learn to adapt to the majority culture, and once you get there, you try to widen the width." She learned how to adapt when she was one of sixteen women in the 120-member class of 1977 at the Tuck School of Business at Dartmouth College.

One of her early bosses had a nick name for her,"PB," for "Pushy Broad."

"I just grinned and bore it," Shea recalls. "You learn not to let stuff like that bug you."

Her experience made her an advocate for family support policies at General Mills. "It's acceptable now to be gone for six months after the birth or adoption of a child (without total pay). If you have a sick child, the company will arrange for someone to come to your house to take care of your child." She described a system of co-mentoring at General Mills: A senior executive will coach a younger person, and she or he, in turn, will let him or her know what people are thinking who are a decade younger. "They each come from a different culture; it can be very powerful for both people," she said.

When women seek her out for advice on which companies to work for, she tells them, "Do not limit yourself. Even if you take time off, remember you still have another twenty-five years of work. When deciding which company to work for, go in with your eyes wide open, look to see if there are other women in management and women vice presidents. See if women are coaching other women and advocating for them."

What's the Best Career: Medicine or Finance?

Some careers for mothers with young children are better than others in terms of flexibility. One of these, much to my surprise, is medicine. *Harvard Magazine* reported on a study that surveyed 6,500 women who graduated from Harvard and Radcliffe between 1969 and 1992. The study found that less than 30 percent of MBAs were working full-time and having children, but 45 percent of the MDs were.[3] It is counterintuitive but true: an MD is more compatible with having a family than an MBA. The reason is that many physicians are working shorter hours, both women and men. The trend is most noticeable in pediatrics, a field dominated by women. A report based on a survey of 1,600 members of the American Academy of Pediatrics concludes that 23 percent were on a part-time schedule in 2006, up from 15 percent six years earlier. Women who worked less reported "greater levels of satisfaction with their work and personal and family lives."[4] All physicians are working fewer hours, according to the *Journal of the American Medical Association*. Average hours dropped from about fifty-five hours a week to fifty-one from 1996 to 2008.[5] Did the increasing number of female physicians influence this trend, or were more women attracted to the field because of the shorter hours? It's hard to know which came first, but the result is that in some fields, the trend toward shorter hours is welcomed by both women and men who want to lead more fulfilling lives.[6]

Wall Street's tough demands on corporate women are highlighted by Geraldine Fabrikant in "The Female Factor," a 2010 piece she wrote for the *New York Times*."[7] She tells the story of Sallie Krawcheck, who was ousted from Citigroup in 2008 during the financial crisis. Six months later, she landed a position at Bank of America, making her one of the few women to have made a comeback after the rampant downsizing of Wall Street at that time. "I don't think I set foot in a restaurant where some woman did not come up to me and thank me for getting knocked around and getting back in," Krawcheck told Fabrikant.

"Women have always been drawn to finance in smaller numbers than men. But after nearly two decades of increased hiring and promotion of women on Wall Street, their ranks appear to be shrinking again," Fabrikant writes. Why? Is it because women's ability is not recognized, or because women reject a 24/7 work week? The answer, most likely, is both.

Women-Owned Businesses

Some women have abandoned the quest to change the corporate culture to meet their needs. They have given up on the long hours, lack of flexibility, and unsatisfying work. Instead, they clear off their desks, walk out, and start their own businesses. "I can't change the world, so I'm just going to get out of it," Robin Grolund, former president of Women Business Owners Network of Vermont, tells me. She had worked for Procter & Gamble, for IBM, and for a small start-up. "I've done it," she says, but "it took me forty-seven years to understand why I wasn't happy all those years." The reason? No flexibility.

"When your child was sick or when you had to do something, you were penalized," she explains. "My mother died six years ago from ovarian cancer. I was [spending time at] the respite house as she was dying and the corporate HR manager came to me and said, 'It looks like you're taking too much time from work.' I worked weekends to make up the time. When the corporation comes to you and basically says, 'We don't care about your life, we don't care about your family,' as a woman, that's just not okay. There are lot of women who stick it out in corporate America, and they get sick and they stifle themselves because of fear."

Grolund helped start the Women Business Owners Network with one goal in mind: empowerment. "Empowerment to me is about helping women take charge of their lives, feeling that they can do things that maybe society says you can't do. They become empowered to start their own business, to have a life that offers them flexibility," she says. "A lot of these women have had very successful careers and then find themselves outside a corporate or an organized environment and wonder how they are going to do this. They have to re-create themselves."

When I ask her whether female CEOs were more sensitive to family issues, she replies, "I think it depends. I see two kinds of women. There are women who support each other, and then there are women who don't. They are the women who say [I] had to fight it, so I'm going to make you fight it. I had to suffer, I was tortured, and I'm going to torture you."

When women-owned businesses grow and succeed they give a big boost to the American economy. Today the estimated eight million majority-women-owned firms have an estimated impact of $3 trillion annually that translates into the creation and/or maintenance of more than 23 million jobs—16 percent of the US total, according to a study by the Center for Women's Business Research.[8] The US Chamber of Commerce reports that between 1997 and 2002, new women-owned businesses grew 44 percent, compared with a 22 percent increase in businesses owned by men. "The overarching shift," according to the study, "reflects the education, experience and characteristics of women at different stages of their lives. It also reflects the lack of opportunities and flexibility in major corporations and large businesses for women," the report concludes.[9]

The downside of the report is that despite growing in numbers, women-owned businesses don't provide large incomes. Just 4.2 percent of all revenue is generated by these companies. Only 20 percent had employees. They are smaller and more likely to fail than those owned by men. The biggest growth deterrent is that women-owned businesses have more difficulty obtaining access to capital. "The major sources of funding that women business owners continue to rely on are personal savings, reinvested business earnings, lines of credit, loans, equity financing and venture capital," according to the National Association of Women Business Owners. Some 65 percent of its membership consider that a major problem.[10]

Despite these realities, and even in a tough economic climate, many believe that the growth potential for women's business remains untapped. As more women seek to be their own boss to find flexibility and a better work/life mix, women-owned businesses are projected to account for one-third of new jobs created by 2018, according to the Guardian Life Small Business Research Institute.[11] That is where the jobs come from, Nell Merlino, head of Count Me In, explains. She has an initiative called "Make Mine a Million $ Business." The reason many women-owned businesses don't grow is that owners "try to do everything themselves," Merlino says. Her company enables women to do the most important thing: how to "hire the right people."

From 59 Cents to 77 Cents: The Ongoing Battle for Equal Pay

For women who choose to stay in the traditional workforce, however, equal pay remains a crucial issue—despite the fact that women and men, regardless of where they fall on the liberal to conservative spectrum, agree on one thing: women should receive equal pay for equal work. In a nationwide poll of all voters, 84 percent responded that they "supported a new law that would provide women more tools to get fair pay in the workplace." Members of all major political parties support improved equal pay laws: Republicans (77 percent), Democrats (91 percent), and Independents (87 percent). When participants were told that the proposed Paycheck Fairness Act "will also make it harder for employers to justify paying different wages for the same work and ensure that businesses that break the law compensate women fairly," 72 percent supported such a law.[12] Equal pay for equal work should be a no-brainer. Unfortunately, it is not.

I recall when women wore green buttons pinned to our dresses with the white number "59¢" on it. That was 1977. The mysterious number, without text, was designed to prompt the question, "What does that mean?" Few knew then that the pay differential between women and men was so wide, that women made just 59 cents for every dollar earned by males doing the same work. If there were a button for 2011, it would read "77¢." Not many people today would have guessed that despite the 18 cent gain (after forty-seven years), a 23-cent gap still exists. When the pay gap is broken down according to race and ethnicity, African-American women make only 61 cents and Latinas 52 cents for every dollar earned by white non-Hispanic men.

The wage gap between women and men is more than a matter of a few cents. It accumulates into a matter of many thousands of dollars over a lifetime. The average pay gap translates into a loss of $10,622 per year in female median earnings.[13] That figure continues to increase over a life span because when women start out their life journey by walking five paces behind men, the distance becomes greater each year, culminating at retirement. The Institute for Women's Policy Research has calculated that a typical woman with a college diploma would lose more than $440,000 in a twenty-year period. This is no mere statistic. A woman approached me at the podium after I had given a speech on women and politics in El Paso, Texas. She wanted to tell me her story. She had recently discovered that a male colleague, doing the same job, had been paid significantly more for many years than she had. "I'm about to retire, and now I'm going to receive a much lower retirement package. I wish I had known that, all these years."

Pay discrepancies contribute to the high rates of poverty experienced by women and children. In our search for practical ways to improve the lives of American families, narrowing the wage gap provides the most direct remedy, particularly for those female heads of households who live on the precipice of poverty. More than one in three of these families with children were poor in 2008.

How can we make progress more quickly to narrow the pay gap? There are two routes—litigation and law. The Lilly Ledbetter Fair Pay Act is a product of both. Ledbetter was a supervisor on the Goodyear Tire and Rubber Company factory floor in Gadsden, Alabama. When an anonymous letter informed her that she was being paid less than equivalent male supervisors, she sued Goodyear. She won, but the company appealed to the United States Supreme Court, which voted 5 to 4 to deny Ledbetter back pay for wage discrimination because she had exceeded the 180-day statute of limitations. The outcry from civil liberties groups was so great that Congress passed the Lilly Ledbetter Fair Pay Act, the first bill to be signed into law by President Barack Obama, on January 29, 2009.

It was hailed as a step forward to assure equal pay, but there was a companion bill that did not make it: the Paycheck Fairness Act, which, as discussed in chapter 9, passed the House of Representatives but failed in the Senate in 2010. That bill would have amended the 1938 Fair Labor Standards Act to make it easier to file sex discrimination cases by putting the onus on employers to prove that pay discrepancies between women and men doing the same jobs were the result of nondiscriminatory business necessities. It also would have prohibited retaliation for sharing salary information with colleagues. The bill further would have provided grants to give women and girls salary negotiation training because studies have shown that the wage gap exists, in part, because women are more reluctant to negotiate higher salaries than men, and when they do, they are perceived more negatively.

Despite support from President Obama, who called it "a commonsense bill," and backing from a wide swath of the public the bill failed because of two opposing views of its potential impact. A report from the Heritage Foundation, a conservative think tank, claimed the bill would allow "government and the courts to dictate business practices" and "would give a windfall to trial lawyers, exposing employers to unlimited punitive damages."[14] The

Women's Media Center, on the other hand, called the act an economic imperative "that is needed now more than ever . . . [because it is] taking meaningful steps to create stronger incentives for employers to follow the law, empower women to negotiate for equal pay and strengthen federal outreach and enforcement efforts."[15]

Senator Barbara A. Mikulski (D-MD) spoke in favor of the bill on the Senate floor. It "makes it more difficult to discriminate in the first place," she said. "It prohibits employer retaliation. . . . Under current law, employers can sue or actually punish employees for sharing salary statements and information with coworkers. This is usually the way that employees find out that they're being discriminated against."[16]

Christina Hoff Sommers, a socially conservative scholar who frequently critiques feminist issues, saw it differently. In a *New York Times* opinion piece, she wrote "The bill isn't as commonsensical as it might seem. It overlooks mountains of research showing that discrimination plays little role in pay disparities between men and women and it threatens to impose onerous requirements on employers to correct gaps over which they have little control." Sommers also contended that the 77-cent wage gap "isn't necessarily the result of discrimination. On the contrary, there are lots of other reasons men might earn more than women, including differences in education, experience and job tenure." Sommers concluded, "The Paycheck Fairness bill would set women against men, empower trial lawyers and activists, perpetuate falsehoods about the status of women in the workplace and create havoc in a precarious job market."[17]

Commentators like Sommers would have us believe that the 77-cent wage gap is more a product of the different choices men and women make than of salary discrimination in the workplace. She claims that we are comparing apples to oranges when coming up with the wage gap. But is this true? The answer appears to be no. The 77-cent figure, as determined by the US Census Bureau, compares apples to apples for full-time, year-round male and female wage earners.[18]

It is more difficult to compare male and female part-time workers because the term "part-time" can cover anything from one to thirty-four hours.

One indicator that the pay gap is genuine is the growing number of employment discrimination cases brought to the Equal Employment

Opportunity Commission (EEOC); it hit 100,000 in 2011, an unprecedented level. One-third of these cases involved discrimination based on sex. An authority on sex discrimination, Joan Williams, told me that these cases have a 50% success rate, which is dramatically higher than most discrimination cases, and that the average recovery is now $500,000.

Clearly discrimination is taking place, but what is less clear is how some women's different work patterns influence wages. Many women continue to take time off to have a family, are more likely to work part-time, and are less aggressive than men in seeking a raise or a promotion. These factors are difficult to tease out from deliberate and persistent gender discrimination. Ironically, when women are the beneficiaries of flexibility they sometimes lose out. Elaine McCrate, associate professor of economics and women's and gender studies at the University of Vermont, explains: "In these jobs, there is a self perpetuating feedback loop. Employers expect women to want reduced hours in order to accommodate family concerns, so they don't invest in women the way they invest in men." Joan Williams calls it "a flexibility stigma," which hits mothers the hardest.

Wage discrimination was charged in the case of *Dukes v. Wal-Mart*, involving lower paid employees. It was the largest employment discrimination class-action suit in American history. The suit was filed on behalf of 1.5 million women who had worked for the company since 1998. The case originated when seven female employees of Wal-Mart realized that men were being paid more for comparable jobs and were getting promoted more often. The Supreme Court threw out the case on June 19, 2011, on a 5-4 decision. The court did not decide whether Wal-Mart discriminated against women, only that the case did not satisfy the rules for class action. Justice Antonin Scalia wrote for the majority that those bringing the case against Wal-Mart could not show uniform discrimination in its 3,400 stores. On the other side, testimony from Professor William T. Bielby stated that Wal-Mart's culture might foster pay and other disparities through a centralized personnel policy that allowed for subjective decisions by local managers, making "decisions about compensation and promotion vulnerable to gender bias."[19]

The culture of gender bias may be the crux of the 77-cent disparity. I remember scanning the newspaper for job listings early in my career. There were two separate columns, one for "Men Wanted" and the other for "Women

Wanted." I never even looked at the "Men Wanted" list. Those separations no longer exist on paper, but they persist in some manager's minds.

High-paid female employees are not immune from pay discrimination. In September 2010, three former female employees at Goldman Sachs claimed "that Goldman intentionally pays its male employees more than their female counterparts, and promotes them more frequently."[20] One of the women was a former vice president, another a managing director, and the third an associate. Their complaint said, "The violations of its female employees' rights are systemic, are based upon companywide policies and practices, and are the result of unchecked gender bias that pervades Goldman Sachs's corporate culture."[21]

The Goldman Sachs case, which is still pending, is not unprecedented in the financial sector. Morgan Stanley paid a $54 million dollar settlement in a similar suit in 2004. And a jury awarded a $175 million settlement to settle a gender-discrimination class-action lawsuit against the pharmaceutical company Novartis, brought by 5,600 current and former female sales representatives in June 2010. "The female workers say they were passed over for promotions and denied equal pay to men, especially when pregnancies were involved."[22]

These examples of successful (except for Wal-Mart, thus far) sex discrimination lawsuits bolster the argument that sex discrimination contributes substantially to the 77-cent wage gap between women and men. Discrimination may not always be outright or even conscious, but it springs from the old stereotypical assumptions about what women and men should and can do. Like a color photograph left too long in the sun, the assumptions are beginning to fade, but the outline can still be deciphered.

Creating Equal Opportunity for Women in Academia and Science

One would expect that academia would be the last place where gender bias would influence pay and hiring practices. The academic world has been seen as a green space where life is fair. If you do well on a test, you get an A. But academia and science stand out as two professional fields where women continue to lag behind men.

In a report prepared for Equal Pay Day (April 11, 2011) titled "Persistent Inequity," John W. Curtis, director of research and public policy for the American Association of University Professors, notes, "There is a common presumption, both within and outside the higher education community, that as bastions of innovation and consideration of ideas and people on their merits, colleges and universities must be at the leading edge of efforts to implement equitable employment practices in their own organizations. Unfortunately the data on gender equity in academic employment do not support this presumption." Progress, he concludes, is actually slow, "*very* slow."[23]

"The numbers have hardly changed in 35 years," Curtis notes. While women comprised 57 percent of undergraduate enrollment and 59 percent of graduate enrollment in 2009, they do not find faculty role models in the same proportion. Forty-two percent of full-time faculty members are female. Only 28 percent of full professors are female. And when women are up for promotion, the process takes longer than it does for men. The good news is that the percentage of female college presidents has almost doubled in twenty years, and four out of eight Ivy League universities are led by women, but the typical portrait of a college president is still male.

On average, Curtis says, the full-time female faculty salary is 80 percent of the average male faculty salary, due to the fact that more women than men are clustered in low-paying and part-time positions. The largest pay discrepancy, when comparing apples to apples, occurs for full professors; women take home 87.6 percent of the salaries that men do. For lecturers, that number is 90.5 percent.

Curtis adds, "A final aspect of the difference in academic employment status is the gendered nature of academic work. Traditionally, the work of faculty members consists of teaching, research and scholarship, and various forms of service. . . . Women faculty members spend a greater proportion of their time on teaching than do men, and even specifically on undergraduate teaching and student advising."

Pay differentials begin right after women and men graduate from college, explain Judy Goldberg Dey and Catherine Hill, in a report prepared for the American Association of University Women Educational Foundation. "All college degrees do not have the same effect. . . . Many majors remain strongly dominated by one gender. Female students are concentrated in fields associated with lower earnings, such as education, health, and psychology. Male students dominate the higher-paying fields: engineering, mathematics, and physical sciences." Aside from the gender that may dominate a particular field, there are stark differences in pay between the genders even within a field. "In education, a female-dominated major, women earn 95 percent as much as their male colleagues earn. . . . Likewise in mathematics—a male-dominated major—women earn only 76 percent as much as men earn. Female students cannot simply choose a major that will allow them to avoid the pay gap," report Dey and Hill.[24]

Women in science meet similar challenges. I first heard about Professor Nancy Hopkins of MIT in 2005, when I read that she had stormed out of a lecture hall where Harvard president Lawrence Summers was holding forth about the lack of women in science. Among the reasons he gave: there may be "innate" differences between women and men. When I spoke to Hopkins she recalled that moment: "I was furious, I was disgusted." What got her so mad? The idea that "women are inferior because of genetics."

Hopkins is a molecular biologist who has won the National Medal of Science and has gained worldwide recognition for her work in genetics. She has also devoted a large part of her career to fighting for equal representation and equal status for women in science. Her mentor was Nobel Prize winner James Watson, author of *The Double Helix*. She says she first became aware of discrimination against women in science when she learned about Rosalind Franklin's contribution to the discovery of DNA—a discovery credited almost entirely to Francis Crick and James Watson.

"Of course what had happened to her is the same thing that happened to me and all of these other women," says Hopkins. "She made a discovery, and without her data they couldn't have possibly made their discovery . . . even if you made the greatest discovery of all time, [as a woman] you couldn't get the credit."

Hopkins spent years researching the role of women faculty at MIT and then decided to do something about what she found. In 1994 there were fifteen tenured women, versus 197 men. She gathered a group of women together, spent several years collecting more data, and made a report to the MIT president in 1999. The group had learned that sex discrimination was widespread. For example, "no woman had ever taken time off to have a child. It was such a stigma." Much has changed as a result of her findings. "Pressure," she says. "Nothing ever happens without it."

The pressure is still on in 2011. Of all academic fields, one would assume that in science and engineering, where results are measurable, success would be based on merit. Not yet. Today, Hopkins says, "about 45 percent of undergraduates majoring in science and engineering at MIT are women, 29 percent of graduate students, and 17 percent of the science and engineering faculty." This is the leaky pipeline, she explained in a keynote address at an MIT symposium.[25] Women drop out along the way, she believes, because of causes that are largely invisible—sexual harassment, a dearth of mentoring, an undervaluing of women's work, unconscious bias and beliefs, and the difficulty of achieving work/life balance. She deliberately decided not to have children in order to devote herself to science. She happily calls herself "a nun of science," but she does not believe that that should be a prerequisite for others.

National statistics about women in science parallel those of MIT. Women start out well along the science, math, and technology pathway but do not show up in proportionate numbers in tenured positions years later. Five women did show up, however, to receive their Nobel Prize awards in science in Stockholm, Sweden, in 2009. Since the prizes were established in 1901, of the 785 awarded, only 40 have gone to women. The 15 percent increase in 2009 was a welcome indicator that women in science have moved forward. But there is more territory to be conquered. Women have not made great inroads in Silicon Valley. Writing on the subject for the *New York Times*, Claire Cain Miller cites statistics from Astia, a nonprofit that advises female entrepreneurs: women own 40 percent of private businesses but create only 8 percent of venture-backed tech start-ups. And, she writes, "for those with a bottom-line approach, analysts say it makes a difference when women are in the garages where tech start-ups are founded or the boardrooms where they are funded. Studies have found that teams with both women and men are more profitable and innovative. Mixed-gender teams have produced information technology patents that are cited 26 percent to 42 percent more often than the norm, according to the National Center for Women and Information Technology.[26]

Now that we know that women's leadership is equal to, or sometimes better than, men's, how do we translate that conclusion into policy? Hopkins has an answer: pressure; keep applying the pressure.

The Power of Law

Whenever strategies for achieving social change come up in discussion, the question inevitably arises: Can laws change human behavior? Or should we wait until people voluntarily change their attitudes, be it regarding African-Americans, women, or gays? History tells us that pressure works best when it has the force of law behind it. Two pieces of legislation have had a direct influence on women's capacity to achieve equality: the 1964 Civil Rights Act, which barred sex discrimination in employment, and Title IX, which was part of the 1972 Education Amendments to the Civil Rights Act. Today Title IX is identified most closely with providing equal opportunities for women and men in high school and college sports. It has changed the lives of millions of women and girls, many of whom would never have kicked a soccer ball without it. But its genesis was not rooted in sports. Rather it was born out of broad-based inequities for females in education.

To put the impact of Title IX in a personal perspective, when I was in high school in Pittsfield, Massachusetts, and then at the University of Massachusetts at Amherst in the 1950s, to my knowledge, there were no women's sports teams. Today, when I ask a class, "How many of you have played sports in high school or college?" almost every hand goes up.

Bernice Sandler, known as Title IX's godmother, says the law has had a wide impact. "Title IX got rid of admissions quotas," she tells me. "My favorite statistic was [that] in the state of Virginia, sometime in the early 1960s, there were 21,000 women rejected for admission to state colleges and universities, and at the same time, no male was rejected." That's not a statistic I could verify, but it is in keeping with the times. "A veterinary school at Cornell University would take two women per year, no matter how many applied," recalls Sandler.

How did she win political support for Title IX? "We used to call ourselves the Mythical Marching Millions," she says. "We had about sixty groups, some like NOW but also American Federation of Teachers. I remember going to a meeting ready to tell people, 'We're ready to lobby, just tell us what to do.' Edith Green [the Democratic congresswoman from Oregon] told us, 'Don't do any lobbying, because people will ask questions and then they'll find out what the bill will really do.' We thought she was wrong. We were very politically naïve, but we listened to her and she was absolutely right."

It was an achievement to get Title IX on the books, but implementation remains the key to its long-term success. Blatant discrimination against women on the playing field or in the workplace has become far less common, but subtle discrimination persists, particularly for moms in the workplace.

The Maternal Wall

When we go back to the impact of "choices," do women actually have choices, or do the realities of combining family and a full-time academic career force many to settle for less by working part-time or not at all? Among women who graduated from college in 1992–93, ten years later, 23 percent of mothers were out of the workforce and another 17 percent were working part-time. Less than 2 percent of fathers fell into the same categories.

Joan Williams has concluded that women are pushed out because employers do not make a sufficient effort to retain them after they become mothers. The wage gap between mothers and nonmothers is now larger than that between men and women, according to some studies.[27] Williams's efforts on "work/life law" show that discrimination against mothers is the strongest form of gender discrimination. She cites studies in which subjects are given almost identical résumés, the only difference being that one, but not the other, lists membership in the PTA; the studies show that the mothers are 79 percent less likely to be hired and 100 percent less likely to be promoted.[28] "It's just dramatic," Williams tells me. "They are offered an average $11,000 less in salary and held to higher performance and punctuality standards. People don't say, 'This is no job for a woman,' but every day of the week they say, 'This is no job for a mother."

A new tool to challenge discrimination against mothers has been issued by the Equal Employment Opportunity Commission: family responsibilities discrimination. It covers such questions as firing or demoting employees when they become pregnant, passing over highly qualified mothers for hire or promotion in favor of less-qualified men or women without children, and firing employees without valid business reasons when they return from maternity or paternity leave.[29] "It's an important development in the law. Now you can litigate these issues in the courts," Williams explains.

The story of women getting fired after taking maternity leave is not uncommon; but most women do not take action. That's why Sandy Stephens, who worked as a housekeeper for the president of Global NAPs Inc., a telecommunications firm in Massachusetts, made news in 2010 when she sued her employer for firing her while she was on leave. Massachusetts law states that women who work full-time for small businesses with at least six employees can get their jobs back after eight weeks of maternity leave. Stephens, though, claimed her supervisor told her she could take a longer leave if she gave birth by Cesarean section. She did have a C section; but when she planned to return to work at eleven weeks, she learned that she had been fired for exceeding the eight-week leave. The Massachusetts Supreme Judicial Court decided in her employer's favor, stating that once a mother is absent more than eight weeks, she is no longer afforded the protections of the Massachusetts Maternity Leave Act.

Women who work for companies with fifty or more employees have a slightly longer period of job protection via the Family and Medical Leave Act, a federal law that protects jobs for up to twelve weeks of unpaid leave for eligible employees. But regardless of employer size, women report that perceptions of them and their ability to do their jobs change dramatically as soon as they reveal they are pregnant. They hit what Williams, in *Reshaping the Work-Family Debate*, describes as "the 'maternal wall'—negative stereotyping and gender bias that mothers experience on the job, often beginning as soon as they become pregnant."[30]

"Sometimes it's more subtle," Williams explains. "It involves what's called 'implicit bias.' For example, there is a case about a mattress saleswoman. Who knew that selling mattresses is really a masculine job? She told her boss that she was interested in being promoted and that she would do whatever it took. He did not promote her and gave her the reason that she wouldn't want to move because she was a mother, and mothers belong at home. It's just an assumption of what mothers want."

"I can't tell you how many women return from maternity leave and, literally, can't find work to do," notes Williams. "One woman said, 'I had a baby, not a lobotomy.'"

How One Woman Coped at Different Stages

Alice Davis, an assistant professor of psychology at a small liberal arts college (she did not want her real name or her institution's published), provides an example of how one female academic coped with managing her career and her family.

The first time I interviewed her in April 2010, she had one three-year-old and was expecting another child. She was optimistic about her school's support for work/life balance because the administration had told her their policies were family-friendly.

The first decision she had had to make was when would be a good time to get pregnant. "I had colleagues who had gone on job interviews when they were pregnant and not gotten the job because they were pregnant. I had colleagues who waited until they got tenure to start their families and then had fertility issues." Another academic told me, "Many women ask themselves what's going to expire soonest, my tenure clock or my biological clock." Davis decided that there is never a great time, so she became pregnant while in graduate school. "You need to decide what you want for your family and make your job work around that," she said. "I got the call to come for an interview for a job the day after I gave birth. So by the time I interviewed my son was six weeks old and they let me be the latest interview of the batch. The baby was colicky, so I ended up bringing my husband and son with me and took fifteen-minute breaks during the two-hour interview so I could pump." Nevertheless, she got the job.

Her chairman and the provost were supportive, giving her a reduced teaching schedule for one semester, which enabled her to care for her first child and share responsibilities with her husband, who then worked from home. Their generation's family life, she noted, was very different from that of their grandparents and parents. When her grandparents had their second boy, she explained, her grandmother had to stay home even though she had a college degree and Davis's grandfather did not. "My grandmother did it, and I'm sure she enjoyed it, but in her later years, she showed a lot of regret and jealousy when I was working and raising kids," recounted Davis. "My husband is different from his family. . . . His grandfather worked all the time and never was involved in child care. . . . With my father-in-law there was a little bit of a shift. But then with my husband, there was a big shift. His father and my father both have commented on what a great dad my husband is."

She appreciated how much things have changed, but said, "It's a good step, but we shouldn't have a parade. . . . Everyone keeps commenting, 'Isn't it wonderful that he changes diapers? Isn't it wonderful that he watches the baby?' I feel like shouting, 'I am here too; I'm doing the same work!'"

Davis called me five months after the birth of her second child to let me know how much her situation had changed. The equilibrium she had found in balancing her career and her family when she had one child was destabilized when she had two. She had been relieved from teaching two courses but was given the new responsibilities of advising students, supervising student research, serving on the curriculum committee, and going to all faculty and department meetings. She had thought that if she arranged for child care for two days a week that would be sufficient. Instead, she found herself needing to come to the office four days a week. Another complication was that her husband had a new job, which meant he was no longer able to work largely from home. She had a new department chair who was less understanding. When she had come up for her three-year pre-tenure review, she was told by her chairman that she didn't have time to be a professor because she had young children. "Then were little things I noticed," recalled Davis. "Committee meetings were between four and six. I teach until four, and have to leave at 4:30 to get to the day care center by five. A more family-conducive schedule for meetings has been brought up many times. They give us lip service. 'We know it's hard, but that's the only time we can do it.' I definitely want to continue teaching and be an academic, but I'm not as positive about the balance, and I'm more cynical about the environment at my institution, [about] the understanding between people who don't have families and those who do."

By the time of our third interview in May 2011, she had settled into a better routine because she had found good child care for her ten-month-old and three-year-old boys, but she continued to face challenges. She had learned that women's ability to integrate their family and work lives depends (in academia) on "who your chair is, when you have a baby, and how well the department is staffed." Her department is one of the larger ones, but she found that the faculty was divided between those who had children and those who didn't. Scheduling a meeting at five o'clock (the most difficult hours for working moms are 7 am and 5 pm) is not gender bias, but for working moms who have to pick up their children from day care precisely at that hour, it's at the very least a damned inconvenience.

She also had noticed a certain reality: It is assumed that when a woman is late for a meeting, she's late because of her children, but when a man is late, it's because he's working on his research. But sometimes a woman is late because of her children and she has a legitimate excuse. "I missed a minor deadline. My child's eardrum had burst and I had to take him to the hospital. My chairman chewed me out for about ten or twenty minutes," Davis said. Yet despite the roller coaster of her career, she remains determined to make it work.

The need for university-wide policies for faculty was made clear to Professor Eleanor M. Miller when she was dean of arts and sciences at the University of Vermont. Inspired by her own experience, she created a family leave policy for tenured faculty. "When I had my children, now twenty-three and twenty-seven, by C-section, I was back at work two weeks later. I was then an assistant professor. I thought it would be easy." It wasn't.

For twenty-five years she had been at the University of Wisconsin at Milwaukee, where she had been the founding member of the women's caucus and associate chancellor for equal opportunity. That position involved her in a tenure case: *Ceil Pillsbury v. State of Wisconsin*. Pillsbury was an assistant professor in the business school and was pregnant with her second child within a two year period before she was up for tenure. A faculty member on the tenure review committee asked her, "Can't your husband keep his pecker in his pocket?" (He later denied having said that; it was his word against hers.) Denied tenure, Pillsbury sued the tenure review committee, accusing them of sex discrimination. The case came up in 1992, the same year as Anita Hill testified against the confirmation of Justice Clarence Thomas. People wore buttons: "I believe Anita Hill and I believe Ceil Pillsbury."

Pillsbury won her case. How long will it take for women and men to win their cases for having a work life that enables them to also have a family life, not only as university faculty and staff, but also as employees who rush off from a meeting, or from the last shift, to pick up a child from day care? How do we create changes, not only in law, but in cultural expectations about the appropriate roles of women and men in the workplace and in the home?

CHAPTER 11

Building a Coalition

When I started writing this book, I believed we needed another feminist revolution to bring about the social and political changes necessary to support the demanding lives of working families in America today.

I was only half right. We need a revolution. But women cannot lead it alone. We have to broaden the feminist conversation to include men, unions, the elderly, the disabled, religious groups, and the unaffiliated. Feminists alone cannot get the job done. They took us halfway there—to greater equality and opportunity. The other half of the journey lies ahead. To complete it, we must link arms with both friends and strangers as we march in step to create a society in which parents can merge their work and family lives without shortchanging the children, the elderly, or the economy.

Who Will March in the Parade?

Who should be invited to the parade? Women and men who understand the necessity of change in stereotyped gender roles, who will advocate for new policies in the front office, debate family roles at the dinner table, and fight for new laws in state capitols and Congress. Some will wear labels identifying themselves as members of labor unions or the AARP, as Christians, Protestants, Jews, or Muslims, or as Democrats, Republicans, or members of the Tea Party. Some may belong to the developing Occupy Wall Street movement; still others will not belong to any organization but will sign up as individuals who have experienced the need for change in their own lives, as they struggle to make the two ends of family and work meet.

There is room in the parade for everyone who wants to march for the protection of the American Dream. For everyone who believes that the promise of America must be kept: to provide a better life for the next generation, which depends on our ability to support our children with both economic security and loving care. One goal need not be sacrificed for the other. Neither can women be separated into opposing factions of stay-at-home moms and working moms and those who aren't moms at all. Most women's lives are fluid; they do not stay in one place for a lifetime. When differences are cast aside and women speak with one voice, their chances of being heard multiply manyfold.

The Role of Labor

Where does the lineup for the parade begin? The labor movement, which played a key role in establishing work/family policies in Europe and in our country in New Jersey and California, is at the head of the line. Their banner is being carried by both women and men, but a closer look reveals that there are slightly more women marching than men. Not a surprise, because the membership of male union members has decreased, due in part to the decline in manufacturing jobs, while female membership has increased, due in part to the growth of service jobs. There is some hope that women moving into union leadership positions may revitalize flagging union membership. There are some firsts: Sandy Pope is the first woman to run for the presidency of International Brotherhood of Teamsters, although unsuccessfully, and Mary Kay Henry heads the 2.2-million-member Service Employees International Union. They have a tough challenge, because total union membership remains at its lowest point in seventy years: at 11.8 percent of all workers. In 1983 it was 20 percent.[1] Because of these declining numbers, nonaffiliated working women and men have to form a larger contingent in the march. The presence of more women in the total labor force augurs well for change.

Netsy Firestein, a longtime union organizer who founded the Labor Project for Working Families, believes that women will account for more than 50 percent of union members in the next five years. "Women make up the majority of workers in the growing sectors of service workers, nursing home workers, and hotel workers," she explains. "Having women in leadership in the unions makes a big difference for work/family issues. Nobody in labor ever says, 'No, we don't agree with these issues.' It's just that they say we have fifty other things that are ahead of you. At the moment it's all about losing jobs and health reform. Our struggle is how we get these issues on the plate so they're not the last to be taken care of."

Are men's attitudes changing? The answer is yes, among younger men, says Firestein. "A lot of the older male leaders had wives at home, so it never struck them. I find that when their daughter enters the workforce, or their daughter has a kid, they get it for the first time. The question is, how do you make this a public issue, rather than a personal issue? That's something we have to challenge and change."

Kate Bronfenbrenner, director of labor education research at the Cornell University School of Industrial and Labor Relations, who has been tracking women's union participation since the 1980s, agrees that the majority of new union members are women, particularly women of color. "They are more active; they are leaders. They are more likely to file grievances, to become stewards, to play a leading role in strikes and be on the bargaining committee. Now are unions giving them a seat at the table once they come in? There has been progress. Not as much as you'd like. The unions that have been most successful at organizing are the ones that have women on staff and women moving up in leadership positions."

There are many reasons that women are more motivated to become organized. Bronfenbrenner sums it up this way: "It's easier for an employer to convince a man not to join the union when an employer says, 'Stick with me, some day you'll make it to the top.' An employer says, 'If you go with the union you'll lose your benefits.' Men are taught in this country you're not a man if you can't do it on your own. Whereas women and people of color have learned that if you make it you need to work collectively. Women have to network for child care, with help from their families, from their neighborhood, to survive. They understand that it took a women's movement to get them where they are. While men have never had a movement so they don't have a collective sense. If you are a white male, you're more likely to be in a job with benefits than if you are a woman. Women gain more from being organized. The difference between union and non-union for women is huge."

One difference for union members is that 90 percent of union contracts have anti-discrimination clauses that enable members to fight discrimination and get quicker results than filing a case with the EEOC (Equal Employment Opportunity Commission), Bronfenbrenner explains. There is an ongoing effort to get parental leave in union contracts. Just 29 percent of manufacturing unions have that benefit. In the public sector the figure is 59 percent.

Bronfenbrenner believes that unions protect workers from arbitrary supervisory power and provide them with some control over their lives. "Unions have to stop fighting among themselves," she warns, if they want to get stronger; and they also need to hire organizers that reflect the workforce.

Male union leadership has historically fought for wages and health benefits. Women are beginning to shift union priorities. "People care about their jobs, but they also care about their families," says Bronfenbrenner. "Trying to be a good parent and do a good job and needing enough income and health insurance and trying to balance all these things is getting harder and harder. We in this country work more hours than people in almost every other country. Where other countries come up with solutions to cut work hours to increase jobs, in this country the solution is to have people work longer hours and have more people unemployed. We're very shortsighted. Those are anti-family decisions; they hurt people's health. We need to put people's health and families and communities first."

Upper-Income and Lower-Income Women—Can They Unite?

Bronfenbrenner agrees that it will take more than union organizing to address family/work conflicts. "It takes a cultural change," she says. She expresses a common complaint heard from the women's movement: upper-class women don't understand working-class women. Class divisions are an old issue that has plagued the women's movement since its inception in the 1960s, but there is an opportunity for a new dialogue today because the dilemmas that families face do not respect class boundaries. High-earning women have more bargaining and negotiating power to tailor their work lives to fit their family needs than low-wage women do, but they, too, have experienced the struggle to combine their career and family lives harmoniously. Frank discussions around the bargaining table and the boardroom table have to take place before women from all ends of the financial spectrum can find common ground.

"Guys still set the norms," says Anne-Marie Slaughter, who recently left her "dream job" as director of policy planning at the State Department—the first woman to have the job—to return to teaching at Princeton. "The longer you work, the tougher you are. There is a 'cultural macho' in these jobs in Washington [and in other fields, including law and finance]. You start with working conditions; the assumption is that you have to be at work all the time. It's just not true. The work ethic was set up by men for men from a time when they worked eighteen hours a day and their wives were waiting for them nervously at home, taking care of their kids. We need to change our assessment of a successful career." Slaughter spent two years commuting from Princeton to Washington and concluded that "it just didn't work. I don't want to not be there for my kids. I had a more prestigious job, but somebody else controlled my time. Now I'm in charge, and if a kid needs me, I'm here, I can dial it up or dial it down. I have what everybody wants: flexibility."

Her former boss, Secretary of State Hillary Clinton, understood her needs. She set an example by leaving the office most nights at 6:30 or 7:00 when she wasn't traveling on a brutal schedule. "Hillary completely understood my decision to leave; she gave me permission," says Slaughter. "A man will say, 'You were making decisions that affected millions of people. Surely that's more important than your family.' But I believe my children will be much better people if I fill my responsibility as a parent." Slaughter has not suddenly become a stay-at-home mom, of course; she continues to adhere to a hectic schedule as a professor and sought-after speaker all over the world—but she controls her schedule.

The personal experiences of high-level women like Slaughter have an impact on middle- and low-income women in two ways: they have an opportunity to modify the male macho work model by example, and they are more understanding of the needs of their employees. When Slaughter supervised a hundred employees as dean of the Woodrow Wilson School of Public and International Affairs at Princeton, her mantra was "family comes first." Similarly, Christina Shea at General Mills found that her personal experiences made her more empathetic than male managers to the women she supervised on the lower rungs of the pay scale. But their good intentions have limits. Women business leaders will still be judged by the same criteria as their male colleagues: how well they succeed in growing the bottom line, not by how much they improve family/work policies. At least not for the short term. The long-term perspective is that the two approaches are integrated—better family/work policies increase the bottom line by retaining a more productive workforce. But the rate of return may differ from one company to another and one initiative to another. Investment in early childhood education will take years to demonstrate results; a flexible work schedule, only months. Dialogue between upper-income women and lower-income women is essential to making a robust and credible argument for long-term investment in family/work policies. Women, whether they are stay-at-home moms, working moms, or part-time working moms, have to join the parade and march to the same drumbeat.

History provides us with two examples of women leaders who bridged the divide between upper- and lower-income women: Frances Perkins and Millie Jeffrey. Perkins was secretary of labor in the Franklin D. Roosevelt administration, 1933–45, and the first female Cabinet member. Her contributions to working women's and men's lives are monumental. She was actively involved in developing the New Deal, Social Security, and the Fair Labor Standards Act, which established the forty-hour week and the minimum wage.

Jeffrey began her career working for the Amalgamated Clothing Workers of America in 1935, became the first female department head of the United Auto Workers in 1945, marched with Martin Luther King, helped establish the National Women's Caucus, and fought for the ratification of the Equal Rights Amendment. She was my hero. She was a slight, small-framed woman who could easily have been overlooked in a crowd, but everyone knew Millie. She was everywhere—whether speaking in an auditorium filled with women activists, at a convention of labor leaders, or at a Democratic National Convention. I spotted her sitting in the balcony of the Vermont State House during my first inauguration as governor in 1985. She had ridden a Greyhound bus from Detroit, Michigan, to Burlington, Vermont, for thirty-one hours to witness a woman raising her right hand to take the oath of office of governor. Millie never lost her ability to speak up for equal justice; she saw no dividing line between empowering women and empowering workers—both women and men.

Nine to Five

Karen Nussbaum, best known as the founder of Nine to Five, an organization of office workers whose story later was made into a hit movie (1980), has been working for women and the labor movement throughout her professional life. She served as director of the Department of Labor's Women's Bureau in the Clinton administration. "When we started Nine to Five it was to organize women in the lower end and office workers. Much to our surprise we found they were the largest sector of the workforce but were totally invisible. We wanted to organize women who may have not have identified with the women's movement but whose lives could be transformed by it. We wanted to expand the women's movement to working women in terms that they found appealing and accessible," Nussbaum says. "When we first started we had to argue that the reason a woman didn't get a promotion was not because the boss was in a bad mood; it was discrimination."

How have things changed thirty years later? "The more things change the more they stay the same," Nussbaum says. "The pressure cooker of discrimination against women in the workplace was released by allowing highly educated women to track into professional jobs. It was a safety valve, and so the impulse to organize was reduced because higher-level women got more of what they wanted, but they got it on an individual basis, rather than a collective basis. Before the mid-seventies, the highest-paid jobs for women were in factories because there were so few women in professional management jobs."

Nussbaum notes that family-friendly benefits exist for only a small percentage of women who work in professional managerial jobs. She sees the entire workforce—women and men—losing ground because of the recession. "What has happened to the vast majority of women workers is the same that has happened to the vast majority of male workers, which is they have lost every basic benefit, as well as never seeing the family-friendly benefit."

She does not believe female managers are any different than male managers. "Corporate policy is to reduce wages and benefits. So if you get a good boss who is a woman they're still operating under a policy where they say they can't pay health care premiums anymore." Despite her pessimism, Nussbaum has not given up. She is executive director of Working America, a community affiliate of the AFL-CIO with three million members. What distinguishes Working America is that it organizes people who work in different places but live in the same neighborhoods, enlisting them by going door to door.

"What's important," says Nussbaum, "is that our members tend to be those that typically do not get involved in anything. They're working-class moderates and are otherwise not part of any organization. So we add new actors to the fight. It is essential if we're going to restore basic working conditions and then finally take up the issues of work and family and opportunities for women."

The potential power of the workforce, unionized and nonunionized, is enormous. Unions, Nussbaum explains, have made a serious effort to deal with family/work issues. "But the pressure on wages and benefits is so strong—especially now during the recession—that it makes it hard to do anything besides protect health care and pensions and not let wages fall too low."

Do work/family issues always have to move to the back of the line, rarely getting their turn? The high unemployment rate that has marked the recession gives employers a credible reason to say, "No, not now." And it gives unions cause to say, "First things first." Have we been too polite in accepting that answer, or is it a matter of timing? Certainly it would be easier to demand paid family leave and universal access to child care when the unemployment rate is low and revenues are high. But experience tells us that opposition to these policies remains strong regardless of the state of the economy. There is never a perfect moment. But change does occur.

The Elderly

The elderly are starting to line up in the parade for work/life policies, right behind younger working women and men. The population over the age of sixty-five is expected to more than double by 2050, creating a policy tsunami that is only beginning to be acknowledged. There are two categories of elderly: those mature adults who remain in the workforce after retirement and do not need assistance, and those who require care.

"We are at a time when we are experiencing a new interpretation of what aging means," explains Marcie Pitt-Catsouphes, executive director of the Sloan Center on Aging & Work at Boston College. "We used to think that we would hit this magic age [of 65] and go from full participation in the labor force and then retire. It was either work or retire. We now have something new, a retirement job, which is not a contradiction; these things can coexist in our lives. It's no longer unusual. There are multiple reasons people work longer, some financial and some nonfinancial."

The necessity to continue to work after retirement, or return to work, has been aggravated by the recession, says Sara Rix, senior policy advisor for AARP. She tells me that the unemployment rate for older workers is at an all-time high. At the same time, slightly more elderly Americans are in the workforce today than before the recession. Women have been hit harder than men, but both groups are feeling a sharp financial pinch.

The elderly have as much to gain as younger working families in three policy areas: workplace flexibility, paid sick days, and paid family leave. Recognizing the importance of these policies for the elderly, the White House invited Jacquelyn B. James, director of research for the Sloan Center on Aging & Work, to its 2010 Forum on Workplace Flexibility. "Older workers are just as interested as younger workers in flexibility," James explains. Her colleague Pitt-Catsouphes agrees: "If we didn't realize it before, flexibility isn't just for parents of young children; people continue to have lives after they have babies."

Like young mothers, older Americans may not wish to work a forty-hour week but may want to, and often need to, continue to work thirty hours a week, either while they are waiting to become eligible for Medicare and Social Security or because of economic necessity. Rather than leaving the workforce, many would continue to work if they had access to flexible hours, part-time schedules, or job sharing. Both flexibility and paid sick days would enable elderly workers to take time off for doctors' appointments or illness without the threat of being fired. Flexibility would also enable their children to take time off to take care of their parents' needs. Employers would be the beneficiaries because this generation of older Americans is the best educated ever, and many are at their peak productivity.

How likely is it that elderly workers would join forces with younger workers to advocate for work/life policies like flexibility? Both James and

Pitt-Catsouphes believe that the country's major demographic shift is producing an "ah-hah!" moment. "People are saying, 'Oh, God,' the landscape is changing and we've got to do something,'" Pitt-Catsouphes says. "This new cohort of retiring baby boomers is powerful, and society has to respond just because of its sheer size."

How fast and how aggressively will this growing group of older citizens demand change? AARP is taking an incremental approach. Spokeswoman Rix has focused on working with employers to voluntarily adopt flexibility policies: "More and more employers are going to acknowledge the benefits; the business case has been made."

Rix supports congressional action on right to request (flexibility) legislation and on making benefits available to part-time workers. "If we had more part-time options with benefits, older workers would stay in the workforce longer," she notes. Employers could retain talented and loyal workers who in the long term are less costly than training new and unskilled workers. The longer workers over the age of sixty-five can remain in the workforce, the less dependent they would be on their families and on the taxpayers. Again, it's a question of long-term vision; we need to recognize the value of long-term investment, whether the subject is early childhood or late adulthood. The up-front costs of flexibility and paid family leave may involve initial expenditures, but the overall gains provide a significant rate of return to employers in increased productivity and greater loyalty. Greater savings for the government are likely if policies like flexibility and paid family and medical leave enable an elderly person to be financially independent or to be cared for at home. When the predictions for dramatic growth in the population over the age of sixty-five and over the age of eight-five come true, the cost of long-term care will place a hard-to-bear burden on all taxpayers. The question is: how will family members provide care when it is needed? According to a report released by the Families and Work Institute, "42% of employed people in the United States (or nearly 54.6 million employees) report that within the past five years, they have provided "special attention or care for a relative or in-law 65 years old or older."[2]

The difference between Grandma having to move to an institution or being able to stay home or with family may depend on whether a daughter or son can take a day or a week off to get a parent or grandparent through a health crisis. It may depend on whether relatives have flexible work hours that allow them to make daily or weekly visits. That may be all it takes to keep Grandma from falling into total dependency and full-time care.

The average cost of nursing home care, according to the National Clearinghouse for Long-Term Care Information, is estimated to be $198 a day for a semi-private room. Workplace flexibility could avoid this cost. The same reasoning applies to paid family and medical leave, which would permit a relative to take a short time off to be at the side of a dying grandparent. As we learned earlier, the experience with the New Jersey Paid Family Leave Act indicates that care for the elderly accounts for the second-highest usage for paid leave.

It is impossible to put a complete price tag on enabling an elderly person to remain independent and give him or her the ability to stay at home. Neither is there any way to gauge the emotional value of being with family at the two brackets of life: birth and death.

"A lot of policies and practices that are good for older workers are also good for working mothers," says Craig Langford, senior advisor for AARP, who was AARP's representative on the 2010 Workplace Flexibility coalition at Georgetown University, noting that, for example, "paid sick days benefit people no matter what their age."

Is there a possibility that AARP would make work/family issues a priority and join a phalanx of flag-waving marchers in the parade for work/life policies? "It hasn't been front and center for us," Langford explains. "The agenda comes from our members; this isn't an issue that has caused a groundswell. Health is a big focus, and there is a lot of worry about Social Security. We look at workforce issues broadly, not on work/life balance."

What would it take, I wonder, to mobilize the thirty-five million members of AARP? They are beginning to see the connection between their concerns and those of younger workers, but they are not ready to jump into the political fray of advocating for broad and often controversial policy changes that might conflict with some of their other views on the role of government in society. Often, they are not conscious of their own contradictions. "Don't let the government touch my Medicare" became one of the jokes during the debate over President Obama's health care reform package as some seniors vehemently defended Medicare—a government program—while they opposed the Obama bill—another government program—with equal passion.

Generations United

In 2011, older Americans demonstrated that they would protect not just the interests of their own generation in regard to Medicare. The legislation proposed by congressman Paul Ryan (R-WI) would have substituted a voucher system for Medicare for people under the age of fifty-five. Those over fifty-five would have been spared, but they were not placated. The outcry was loud enough that many politicians either denounced the idea or distanced themselves far from it.

Not all over-age-sixty-five citizens are motivated by self-interest, according to Mary Catherine Bateson, seventy-one, a writer, cultural anthropologist, and daughter of anthropologists Margaret Mead and Gregory Bateson. She is best known for her earlier book about women's changing lives, *Composing a Life*. Her most recent book is *Composing a Further Life: The Age of Active Wisdom*. "The assumption is that older voters care only about their own entitlements—this is demeaning," she says. She is embarking on creating a new organization, Generations United. "It is primarily focused on seniors advocating on behalf of kids. Our motto has been, 'I'm voting on behalf of my grandchild.' We claim the right to have a voice, not to be marginalized, speaking for the future, not the past," she explains. The group originated when graduates of the feminist movement, including Rep. Patricia Schroeder, columnist Ellen Goodman, and vice presidential nominee Geraldine Ferraro—who had fought for women's right to work and be productive—decided they did not want to limit their options after retirement. "We're drawing on the model of the women's movement to get people thinking beyond the stereotypes that are controlling them," says Bateson.

The average life span is approaching eighty, she explains, almost twice what it has been throughout human history: children, parents, grandparents, and great-grandparents now live in one community. "We are living longer and healthier. We are in a new stage of adulthood; it can be an extraordinarily productive time."

When I ask Bateson whether the elderly could ally with younger voters on issues that affect younger families and children, she has no doubts. She envisions that Generations United will form chapters state by state. For example, she will ask older voters to look at a school bond issue in their community "with a different set of eyes, not only, 'How does this affect me?'

but 'What are the implications of this vote for the future of the community I care about?' The reality is that grandparents and great-grandparents are invested in the future, they care about the world they live in, and about their children who will raise their grandchildren."

Is this perspective on our growing aging population too idealistic to be translated into political action? Politicians of both parties know they get a knee-jerk reaction when they fan the flames of fear over cutting Medicare or Social Security. Why go further if they know that this is a proven vote getter and that voters over the age of sixty-five will turn out on Election Day in far greater numbers than younger voters?

At the age of seventy-eight, I share Bateson's views about the future. It is hard to know how many of us "seniors" feel the same way because our spokesperson continues to be the AARP, a large, well-organized, well-financed organization that, like the US Chamber of Commerce, claims to speak for all. Generations United is unlikely to achieve equal volume, but it will enlarge the conversation.

While AARP is not prepared to advocate for legislation like paid family leave, it is comfortable working with employers to encourage them toward innovative employment practices. For example, *Working Mother* magazine publishes a list of "best companies to work for," in this case the best employers for workers over age fifty, recognizing "innovative policies and best practices in talent management. These organizations are creating roadmaps for others on how to attract and retain top talent in today's multigenerational workforce."[3]

The Sandwich Generation

An increasing number of families find themselves struggling with caring for children and simultaneously caring for elderly parents. They are known as the "sandwich generation." Stephen Miller, writing about the eighth annual MetLife Study of Employee Benefit Trends, notes, "While 45 percent of working parents are very concerned about having more time to spend with their families, that percentage jumps to 72 percent for those who are simultaneously balancing parental and caregiving responsibilities."[4] And according to a 2010 study by the Families and Work Institute, 42 percent of workers had provided elder care over the past five years. Of those caregivers, 46 percent of women and 40 percent of men also had children under the age of eighteen at home.[5]

Do we really need workplace flexibility and paid family leave laws to enable family members to provide the love and care that can keep the elderly where they thrive best (and cost the least)—at home? Or are employers implementing such policies without federal requirements? Many employers claim they are implementing these policies on their own on a case-by-case basis. But are they? "Employees providing eldercare reported less access to the flexible work options needed to fulfill their work and personal needs compared to those employees providing childcare or those with no dependent care at all," according to a study.[6] In all industry sectors combined, "only one-third of employers (31%) felt they had established options for employees to work in a flexible manner 'to a moderate/great extent.'"[7]

Men Join the Parade

The argument against government mandates and in favor of voluntary family/work policies is difficult to support with these modest figures. But what if there were a new infusion of support from the second largest sector of the population: men? If a significant number of them joined the work/life success parade, would their voices drown out the naysayers?

Joan C. Williams believes that men provide an essential component of a new family/work coalition because they too are experiencing not only the stress and frustration of combining work and family but, sometimes, the discrimination of being a dad with caregiving responsibilities. "All fathers," she writes, "are not equal. Breadwinners married to homemakers earn 30 percent more than those in two-job families and encounter favored treatment at work. . . . In sharp contrast, a father who discloses that he has family care responsibilities faces sizable job risks. One study found that men are often penalized for taking family leave, especially by other men. Another found that men with even a short work absence due to a family conflict were recommended for fewer rewards and had lower performance ratings."[8]

More and more men want to enjoy both the joys and responsibilities of parenthood, concluded a 2011 family survey of nearly a thousand white-collar fathers in large corporations, titled *The New Dad: Caring, Committed and Conflicted*. "In spite of their high aspirations and degree of satisfaction with their careers, most fathers did not view their work as the center of their existence."[9]

When fathers were asked how they see their responsibilities to their children, on a scale ranging from "earning money to meet my child's financial needs" to "physically/emotionally caring for my child," the vast majority (70 percent) of respondents chose the middle ground: "both caring for my child and earning money to meet his/her financial needs." And the fathers surveyed said that the three most important aspects of being a good father were "provide love and emotional support"; "be involved and present in your child's life"; and "be a teacher, guide and coach."[10]

The survey indicates that fathers would like to participate much more in their children's care than they actually do. Can that desire, tinged with guilt similar to what working mothers experience, pull them into the parade to march with women, labor leaders, and the elderly? Most dads today don't want to be like their fathers who arrived home in the evening when their children were already asleep and left in the morning before they woke up, with no time for bedtime stories, or hugs and kisses. When men join forces on issues that have been traditionally led by women, they get double points, just as they receive inordinate praise when they do the dishes or the laundry. When my then husband changed my son's diaper on a park bench at the zoo in Bern, Switzerland, many years ago, he got some stares and several approving smiles. They assumed, rightly, that he was an American.

When men joined Catalyst Canada in Montreal on June 7, 2011 for a forum on "Engaging Men as Diversity Champions," it was worthy of a press release. When congresswoman Rosa DeLauro handed the podium to a male colleague to speak on paid family leave, his words resonated in the hall more than hers. It's a stark truth—when unexpected voices join the usual chorus, people listen. It is time to reach out to men, both as employers and as employees, as fathers and as grandfathers, because the advent of the increased number of two-wage-earner and single-head-of-household families affects all family members, women and men, the young and the old.

Can Conservatives Join the Cause?

The largest divide on family/work policies that involve legislation is between liberals and conservatives. Is there any possibility that enough common ground can be staked out on selective issues to form an alliance? The question is particularly difficult to answer when the country is sharply divided on the role of government itself, both in terms of its role in private lives and in regard to spending and taxation. Could the "family values" community send a few people to join the work/family parade? In the course of writing this book I made several requests to speak with a leader of the Christian Coalition that went unanswered. Yet I am not ready to give up hope. The early childhood program in the Evangelical stronghold of Oklahoma provides one example of how conservative and progressive groups can agree on the need for early childhood education. The door remains open—if just a crack—to a new dialogue on government participation in this and other family/work policies. If we could abandon the divisive rhetoric, often fanned by ambitious partisan politicians on both sides, and focus on the stories of working families' struggles to support and care for one another, we could start a new conversation. Conservatives tend to demonize all new government programs as "socialism." Progressives tend to mock "family values" espoused by conservatives. How can you support family values when you wish to cut programs that help children? We're the ones who have real family values, they say, because we support education and health care. Admittedly, there are two definitions of family values, one espoused by the right, the other by the left. But we have not made an effort to begin a dialogue on the basics: what do families need, from the youngest to the oldest? There is nothing to be lost by reaching out.

We assume when we speak of large sectors of the population that they are homogeneous. When we speak of employers, we think of the US Chamber of Commerce; when we refer to the elderly, we think of AARP. The evidence I have gleaned while writing this book proves that particular constituencies do not march in lockstep. The growing number of outliers who are making changes may now be considered pioneering but soon may become commonplace. The challenge is to identify those who have broken away from the stereotypical configuration of family and work, bring them together, and encourage them to speak as vociferously as those they left behind.

The Religious Community

Mention the religious community, and the conclusion is that regardless of denomination, religious leaders are more traditional than transformational. "The assumption is that we're only interested in criminalizing abortion and preventing gays from marrying," says Jennifer Butler, a Presbyterian minister who is founder and executive director of Faith in Public Life, formed during the 2004 election cycle to provide an alternative to the voice of the Christian Right. She was also a member of the Workplace Flexibility 2010 coalition at Georgetown University. "People of faith are concerned with all kinds of social justice issues," she explains.

Faith in Public Life provides a media strategy for faith groups that aren't being heard, from Protestants and Catholics to Jews and Muslims, "because they don't have a big enough megaphone," unlike ultra-conservative religious activists such as Glenn Beck, Rush Limbaugh, and James Dobson (who heads the right-wing Focus on the Family), Butler says.

I ask Butler where she places Faith in Public Life on the spectrum of religious organizations. "I say moderate and progressive. The reason I say 'moderate' is that some of the communities we work with may not be liberal across the board on every issue. For example, the African-American community can be reticent to take on gay marriage. The Latino community and white Evangelicals may not want to take on climate change legislation and would call themselves pro-life. The moderates that we work with in those communities want to see some sort of common ground. They are willing to talk about solutions. They have a different ethical position on when life begins, but they are willing to sit with the choice community and talk about solutions."

She estimates that these moderate groups represent approximately 75 percent of the religious community, which as a whole is "compassionate and believes in love thy neighbor and wants to make a better world." Some African-American members of the Evangelical community are moderate because of "their history of struggle and the challenges they face. They are more supportive of the role of government because of the civil rights legacy and what it meant for their communities."

The Shriver Report (2009) notes that there is a "correlation between women's rising workforce participation and decreasing religious activity," but the exception is female African-Americans. "Women outnumber men in virtually every Christian tradition. . . . The numbers are highest for African-American women: 60 percent of those affiliated with historically black churches are women. In fact, African-American women are the most religious of all Americans."

The Shriver Report's focus groups on women and religion indicated a contradiction: "For some religious institutions, the reality of working women's lives has exposed a discrepancy between their beliefs and day-to-day practices. On the one hand, they maintain a firm belief in the spiritual superiority of the 'traditional family' and the primacy of women's domestic role, yet they offer programs to accommodate working mothers and blended families. Child care programs, especially, are growing across faith traditions, so that at least one-quarter of children in child care centers are in programs located in churches, synagogues, and other places of worship."[11] For religious groups, recognizing the day-to-day needs of working parents may be the first step in transforming family values into action.

I ask Butler whether she sees the Christian Right definition of "family values" evolving in that direction. "We want to see that happen. We are fund-raising right now to bring those religious leaders together. Traditionally there hasn't been money or support for these groups [moderate] because they are seen as the enemy. People do not see the complexity and nuance among them. I think the coalitions and relationships haven't been built." Some religious leaders, she believes, have been working all their lives to help the Evangelical community "expand their notion of family values to include economic needs and economic justice issues."

A self-identified feminist, Butler concedes that "at first I was afraid of these people [the religious right], but then I learned that they are wonderful. They have fire in the belly about this and they want to work on it. Both sides need to embrace family. We usually talk about the working family if we're talking about labor, or the single-parent family if we're talking about feminists. But let's just talk about the family. If we want to make headway on policy issues like work/life balance, we have to avoid politicizing families. What I want is to prevent these wedge issues from being there and splitting people off."

Is that the key to forming a broad coalition on family/work policies to avoid the areas of disagreement and cultivate the common ground? The religious community has the potential to become a strong ally; it is not as homogeneous as it may first appear. Those who have the loudest voices do not speak for the majority. The challenge is to mobilize those with moderate views to speak loudly enough to be heard above the right-wing diatribes. They can express the needs of working women and men who struggle with meeting their responsibilities to their jobs and their families every day. Religious faith and political activism need not conflict; one can inspire the other, as they have throughout history.

Health Care and the Sisters

Sister Simone Campbell's role in the final hours of the 2010 health care reform debate provides an example. Campbell is executive director of Network, a national Catholic social justice lobbying group, and President Obama told her at the bill signing ceremony that her support for it had marked the tipping point. The wheels of legislation had gotten stuck on the muddy issue of abortion. Campbell and fifty other nuns wrote a letter to the members of Congress in support of the Senate version of the bill, confident that the bill would pass muster with Catholic beliefs. "We write to urge you to cast a life-affirming 'yes' vote when the Senate health care bill (H.R. 3590) comes to the floor of the House." She listed the bill's benefits, including $250 million in support of pregnant women. "This is the REAL pro-life stance, and we as Catholics are all for it."[12]

The US Conference of Catholic Bishops disagreed. And Rep. Bart Stupak (D-MI), was not pleased with the sisters. "With all due respect to the nuns, when I deal or am working on right-to-life issues, we don't call the nuns," he said on MSNBC's *Hardball*. The nuns, however, called him—literally, with nuns from Stupak's district calling his office. "Who's been on the ground, in the field? Who knows the struggles people have to deal with? It's the sisters," one retorted.[13]

Campbell, who is pro-life, comments to me, "Poor man, he got himself in trouble." Her position was fortified by the Catholic Health Association and Catholic hospitals, which also supported passage of the bill. When the bishops opposed it, she says, "I was shocked. All of us sisters have done the work with those in need; we know the anguish. It was not a trade-off between living folks and potential folks." She explains her difference with the bishops this way: "We're hands-on people, working with the people. The bishop's role is to care for institutional life, administrating, fiscal responsibility, finding priests. Most of the bishops don't have free hours in the rectory to talk to the folks in crisis."

She told the *New York Times*, "When I read the Gospel, where is Jesus? He's healing the lepers. It's because of his Gospel mandate to do likewise that we stand up for health care reform."[14]

As an outspoken leader of Network, she notes that the church is "investigating all of us. Luckily I have faith. My life is deeply spiritual." I ask if the church would ever ordain women. "Eventually; it takes forever. Hierarchy doesn't understand that women are moving forward everywhere. If it took the church three hundred years to say that Galileo was right, the church is not going to change quickly."

Sister Campbell's open disagreement with the bishops provides insight into the power of religious leaders who defy stereotypes. They are not paralyzed by ideology but are motivated by practical experience, which gave them a different perspective from that of the bishops. The sisters were the ones who stood at the bedside, holding the patient's hand. They did not disagree with church leaders in silence, which would have been the expected form of dissent. Instead they spoke out—and that made the difference.

"Breaking away from stereotypes," Mary Catherine Bateson observes, is the key "to the liberation movements of the twentieth century." She names the women's movement and the civil rights movement as examples. I would add to the list the lesbian and gay rights movement and the disability rights community, which succeeded in passing the landmark Americans with Disabilities Act of 1990. Each group has defied common assumptions about their place in society.

Gay and Lesbian Rights Movement

Can we find an analogy between the movement for working families and these transformational periods in recent history? I believe we can. The gay and lesbian rights movement provides an example of how stereotypes can change in a short period of time. In an op-ed piece for the *New York Times*, columnist Frank Bruni wrote about his college experience in the mid-1980s: "Same sex marriage? I don't recall our talking—or dreaming—much about that. We considered ourselves realists. Sometimes idealists. But never fantasists. As it happens, we were pessimists, and underestimated our country's capacity for change."[15]

I saw the evolution from when I was governor in 1987. I spoke at the first gay pride parade in Burlington, Vermont, becoming the first Vermont politician to do so. The *Burlington Free Press* printed a photo of me at the podium on the steps of the Unitarian church, in front of a large overhead banner lettered with the words: "Gay Pride." The photographer had made sure that the print on the banner was larger than me so that readers could decipher it. My next event that day was a Memorial Day ceremony in the park square of the nearby town of St. Albans. As I stood with the decorated veterans and saluted the flag, I knew that within one hour's time I had stepped into two different worlds. The next week I was told that my photo had been scotch-taped to a cash register in a country store with a red circle and slash scrawled on it.

In the year 2000, Vermont became the first state to adopt a civil union law with bipartisan support. About a dozen legislators voted for the bill, knowing that they might not be reelected if they did. About six of them lost their seats. Yard signs had sprung up throughout rural Vermont: "Take Back Vermont." No one knew the precise meaning, but the intent was clear: repeal civil unions.

Repeal efforts failed, and nine years later the state passed a gay marriage law, overriding the governor's veto. This time there was no backlash. At the time of this writing, Vermont is one of six states (along with Connecticut, Iowa, Massachusetts, New Hampshire, and most recently New York) plus the District of Columbia to make gay marriage legal. These states are not typical of the country; forty-one states ban gay marriage. The national debate has been far more contentious, but the direction is apparent—gay and lesbian Americans are moving closer to the norm. A *Newsweek* poll found that voters are in favor of "hiring" gay and lesbian people as major officeholders, even though they are still divided on whether homosexuality was a sin.[16]

Gay and lesbian candidates are being elected throughout the country, including in the more traditional South. For example, in 2009 Annise Parker was elected mayor of Houston, which became the largest city in the United States to elect an openly gay mayor. How did the gay and lesbian revolution come about? How did this group—once considered abnormal and even criminal—become mainstream? Voters began to shed their stereotypes about gay people when their sons and daughters, neighbors, and co-workers came out. No longer were they the "other"; they had become more like us, with similar hopes and fears. In Vermont, the decisive moment occurred during the legislative debate before the vote on civil unions. Rep. William (Bill) Lippert, an openly gay legislator, stood up on the floor of the House and asked his colleagues to support the bill. He told his story, and his listeners in the well of the House were moved. They saw him not as a homosexual, but as a colleague whom they knew and respected. In New York, Governor Andrew Cuomo and Mayor Michael Bloomberg both had personal reasons for advocating gay marriage. Cuomo's companion, Sandra Lee, has a gay brother; Bloomberg has a lesbian niece.

Initially supported by liberals, gay and lesbian civil rights have become a bipartisan issue. Gay and lesbian Americans are in a higher income bracket than average Americans, and they are generous campaign contributors. The largest donors to the New York same-sex marriage campaign were Republicans, who were brought into the battle at the behest of the governor. Why did they respond? "One major reason was that the wish and push to be married cast gay men and lesbians in the most benign and conservative light imaginable, not as enemies of tradition but as aspirants to it," writes Bruni.[17]

In its early days, the movement had to be more cautious. Tim McFeeley, who in the early 1990s was executive director of the Human Rights Campaign, an advocacy group for the gay and lesbian rights campaign, says that they were careful with labels because though they wanted "to attract a broad following, people weren't ready yet for the real thing." McFeeley would tell a gay candidate to say not that he had a "boyfriend' but that he was "in a relationship." This calls to mind the New Jersey family leave law, in which the program was called family leave insurance program, not paid family leave, a small but significant difference. Wording, I am reminded, is important.

The Disability Rights Movement

The Americans with Disabilities Act was signed into law in 1990, but advocacy for the disabled began years before, explains one of its prime movers, Judy Heumann, who served with me in the US Department of Education as assistant secretary of special education and rehabilitation services, when I was deputy secretary. She is now special advisor for international disability rights at the State Department.

"In the 1960s and '70s we saw a spike in the development of disability organizations that dealt with single disability issues, such as epilepsy and polio," says Heumann. "We were influenced by the civil rights and women's rights movements, but we in the disability community were considered outsiders to these movements, even though we learned from them. Younger members of the community were redefining disability and moving away from the charity approach, asking people to give money for a cure for a certain disability. We focused on discrimination in employment and education, not being able to get on buses, cross the street, or read sign language."

Their goal, she says, "was to be able to move into the world of work." Cross-disability organizations were first started by students at the University of California at Berkeley, and according to Heumann, they played a strong advocacy role. "They started a wheelchair repair program. [Normally] when a wheelchair was broken, you had to give the chair to a company and it would take a week for it to come back. What started to happen is that non-students who needed a wheelchair started to come to the wheelchair repair program for help."

When Medicaid started to fund home supportive services such as cooking and bathing, "a coalition started to evolve between the emerging cross-disability movement and the senior movement. It was a very effective body; it embraced so many people. It's a coalition that has lasted over the years, beginning at the city, county, and state level. Our individuals come from all walks of life," Heumann says. "The [Washington] DC consortium for citizens with disabilities was formed, which included a hundred organizations which worked on ADA [Americans with Disabilities Act]. We had to learn how to compromise and how to work together. Looking back, ADA in 1990 was the result of a coalition work that took place over the last two or three decades. Coalitions allowed people to get a better understanding of the commonality of needs and solutions. Both the elderly and the disabled suffered from stigmas. Their goal was to be able to stay in the community and to change the perception of disabilities from a medical issue to a civil rights issue."

Strong support came from several key senators, including Ted Kennedy (D-MA). A private citizen, Justin Dart, called the father of the Americans with Disabilities Act, became a passionate and effective spokesman. He went on tours around the country, bringing disabled people with him to provide testimony, which gave the disabled community not just numbers, but names and faces.

In retrospect, Heumann concludes, it was both a top-down and a bottom-up strategy. As a result the disabled are now part of communities from which they were once barred. Her own experience as a wheelchair-bound person has changed. "Parents who have children interact with me now. In the past they would pull their kids away and not let them engage. Now they let them touch the wheelchair and talk to me."

The power of coalition building and garnering support from individuals from "all walks of life" has transformed the lives of disabled Americans, says Heumann. Today, children who might once have been kept in outsized cribs in the attic are receiving an education and the capability to contribute. The transition has not always been smooth. When large institutions for the mentally ill were closed down in the 1970s and '80s and many patients were placed in group homes, and when disabled children were first "mainstreamed" into public school classrooms, there were loud and frequent objections—to both the cost and the consequences of these changes. Few, however, would now wish to turn the clock back.

Each of the transformative rights movements of the twentieth and early twenty-first centuries—civil rights, women's rights, gay rights, disability rights—was made possible because slogans and stereotypes were replaced by personal stories and fresh facts that pushed aside old assumptions. Strong coalitions were formed, and each group had a few focused and courageous leaders who had broken away from the pack mentality that had once dominated the conversation.

How do we elevate the work/family debate to that level? How do we enable the personal stories of working women and men, and the children and elders they care for, to be taken seriously, to be not marginalized as "them" but accepted as "us"? How do we stop ghettoizing the work/family debate into small communities with special interests, and begin to break down the walls that separate women from men, working moms from stay-at-home moms, union members from nonunion workers, the elderly from the young, and one religious group from another? It is time to give the signal to strike up the band and march in unison.

CHAPTER 12

Child Poverty

There is a direct relationship between the lack of enlightened family/work policies and child poverty. The impact is felt in several ways—on parents and on children. Without paid family leave and workplace flexibility, parents find it more difficult to enter and stay in the workforce. The loss of a paycheck, particularly for single parents, can thrust them into poverty. Income is further eroded by the expense of child care. And without quality child care and early education, children are more likely to repeat their parents' cycle of poverty because they lack the skills that would enable them to effectively cope with society's daily demands.

To reduce poverty, we have to learn to think differently about children; they are not only "their" children, they are "our" children. We cannot escape the well-worn cliché that our children are *our future*. If we cast off our children, we will be like farmers, eating our seed corn.

It is not easy to slough off stereotypical thinking, but we have done so many times before. There was a time when employers believed they could not survive without the labor of children. Massachusetts was in the vanguard when it limited child labor to ten hours a day in 1842. Factories moved south to avoid child labor laws in the north. It was not until 1938, with the passage of the Fair Labor Standards Act, that child labor was outlawed everywhere. Two earlier efforts to pass a constitutional amendment regulating child labor had failed. Factory owners were certain that they could not make a profit unless children, as young as nine or ten, worked twelve or fourteen hours a day in mills, factories, and mines. We have the sad photographs to prove it.

Child poverty today is not as easy to photograph and arouse anguish, but it exists to a degree that should shock us as much as seeing a gaunt and gray barefoot ten-year-old, circa 1850, clothed in rags standing next to a whirring factory machine. Nearly a quarter of US families with children under the age of six live in poverty today. More disturbing, the child poverty rate in America is going up, not down, aggravated by the recession, but not entirely a result of it. Today it is the highest it has been in two decades, at 22 percent.[1] Children are often reduced to poverty because mothers continue to be paid less than women without children; childless women make 90 cents to a man's dollar, while mothers make 73 cents. Single mothers make less, just 60 cents, and African-American mothers even less than that. In 2007, children living in households headed by single mothers were more than five times as likely to be living in poverty as children living in households headed by married parents—42.9 percent compared to 8.5 percent. For Hispanic single mothers the figure was 51.4 percent; for African-American single mothers, 50.2 percent.[2]

As the current recession is prolonged keeping unemployment high and both the federal government and the states enact budget cuts that weaken the safety net, new and more disturbing poverty figures are released almost weekly. The most recent finding of the US Census Bureau, as of December, 2011, reveals that nearly 1 in 2 Americans are now either poor or low-income, (defined as earning between 100 and 199 percent of the poverty level). Fifty-seven percent of the nation's children fall into this category.[3]

Poverty Rates Declined for the Elderly but Rose for Children

While childhood poverty rates have soared, older Americans' poverty rates have declined. The reverse was true in 1950, when the poverty rate for the elderly exceeded that for children. As Charles Blow notes in an op-ed piece of the *New York Times*, "According to data from the Census Bureau, the percent of people ages 18 to 64 who were living in poverty in 2009 was higher than it had been in any year since 1959, while the percent of seniors living in poverty was lower than it had been in any year since at least 1959."[4] What changed? Social Security and Medicare, two hugely popular and expensive government programs, have kept millions of aging Americans out of the reach of poverty. And though consensus on poverty levels can be difficult to achieve—a November 2011 report that took noncash benefits such as food stamps into consideration concluded that poverty rates were somewhat higher for the elderly and lower for children than was previously thought—the overall rate for all groups continues to rise.[5]

The most effective program to reduce poverty for both the elderly and children has been the earned income tax credit—through which low- to moderate-income individuals and families can qualify for tax refunds—but it reaches only a segment of the population and varies from state to state because states can supplement the federal program. Some cash-strapped states have shrunk this benefit. Michigan reduced its credit from $432 a year for an average family to $138 a year.[6] Other programs that offer assistance for struggling families include Temporary Assistance for Needy Families (TANF), though its benefits are available only for a short time and then are cut off forever. The Food Stamp Program (a.k.a. Supplemental Nutrition Assistance Program or SNAP) is one of the most important programs for reducing child hunger. Not surprisingly, due to the recession, usage is on the increase; the recipient population grew 70 percent in the last four years. Food stamps are used by 46 million Americans or 15 percent of the population. Equally alarming is the revelation that 49 percent of all children born in the United States receive nutrition assistance through the WIC (Women, Infants, and Children) program.[7]

There is no point in pitting the elderly against children; members of both groups need help to push back poverty. It is fair to ask, however, why do the elderly receive so much government help, and the children much less? The answer is clear: the elderly, through AARP and by individual action, have formed a powerful and effective lobby. They speak with one voice—loudly, consistently, and effectively—and they are faithful voters; they turn out in greater numbers than any other segment of the population. No wonder that proposing changes in Social Security and Medicare is called the third rail of politics. Even in a time of serious budget cutting, Congress has experienced great difficulty in addressing fiscal challenges in sustaining these entitlement programs. They know where the votes are.

When I campaigned, I, like every other politician, went to every senior citizen center I could locate—and stayed for lunch. I also visited child care centers—but not for votes; they weren't there. It will be difficult to make the lobby for children and families as powerful as the lobby for seniors because, today, it has neither the time nor the money to organize as effectively. Neither does it have the same gravitational pull on public empathy or the ability to cross economic divides. Somehow taking care of Grandma—regardless of her income—has more appeal than taking care of poor little Joey or Suzie, especially when the blame for their impoverishment can be placed on their parents. The staying power of programs for the elderly is buttressed by the fact that every American over the age of sixty-five is eligible for them. They are not and never have been programs for the poor. They are entitlements, not only in dollars, but in intent—old people should not suffer; old people are entitled to receive our help. They took care of us; now it's our turn to take care of them. It is time to achieve a similar sense of entitlement for children—children should not suffer; children deserve protection from hardship, because they do not have a choice of who their parents are, whether they are rich or poor, educated or not. We have to broadcast that the long-term consequences of child poverty are severe and lasting. In depriving our children, we deprive ourselves of future educated, healthy, and tax-paying citizens.

Citizens are most dependent on government assistance at the two most vulnerable stages in their lives: childhood and old age. This is when domestic spending in most countries reaches its apex.

Highest-Income Countries = Lowest Poverty—Except for the United States

It stands to reason that poor countries would have proportionately more poor children and rich countries less. Not so in the United States. According to the Luxembourg Income Study, which measures child poverty in thirty developed countries, "The U.S. emerged as a marked exception, with a substantially higher level of child poverty than its national income would predict."[8] The United States continues to believe in the "trickle down" theory, which maintains that the "high level of income inequality in the U.S. generates favorable levels of economic growth, which in turn raises the standard of living of the worst-off Americans, relative to their European counterparts," the study states.[9] Recent poverty figures do not support that belief. Most disturbing is the finding that children younger than six are more likely to be poor than older children.

Poverty, according to the Luxembourg Income Study, is defined as disposable household income of less than 50 percent of median household income. Which countries have the lowest child poverty rates? Denmark, Finland, and Norway top the list at 3 percent; Sweden has 4 percent; the Netherlands has 6 percent. And a large group of non-social-welfare states do far better than the United States: the Czech Republic, Slovenia, Taiwan, and Belgium are at 7 percent, less than one-third the rate in the United States. Three other countries are at 8 percent: Austria, France, and Hungary. We have the highest rate among the thirty countries examined, exceeded only by Russia and Mexico, as determined by the study.[10]

Our relative standing compared to other countries is impossible to justify and difficult to explain. One conclusion is that the "trickle down" theory is as outmoded as the belief that the world is flat. Another conclusion is that we make it hard for parents, particularly single mothers, to work, even when they have a strong desire to do so, because of lack of affordable child care and flexibility. It is time we moved on and examined why the gaps between the super rich, the middle income, and the poor continue to grow and take serious steps to narrow them.

The Nordic countries are in the low single digits of child poverty because their "institutional design is both strongly [income] redistributive and most highly associated with structural features that encourage and enable maternal employment; both elements shape the prevalence of child poverty."[11]

Other figures are more alarming. A report on the impact of the 2011 recession on America's children, issued by the Children's Defense Fund, tells us that number of children living in poverty has increased by four million since 2000, and "the number of children who fell into poverty between 2008 and 2009 was the largest single-year increase ever recorded." The report also notes that "the number of homeless preschool-age children increased by 43 percent in the past two years. The number of homeless children and youth enrolled in public schools increased 41 percent between the 2006–2007 and the 2008–2009 school years." And it goes on to say that "during 2009, an average 15.6 million children received food stamps each month, an increase of 65 percent over just 10 years."[12]

Equally disturbing was an August 2011 report on how children have fared during the recession from Kids Count, a project of the Annie E.

Casey Foundation. Patrick McCarthy, president of the foundation, told Judy Woodruff on *PBS NewsHour* that 31 million children in the United States are "two or three paychecks away from economic catastrophe."[13]

Influences on Poverty

Studies have shown that family structure, labor market income, and the educational level of the household are key factors that influence child poverty. These findings argue for more investment in education—the key to higher earnings. Instead, we are moving in the opposite direction. The projection for the future is grim. Data from the nonpartisan Center on Budget and Policy Priorities points out that thirty-eight states have made deep cuts in their 2012 budgets in K–12 education, higher education, and health care.[14]

Why is the American public not outraged by US figures? In part, because we don't see the faces behind the numbers. Statistics have no conscience. We can push the delete button and be free to roam. We see photos of the starving children in Somalia, bones protruding, and we send help. Most of us don't see the children who have potato chips and soda for breakfast. Teachers, doctors, nurses, social workers, and caregivers cannot shrug these figures off because they see these children and know their stories, but most Americans do not. We do not see them because they are literally out of our sight.

When I served as deputy secretary for the US Department of Education from 1993 to 1996, I saw the faces of poverty in every inner-city school I visited—Chicago, New York, Boston, Los Angeles, New Orleans, Philadelphia, and on the back roads of Vermont. I had to get off the highway to find them. The people who went straight home on a six-lane throughway to the suburbs never encountered them. They did not see what I saw on my way to a school in Philadelphia: street after street of slouching young men with nothing on their hands but time; curb after curb piled high with garbage in front of houses that no one would choose to live in. I went there at the behest of the Clinton administration, which sent Cabinet members out from Washington to make the case against the proposed reduction in school lunch programs championed by Republican Speaker Newt Gingrich, as part of his ill-fated Contract with America.

The Philadelphia school was the only building in the neighborhood that looked intact. When I entered the kindergarten room, there were dozens of small five-year-old children—some with pretty ribbons in their hair—eagerly holding their hands out to the teachers to receive a packet of free school lunch. I felt a sudden rage. "They want to take this away from them," I asked myself, "when this is all they have?"

I could not believe what I was seeing when I visited a high school in New Orleans in a neighborhood called Desire. No one would desire to take the street car there unless they had no other choice. These children did not. The principal pointed out the bullet holes in the walls, told me about the leaky roof, and expressed concern about how many girls had become pregnant that year. Most of the children came from the nearby housing project, also named Desire, that was so dilapidated that it redefined the word "slum." "War zone" would have been a more apt description. When I got back to Washington I described my visit to HUD (Housing and Urban Development) secretary Henry G. Cisneros, and he agreed to tear the Desire housing complex down. I did not know where its residents would be relocated, but I was relieved that they would no longer be living in Desire.

If the men and women in Congress had witnessed these scenes, could they have proposed these cuts for hungry children? I believe the answer would be "no." We succeeded in defeating the cuts that time, but providing a safety net for the poor is never a settled issue. In the budget battles of 2011 nutrition programs for pregnant women and food stamp programs for struggling families were once again vulnerable. Why?

The British Example of Reducing Poverty

Americans can turn their eyes away from the poor because many believe the poor have themselves to blame; they believe that the poor are either lazy or stupid. Complacency sets in with the assumption that "the poor will always be with us." There is not much to be done about poverty in a capitalistic system, we surmise. Our only recourse is to submit to social Darwinism let the fittest survive. But research tells us otherwise.

"For many children, their risk of living in poverty is strongly shaped by the design of their countries' instruments of redistribution," the Luxembourg report states. In other words, public policy matters. For example, the study found that the poverty level in England was 34 percent—higher than in the United States—before accounting for tax credits and income transfers, but after these policies were put in place, only 19 percent of England's children qualified as poor. In contrast, in the United States, the before and after stories are different. Before taxes and transfers, 25 percent of our children were poor; afterward, the poverty rate was reduced only slightly, to 22 percent.[15]

The English figures prove that poverty rates can be reduced if leaders make a serious, long-term commitment to do so. It is the only proper economic and moral choice for an affluent nation determined to be number one in the world. Continuing on the same road of deliberate indifference could, as columnist Charles M. Blow writes, lead to a "lost generation."[16] We cannot escape from the reality that it will be our generation's great loss as well.

The difference between the United Kingdom and the United States is that in 1999 Tony Blair's Labor party government embarked on a twenty-year plan to eliminate poverty. By 2004 he reported a 23 percent reduction. What is happening under the Conservative leadership of David Cameron, who has initiated drastic cuts in domestic spending? Cameron has vowed that no children will be made poor as a result of budget cuts, explains Jane Waldfogel, professor at the Columbia University School of Social Work and author of *Britain's War on Poverty*. Cameron's government is committed to protecting children in tough economic times, she says, and "the United States can learn from Britain." Rather than reducing programs like paid maternity leave, Cameron is extending it to fathers. The voucher program to enroll all children in preschool will be extended to all three- and four-year-olds, rather than only the most disadvantaged. Two-year-old disadvantaged children will be added. Such commitment to reducing poverty by both liberal and conservative governments, in good times and in bad, made it possible for Britain to cut its child poverty rate in half. In contrast, the recession in the United State has thrust millions more children into poverty. England differs from the United States on several fronts: the minimum wage is $9.70 an hour, compared to ours at $7.25, tax incentives encourage parents to go into the paid labor market, parents have access to universal preschool, and workers have the right to request flexible work schedules.

What actions would Waldfogel recommend for the United States? "We fought the war on poverty and poverty won," she says. "This is not rocket science. If we have the political will, we know what the tools are: a higher minimum wage, larger tax credits, and universal pre-school." (In the War on Poverty during the Lyndon Johnson administration, poverty was reduced during the 1960's, reaching a low of 11.1 percent in 1973 then began climbing again.) She believes that racism underlies some of the United States' tendency to neglect the needs of poor. Poor children in England are usually depicted as white, as if they stepped out of a Charles Dickens novel; in the United States they are often depicted as black or brown. White policy makers may find it more difficult to identify with these poor children than with red-headed Little Orphan Annie. Consider the breakdown, by race, of children living in poverty:

All children: 20.7[17]
White only, non-Hispanic: 11.9
Black: 35.4
Hispanic: 33.1
Asian: 13.3[18]

There is no doubt that poverty often hits black and Hispanic families the hardest. For example, babies born to black women are up to three times as likely to die in infancy as those born to women of other races.[19] But these percentages give the impression that there are more African-American children who are poor than white children. In actual numbers, however, whites comprise the largest group of low-income children: 11 million live in families with incomes twice below the federal poverty line.[20]

Reducing Poverty in America

If we could provide a combination of paid family leave, which would enable mothers and fathers to care for their children in the first year, with subsidized care for two- to five-year-olds, poverty in this country would be substantially reduced. Child care costs are a relatively new expenditure for working families because some thirty or forty years ago, mothers were less likely to be in the workforce. These costs have subtracted a large chunk of their income, varying from city to city and from one type of care to another. Center-based care averages $11,666 per year but ranges from $3,582 to $18,773, usually amounting to 30 percent or more of an annual salary. Infant care can be as high as $2,000 a month. I met with several mothers on the University of Vermont staff who regularly compare experiences in a weekly "mothers' group." Child care was their big issue. "Finding good child care is a full-time job," said one mother. "Paying for it is equivalent to a mortgage payment," said another.

These expenditures have the effect of a hidden tax on working families. The annual cost of center-based care for a four-year-old is more than the annual in-state tuition at a public four-year college in thirty-three states and the District of Columbia, according to the Children's Defense Fund study.[21] Reducing or eliminating child care costs would have three poverty-reducing results: 1) poor families would have more disposable income, which could lift them from a minimum wage standard to a livable wage; 2) parents would have an easier time obtaining and maintaining employment; and 3) parents could afford higher-quality child care, which would better prepare children for school and for adulthood.

The Cost of Poverty

What is the cost of poverty? It is not cheap. Poor children have lower reading scores, poorer health and social behavior, and considerably more stress in their often uprooted lives. According to a brief from Child Trends, a nonpartisan research center, "Studies find that those who experienced persistent poverty as children are much more likely to be poor as adults than those who were not poor in childhood. . . . In the long run, childhood poverty poses economic costs to the United States through reduced productivity and output, the cost of crime, and increased health expenditures. Children who grow up in poverty are more likely to have low productivity and low earnings relative to children who did not grow up in poverty. It has been estimated that the reduced productivity lowers the gross domestic product by 1.3 percent annually."[22] Gøsta Esping-Andersen provides a higher estimate: "Recent calculations show that the societal cost of child poverty in the United States is equal to 4 percent of GDP, due mainly to the link between poverty and school outcomes, health and criminality."[23]

Looked at from another perspective, if women could be fully employed at the same level as men, the gross domestic product would grow as much as 9 percent, according to a study by the World Economic Forum. How much would some of these programs to alleviate poverty cost? Twelve weeks of paid family leave through an employee-funded insurance program would cost each worker $10 a month, according to Heather Boushey, of the Center for American Progress. A full year of leave for every working parent would cost the country just $25 billion, according to Jane Waldfogel.[24] (And note that some observers have concluded that it is easier for employers to replace a mother who has a year-long leave than to find a replacement for a few weeks or months.)

What Has Happened to the American Dream?

If funding is not the major obstacle, why aren't we swinging into action? In addition to shielding our eyes, we continue to believe that a dose of honest hard work and an ounce of ambition will enable anyone who really wants to move up and out of poverty to do so. If the United States has a common credo, it is the American Dream. We continue to adhere to it despite growing evidence that it is no longer universally accessible. There is an increased concern that many members of this generation will *not* be better off than their parents.

I find myself reluctant to let the American Dream go because I am a product of it. When my widowed mother brought my brother and me to the United States from Switzerland in 1940, at the outbreak of World War II, she was inspired to make the sea voyage on the S.S. *Manhattan* with her two young children because she harbored the same ideal that immigrant parents still cling to today: "Everything is possible in America," my mother told us. We believed her. It turned out that she was right. I was able to work my way through college by waitressing every summer. This was before there were college loans and grants, but tuition was low. I received an excellent education at a public university, the University of Massachusetts, followed by a scholarship to the Columbia School of Journalism, and later, a master's degree in English literature from the University of Vermont.

When I served as US deputy secretary of education I was able to tell my audiences, "I grew up with a single mother and my older brother and couldn't speak English when I arrived in America; education is what made the difference in my life, and it will make all the difference in yours." Heads nodded.

My belief in American upward mobility was reconfirmed when I returned to Switzerland as the American ambassador in 1996. I began to muse, what would my life have been like if my mother hadn't brought us to America? I doubted that I would have had the same opportunities. Switzerland, like most of Europe, is a more class-conscious and money-conscious society. Family background is important. When I was being interviewed by the *Neue Zurcher Zeitung* (New Zurich Newspaper) editorial board shortly after my arrival, the editor's first question was, which neighborhood had we lived in? He nodded approvingly when I told him the Dolderstrasse, a fine neighborhood. I had passed scrutiny.

Upward Mobility: United States Ranks Number 8

Therefore it came as a shock to learn that the United States provides less upward mobility than seven other developed countries. Once again we are not number one, but rather number eight, behind Denmark, Norway, Finland, Canada, Sweden, Germany, and France, according to a report from the Economic Mobility Project.[25]

France, home of Louis XVI and Marie "let them eat cake" Antoinette? How could they offer more upward mobility than we? How could socialist countries like Sweden and Denmark provide more upward mobility than the capitalist United States? Are we not the premier land of opportunity, the Mecca for immigrants worldwide?

The report measures economic mobility by trends in personal or family incomes and focuses on "*intergenerational mobility*—the extent to which children move up or down the income spectrum relative to their parents' generation." What does a reduced pace of upward mobility mean for child poverty? "This means that one of the biggest predictors of an American child's future economic success—the identity and characteristics of his or her parents—is predetermined and outside that child's control."[26]

Despite the hard facts that tell us the American Dream has moved farther from our grasp, the report indicates that Americans refuse to believe these findings. No doubt few are aware of our ranking as number eight. Unlike our global counterparts, the Economic Mobility Project report tells us, Americans are wildly optimistic about "being able to control their own economic destinies through hard work, less likely to believe that coming from a wealthy family is important to getting ahead, less likely to think that differences in income within their country are too large, and less likely to favor the government's responsibility to reduce these differences." They seemed undisturbed by the fact that "between 1978 and 2005, CEO pay increased from 35 times to nearly 262 times the average worker's pay. Said another way, by 2005, the typical CEO made more in an hour than a minimum-wage worker made in a month."[27] American romance dies hard, but there are new signs of discontent as the gap continues to grow. The winds of autumn in 2011 brought us the national Occupy Wall Street movement, with its slogan: "We are the 99 percent." It put the spotlight on America's huge income disparities between the very rich 1 percent and everyone else, bringing these figures into the public conversation for the first time.

There are some contradictions: "Perhaps driven by widening inequality and a concern about the fairness of the game, there is a tangible and growing sense of pessimism among the American public. In exit polls after the 2006 election, less than one-third of the voters said that they thought life would be better for the next generation."[28] Americans, it seems, can be mental jugglers, holding two opposing beliefs at the same time. By 2011, the Occupy Wall Street movement had touched a sensitive chord: 43 percent of Americans "agree with the views of the 'Occupy Wall Street' movement, according to a new CBS News/New York Times poll that found a widespread belief that money and wealth should be distributed more evenly in America."[29]

The implications of the Economic Mobility Project report, among others, are clear: First, poverty or the lack thereof is not entirely within the control of the family, least of all by the children. Second, the two-wage-earner family provides the best bulwark against poverty. As a country we must do a better job of supporting that family. Only then can we begin to restore the American Dream to its true meaning—that every American, regardless of where he or she has started out, can through perseverance and hard work climb step by step out of poverty and into the middle class. If we do not act now, we face the sad prospect of dooming a high percentage of our children to poverty; that is not only an unjust waste of human potential, it is a dangerous economic policy that will impact the well-being of every American.

CHAPTER 13

How Do We Win?

I received my first lessons in advocacy when I was a young mother and a member of the League of Women Voters in the 1960s. The League taught me this: before you take a position, do the research and get the facts. I was thoroughly bored by the lengthy discussions of facts and figures in support of a new sewage treatment plant for the city of Burlington, Vermont. But we got the plant.

The facts, figures, and research on family/work policies have been accumulating over the last fifty or more years by universities and children and family advocacy groups. Without them, we would not be where we are today: on the precipice of fundamental change. But there is more to be done. We must find new and innovative ways to inform lawmakers and the public about the impact of family/work policies on today's families. We have to bolster the economic argument made by economist James Heckman: that long-term investments provide a significant rate of return, not only in dollars saved, but in lives transformed. We have to translate the scientific arguments about early brain development into lay language that is easily understood. Business leaders need to receive specific information about how family-friendly policies will raise, rather than reduce, their bottom line. In short, they need to be given proof that these policies are *good for business*, as well as for families.

And we must make a moral case—the most difficult of all—that our generation has a responsibility for the well-being of the next. Just as we erased the stereotypes we once held about the potential of Americans with disabilities, we must discard the stereotypes we have held about families—who works, who doesn't, and how we provide security for both the youngest and the oldest among us.

Where's the Road Map?

Armed with the facts, there is a second challenge we must face for these policies to be heard above the din of the naysayers—how to counter the influence of money in politics. The advocates have had neither the money, the time, nor often the skills to be as well organized as the opponents. One glance at the power equation reveals that children and family advocacy groups look like political midgets compared to the giant US Chamber of Commerce and the Business Roundtable, who presume to speak for all businesses.

Advocates have yet to find a megaphone that can drown out the voices that have shouted "job killer" at every family/work proposal. Each separate group of child advocates can be marginalized for not speaking for the majority and, therefore, easily dismissed. Once again, we can learn from the Americans with Disabilities Act. The hundred separate organizations, each with their own agenda—the hearing impaired, the blind, polio victims, the wheelchair bound—got together under one umbrella, and their combined forces cleared the road to success.

Creating unity will take work. The problem is not always that there are too few voices for family/work policies. In some areas, there are too many. In the state of Vermont there are more than a dozen nonprofit organizations and a number of state agencies that advocate for affordable, quality child care and early education. Even the experts I spoke with, like Cheryl Mitchell, former deputy secretary of the Agency of Human Services, had difficulty keeping track of all the agencies and their related programs.

Where's the road map? I ask Mitchell. "It's more of a path through a thick jungle," she replies.

When I was governor I sought to bring together all children's advocates within the Vermont government and build a coalition of advocates outside of government. Twenty-five years later, the effort continues without notable progress. There have been successes in some areas, such as the child care coalition called Kids are Priority One, and the Parent-Child Center in Middlebury, Vermont, founded by Mitchell. I was so impressed with my visit to the center, that as Governor, I established similar centers throughout the state. They have become the focal points for social services for the entire family. I ask her, why can't child advocates who share similar goals get together and speak with one voice instead of each going after their own piece of the pie?

"There is a scarcity mentality that there is not enough money to go around," Mitchell explains. "They think their issues are the most important ones, and they can't wait." When new funds become available for child care, there is a struggle to decide whether to increase salaries for staff or reduce costs for families, she explains.

Her words remind me of the lack of cohesion that helped sink the universal child care legislation vetoed by President Richard Nixon. The conclusion is clear: advocacy groups must learn to unite and speak with one voice.

Uniting Advocacy Organizations

There are many organizations, such as the National Partnership for Women and Families, and the Sloan Work & Family Research Network at Boston College, that have done important research and advocacy work for families. The Internet is expanding their reach. Long-standing national organizations like the American Association of University Women have become increasingly active, engaging their members by e-mail to support legislation such as the Paycheck Fairness Act, which would increase the likelihood of working mothers increasing their pay. Organizations that once successfully led the charge for change on women's issues, such as NOW, while still engaged in the battle for choice, seem irrelevant to many young women who see them as part of their grandmothers' generation. Today, women are less likely to attach themselves to feminist organizations and more apt to join professional organizations that further their careers and speak directly to the issue of work and family.

That list is long. A sampling includes the Caucus for Women in Statistics, the Association for Women Geoscientists, the Women Business Owners Network, the Committee on Gender Equity in Anthropology, the American Medical Association Women Physicians Congress, and Women of Wind Energy. The fact that women continue to form women's organizations within their own professions indicates that the goal of gender equality has not yet been met. Women in Physics, for example, issued a paper titled "The Art of the Impossible: Balancing Physics and Family," and Sociologists for Women in Society issued "How the Balancing Act Disadvantages Women in the Workplace."

The Tea Party, the Arab Spring, and Occupy Wall Street: The Surge in Direct Action

Just when I thought that organizing through social media had dispatched old-fashioned marches and protests to the rubbish heap of history, the Tea Party, the Arab Spring, and Occupy Wall Street sprang up, seemingly out of nowhere. As I was trying to cross Pennsylvania Avenue in Washington, DC, in 2009, I had to thread my way through the first mass parade of Tea Party marchers. I was shocked by the angry signs and shouts, and said to myself, "This will never last." I was wrong.

Protests were back, abetted by social media. Since then, with the emergence of the Arab Spring, we have learned that Internet information outlets have often become the medium for social change. No longer is there a choice between communicating the message through the Internet *or* marching in the streets; the two walk in tandem. The Internet has enabled protestors to move from the passive stage of text messaging to the active stage of putting their bodies on the line. It has also allowed video clips to travel widely and quickly, directly from the scene, shaping public opinion. When surging unarmed crowds were fired at by well-armed soldiers during some of the Arab uprisings, their shots were literally heard around the world.

The global revival of old-fashioned protest movements was unexpected and surprisingly effective in some countries, like Egypt and Libya, bringing down long-standing, deeply entrenched dictatorships. Almost all of the Arab countries have been washed by the waves set off by a pebble dropped in the pond of Tunisia, when one merchant immolated himself in protest against police authority. The rivulets were felt across Europe and America as well. As I write this, Occupy Wall Street encampments in the United States have been torn down in most cities. The next question is: will this largely liberal movement survive the winter and evolve into a political movement to become a progressive counterbalance to the conservative Tea Party? Will it focus on one issue, such as campaign finance reform to curb the power of money in politics which affects all other issues? It is too early to tell. What we can tell is that protest has, once again, become a tool for change. Showing up matters.

Can we skim off some of the energy of the Occupy movement and use it to jump-start a call for new family/work policies? Scanning the faces of the occupying crowds indicates that the movement—while determined to be leaderless—nevertheless appears to have a majority of male spokesmen. Should we promote more female leadership within, or should working families stage their own marches? We may need to do both.

Internet Outreach and MomsRising

It has not yet staged a protest in the streets, but MomsRising is a highly effective Internet organization, cofounded by Joan Blades (who was also cofounder of MoveOn.org) and Kristin Rowe-Finkbeiner, author of *The F-Word*. Together they wrote *The Motherhood Manifesto* in 2006. They decided to donate their book proceeds to an organization that spoke to their cause. Finding none, they started MomsRising, which now partners with more than a hundred organizations and has a membership of over one million and a social media reach of over three million.

MomsRising enables its members to respond instantaneously to calls for action, online. For example, for the health care reform bill the group made 600,000 constituent contacts on the ground and online in the months leading up to the vote. "They had meetings in Senate offices in every state, made phone calls, shared stories," Rowe-Finkbeiner explains. "We hope to build a huge group of engaged citizens that are thinking long term. I think parents are good because they think about the future when they think about their kids. We try to meet people where they're at. Young mothers are just overwhelmed with how busy they are."

Cofounder Blades explains, "three-fourths of the moms are in the labor force, juggling many roles, so they can't physically be in the nation's capital, but they can send messages." Sometimes they send messages in unique wrappings that get politicians' and the media's attention. They sent fortune cookies, apples, and even decorated diapers with the message that the current health care system stinks and we need a change.

Some have criticized MomsRising for focusing only on moms, to the exclusion of dads. When asked, Rowe-Finkbeiner responds, "We feel that anyone with a belly button and anyone that has ever had a mother needs to be engaged and involved in these issues." So far, 5 percent of the group's membership is men.

This is its mission:

M. Maternity and paternity leave
O. Open flexible work
T. Toxic free families
H. Health care for all
E. Early care and education
R. Realistic and fair wages
S. Sick days, paid

Blades best summed up its mission: "We're working on economic security and fairness for families."

In 2010, when budget cuts were proposed by the Republican-controlled US House of Representatives, MomsRising sprang into action. Joan Blades penned a letter for members to send to their congressional representatives that said, in part, "We often hear from our political leaders that 'Governments need to budget like families do.' You're right! Congress needs to start budgeting like real families and put our nation's kids first!"[1] Joan Blades understands what is at stake for the country if cuts to social programs are enacted. She asks me, "Who is going to pay our Social Security when we're older? If these kids don't have good jobs and we don't have a good economy, then my Social Security is in jeopardy." She elaborates, "It [present policy] is ultimately going to kill us because we are not taking care of our kids. They are the engine of our economy; if we don't invest in them, we're not going to be competitive."

Head Start and food stamps were spared in that budget confrontation, but not necessarily in the next.

MomsRising is using its ability to mobilize a constituency that would not be heard without access to the Internet. Can we build on that model to mobilize a larger constituency?

Time for a Family/Work Agenda

When I described the subject of my book to a friend, she responded, "I'd like to get involved in those issues, but where can I begin? What organization could I join?" I suggested MomsRising, but realized that was not what she was looking for. She wanted to do more than send e-mails to her congressman or congresswoman. She wanted to become fully engaged in family/work policy advocacy. How could I point her in the right direction?

Thus far, the agenda for family/work policies has been narrow: one battle at a time, such as paid sick days in Connecticut and paid family leave in New Jersey, with the hope that these victories will spread to other states and eventually pave the way for federal legislation. It is time to promote the concept that all family policy changes need to be integrated into one agenda, following the different stages of a child's life. It must begin with home visitation from nurses or other professional staff for all new parents, continue with paid family leave and workplace flexibility, be followed by affordable quality child care and early childhood education, and conclude with after-school care for children up to the age of twelve. That is the ideal.

Political pragmatism tells us we have to take one step at a time because the political system cannot digest such a large meal. Progress has been painfully slow. We must work on individual and comprehensive policies at the same time. We must describe the big picture to enable the public to visualize how these policies are integrated, and how, when they are combined, they would improve the lives of all working families. Each group that advocates for one policy must assume responsibility for placing it in a larger context. Workplace flexibility and paid sick days must be partners, and both should embrace paid family leave. Quality child care and early childhood education run into one another like watercolors on paper. Today, all the advocacy groups are competing for the same dollars. They cannot afford to compete against one another any longer.

I learned the importance of having all the stakeholders in the room when I chaired the Vermont House Appropriations Committee. Previously, each higher-education constituency had testified separately for their slice of the pie, whether it was the Vermont Student Assistance Corporation (a public nonprofit providing students with financial aid), the state colleges, the private colleges, or the University of Vermont. With everyone in the room at the same time, they had to listen to their colleagues and learn to make the case not only for themselves, but for the entire higher education budget.

All for one and one for all is the most productive strategy, even if it involves greater risk. A common call for action will lead to a concentrated message, which is more difficult to sideline than separate demands. Admittedly, it is not easy to compromise, even among friends, but putting aside individual interests and pledging allegiance to a common goal is more likely to result in a win–win scenario.

The Search for Bipartisan Support

Senator Bob Casey (D-PA) is ready to pick up the mantle left behind by Senator Ted Kennedy (D-MA) on children's issues, including state grants to fund early education programs. Casey says he was inspired to be a child advocate because he believes "every child is born with a light inside them; some need a little help that we can provide. Every child needs to reach his or her potential." He stresses that in debating budget cuts, "we have to make sure that we don't injure children." He also acknowledges that the bipartisan spirit that enabled the Congress to pass legislation providing children's health insurance has begun to fray. He has not succeeded in getting one Republican senator to cosponsor the Continuum of Early Learning Act 2011, which would promote quality and coordination of early learning programs. "So far we haven't achieved that. We're still working on it."

He remains optimistic. "Children's programs are still popular. They have proven to be successful. In addition to shared values, it's smart economics. It's a job creation issue. Businesses in my state have come to the table. They tell us, 'We've got to invest in kids.' They understand the benefits of early learning and care. Some senators who support it have not been vocal."

"Why?" I ask.

"Any new spending is considered by definition a mistake," he replies.

So, how can voters help politicians become vocal?

Make family/work issues a top campaign issue. Question every candidate for public office about where she or he stands on child care, early childhood education, paid family leave, and workplace flexibility.

Hold elected officials accountable. Let them know that pro-family rhetoric should translate into support of policies that improve the lives of children and families.

Organize the unorganized to support or oppose candidates on the issues. They have to be convinced to take time out of their already overbooked schedules to send an e-mail, make a telephone call, write a letter to their representatives, and, most importantly, vote.

When "60 Minutes" reported on the "Hard Times Generation" in Florida, Scott Pelley portrayed a single out-of work widowed father who spent nights looking for a safe parking space for his yellow van because the homeless shelters were full. It was his two children who were impossible to forget. They were shown getting ready for school in a gas station bathroom, and—because there was no place to cook—relying on tin cans for food. The articulate young girl, Ariel, told her story so stoically that two weeks later, "60 Minutes" reported that viewers had responded by giving or promising one million dollars to help the homeless in central Florida. Three colleges offered full scholarships for the children. No longer were these children statistics, they were a family who broke our hearts.[2]

Lawmakers have to be exposed to these realities that low-income families face. They have to see the signs of poverty—to believe that it exists. It is easier for a congressman to sit down with the US Chamber of Commerce, enjoying a good lunch, served on a white tablecloth, and chatting comfortably with lobbyists, than it is to meet with a child care director, squeeze into a tiny chair, play with blocks, and munch on peanut butter and crackers. Most members of Congress have no experience with economic scarcity. Their salary is $174,000 a year. Forty-four percent of the members of Congress are millionaires. They have all the benefits that many Americans lack—high salaries, quality health care, and the opportunity to take paid sick days (or fund-raising days) off without fearing the loss of their jobs. The income gap between lawmakers and their constituents, while always significant, has widened dramatically in the last six years. The median net worth of members of Congress tops $900,000[3] and has increased 15 percent from 2006 to 2010. That figure dropped 8 percent for all Americans in that same period. It should not be surprising, then, that so many members of Congress stand ready to slice into programs that sustain poor Americans.[4]

The message from working families must be as tough as that of the business community: our vote depends on your support for our issues. We will no longer settle for soothing words like "This is not the right time," or "I would love to support you, but . . ." Politics is always a question of making tough choices, in good times and bad.

Dealing with Competing Interests

Politics is about competition. The first round of competition is obvious—getting elected. The second round of competition is less visible—how to deal with competing interests, how to find a spot near the top of the agenda. That's where democracy's toughest battles are fought: in determining what will get done. Remember the old diagrams that used to portray how a bill becomes a law? If you concentrated and went very slowly and carefully, it would be possible to follow the diagram's circuitous route from bill to law. Today, that course is impossible to chart and navigate because it has become an obstacle course, one that only lobbyists are trained to follow, and it is more often designed to impede the process than smooth the way.

Fierce partisanship and limited dollars are major impediments of progress. Nevertheless, the agenda is more fluid than the public realizes, even in hard times. Strong political pressure can make an issue move from the "fail" side of the ledger to "pass," and back again. As a state legislator, I learned that when a program was convincing and had a vocal constituency, we somehow "found" the money and shifted other parts of the budget around to accommodate it. What constitutes pressure? Lobbyists, of course, with their financial firepower to elect and influence lawmakers, usually outweigh more poorly funded nonprofits and citizen activists, but not always. The success of the civil rights movement and the disability rights movement reminds us that occasionally the most powerful do not prevail.

The barriers to family/work legislation have not been put up only by conservative lawmakers. While liberals have not been vocal opponents, neither have many been strong advocates. Democrats continue to miss the opportunity to take the initiative either because they fear being called socialists or big spenders. Republican *New York Times* columnist David Brooks points out in a recent column that capitalism cannot work without also dealing with social decay. Referring to Adam Davidson's article "Making It in

America" in *The Atlantic*, he writes, "If President Obama is really serious about restoring American economic dynamism, he needs an aggressive two-pronged approach: More economic freedom combined with more social structure; more competition combined with more support." That social structure includes "better treatment for superstar teachers, more childcare options and early childhood education" Brooks writes.[5] Mona Harrington writes in *Care and Equality*, "The family must become a liberal issue. And the basis for a new liberal family politics should be outright, enthusiastic, unabashed support for families. . . . . However, [liberals] must be prepared to do this against inevitable conservative denunciations framed, as they always are, in moral terms, with conservatives positioning themselves as the defenders of morality and picturing liberals as libertines, abandoning it. A new liberal family politics must reframe this old argument. It must refute the claim of conservatives to be the sole guardians of the country's morality."[6] What would happen if more politicians of both parties and at both ends of the conservative–liberal spectrum ran on a "sensible family politics" platform of paid sick days, paid family leave, workplace flexibility, and early childhood education? I am convinced that these issues could be decisive in determining the outcome of many close elections.

The Role of the Private Sector

In our emphasis on the public sector, we cannot ignore the importance of the private sector to enact family/friendly policies. The family/work policies at Deloitte and Ernst & Young can be models of excellence. Business leaders are persuasive precisely because they speak from their experience. When they report that family/work policies improve the bottom line, their peers listen. The work of Brad Harrington, at Boston College, has focused on informing employers how to implement workplace flexibility and fills in an important piece of the work/family puzzle. While many business leaders will remain in lockstep, opposing these policies as "job killers or worse, socialism," others are beginning to see the positive side of the equation. When Rob Grunewald, associate economist at the Federal Reserve Bank of Minneapolis, spoke at a Vermont Business Roundtable conference on the importance of early childhood education, I sensed that the business community was en route to enlightenment. Whenever we can work with employers as partners, rather than enemies, we should eagerly engage in a joint effort. But our patience for change cannot be infinite. Private action alone will not enable us to achieve our goal.

Making a Difference: Women Lawmakers

Female lawmakers, as I have noted earlier, are somewhat more likely than men to support family/work policies, but because of their small numbers the political arena remains largely a boys' club, where the game is played according to their rules. It is symbolic of women's second-class status in the House that it took ninety-five years from the time the first woman was elected to Congress for congresswomen to obtain their own restroom near the House floor. For all those years in between they had to take a long walk through Statuary Hall to reach the Lindy Claiborne Boggs Congressional Women's Reading Room.

Even today the mostly male politicians comfortably schmooze with one another, not only in the men's room, but in the hallways, on the golf courses, and everywhere else they gather. Only when we achieve a significant increase in the number of female lawmakers will the ladies' room become a caucus for family/work policies, equal in power to the men's room caucus.

I believe that if we elected more women to political office, work and family policies would be viewed differently than they are today—not as benefits for the few, but as necessities for all. Ever since I was first elected to office in 1972, I have been an advocate for women in politics because gender balance and diversity are essential ingredients of democracy. That is why I wrote *Pearls, Politics, and Power*: to demystify politics and to demonstrate that when women are at the table both the style and content of politics changes. Senator Kirsten Gillibrand (D-NY) agrees. She launched a campaign called "Off the Sidelines" to encourage women around the country to run for Congress. Gillibrand believes more women in politics would change the combative tone of the male-dominated system.

Gillibrand contends that it should be "a source of concern to women that the issues that are important to them—like workplace discrimination and access to child care—are being decided by lawmakers who are almost exclusively male," she told the *New York Times*.[7]

It is tempting to have second thoughts about encouraging more women to run for office since the emergence of former Alaska governor Sarah Palin and Rep. Michele Bachmann (R-MN), both Tea Party conservatives who do not believe that government should get involved with working families or much of anything else. The emergence of conservative Tea Party women should not come as a surprise. When women are encouraged to run for office, they, like male candidates, will represent a broad spectrum of views. Palin and Bachmann proudly promote themselves as raising children completely on their own. Although they distance themselves from feminism, neither woman would be in the position she is in today if it were not for the feminist movement. Palin's mascot, the Mama Grizzly, is a powerful fighting symbol. But unlike earlier feminists, Mama Grizzly is not fighting for herself; she's fighting to protect her cubs. Palin and Bachmann promote themselves as mothers first, politicians second. They stand up and roar against any predator, which, in their view, is primarily the encroaching federal government. Perhaps we are focusing a great deal of attention on these two women because they represent a new female conservative politics. There is also no doubt that they have succeeded in marketing themselves effectively. Whether Tea Party candidates are good or bad for feminism is still up for debate, but on one front Sarah Palin has made a positive contribution—motherhood. Palin brings her children in front of the cameras. Some argue that she is exploiting her children. I do not. She is saying, I can be both a politician and a mother.

Times have changed. When I ran for a seat in the Vermont legislature, my informal kitchen cabinet advisors debated whether I should feature the usual candidate family photo in the brochure, with my husband and four children. It was considered risky because it might provoke the question—usually unasked, but sometimes asked— "Who's taking care of the children?" The family dog, however, could take center stage. Bonnie was a winner.

Today, the maternal wall still exists for women in the workplace, but not in politics—at least not much. In fact, when Republican Mary Fallin ran against Democratic lieutenant governor Jari Askins for governor of Oklahoma, the question raised in a debate by a blogger was: "Does being a mother make you a better politician?" Fallin claimed, "I think my experience is one of the things that sets me apart as a candidate for governor." Being a mother, having children, raising a family, she stated, is an important credential.[8] She won against her single, childless opponent.

I find myself asking the question that I didn't want anyone to ask me when I was running: how do women like Palin and Bachmann do it? Palin denies that she has household help, but she can drop her youngest, Trig, at one of two sets of nearby grandparents whenever she needs to, as portrayed in the television series, *Sarah Palin's Alaska*. Every working woman in America would be thrilled to be in her situation. Her mothering experiences do not resonate with the lives of most women who face a constant struggle not only to make financial ends meet, but to make their conflicting roles as mother and wage earner meet.

Everyone needs a support system. I probably could not have run for office without my then husband's support, both financially and emotionally. The hard part was trying to be in two places at once: at home with my children and in public life with my constituents. How did I do it? Gradually. The Vermont legislature is a part-time citizen legislature that meets from January to May. Commuting time between my home in Burlington and the capitol in Montpelier was forty-five minutes when there wasn't a snowstorm. I could get home for dinner most evenings. When I became the Democratic whip and chaired the Appropriations committee, my schedule became more demanding. I put together a patchwork of caregivers who were there when my children got home from school. Friends and neighbors helped with carpools. And then my children started to grow up. When I was elected lieutenant governor I could still control my schedule. By the time I was elected governor in 1984, three of my children were in college and my youngest was in high school.

Today, the electoral playing field for women is almost level, particularly for legislative races. When women run against men they stand an equal chance of winning, if the surrounding circumstances are the same, such as if both are running for an open seat or both are running against an incumbent. Women often, however, get special treatment, more so when they run for executive positions, like governor or president. Hair, hemlines, and husbands continue to burden women on the campaign trail. They have to lug that extra piece of baggage to every stop.

Women Making a Difference

Hillary Clinton, as secretary of state, is the most admired woman in America. When she was a candidate for the Democratic Party's nominee as president, her abilities were less well recognized because politicians tend to be portrayed as two-dimensional caricatures, like stand-up cardboard cutouts. Clinton was often described as being too tough or too soft; too strong or too weak. Never quite right.

As Jonathan Alter observed in *Vanity Fair*, "One of the least noticed changes in American public life is how [Clinton] has been transformed from a subject of constant gossip and calumny into a figure of consequence and little controversy."[9] She is the third woman to hold the office of secretary of state, following Condoleezza Rice and Madeleine Albright, but she is the first secretary to demonstrate subtle gender policy differences. One of her first actions was to appoint Melanne Verveer ambassador-at-large for global women's issues. Clinton has been a consistent spokeswoman against violence against women and for worldwide gender equality. Perhaps that's the prerogative of the third woman to be in that position.

Other women continue to receive recognition for being "First." That distinction was earned by the three brave women who as a group received the Nobel Peace Prize in 2011: Liberian president Ellen Johnson Sirleaf, Liberian Leymah Gbowee, and Tawakkol Karman of Yemen. "We cannot achieve democracy and lasting peace in the world unless women achieve the same opportunities as men to influence developments at all levels of society," said Nobel Committee chairman Thorbjorn Jagland in Oslo.[10]

"I urge my sisters, and my brothers, not to be afraid," Sirleaf, an extraordinarily courageous leader, told the Nobel audience, "Be not afraid to denounce injustice, though you may be outnumbered. Be not afraid to seek peace, even if your voice may be small. Be not afraid to demand peace."[11]

We are accumulating more information that women not only lead and legislate somewhat differently than men, but that they are also better at it, according to a recent study published in the *American Journal of Political Science*. They sponsor and co-sponsor more bills, get more bills passed, bring home more dollars ($49 million on average per district), and work harder. Ohio State political scientists Craig Volden and Alan Wiseman "tracked every bill introduced between 1981 and 2009, and found that those sponsored by women survived deeper into the legislative process, garnered more press attention, and were more likely to be deemed 'important' overall." As a result, the authors of the study conclude that "it's the women themselves—specifically, their skills at 'logrolling, agenda-setting, coalition building, and other deal-making activities'—that are responsible for the gender-performance divide."[12]

It would present a pleasant change to watch a gender-equal Congress at work, compared to the testosterone-dominated, dysfunctional Congress today, which is the target of growing public disdain and distrust. An observer of the prolonged debt ceiling crises commented on CNN, "Yes, over the past three weeks, we've seen just about every act there is to this political theater and, staying true to the time of Shakespeare, it seems every character is played by a man. Odds are that if there were more women in these discussions, the crisis would have been resolved by now."[13]

The Women's Vote

How do we translate the vision of a gender-equal Congress into reality—and then make that translate into progress for working women and families? More women must run for office, and more women must vote. The answer is simple. Implementation is complex. Studies indicate that women are 50 percent less likely than men to consider running for office. They tend not to see themselves as future lawmakers because they underestimate their credentials and are less likely to see the political arena as a place where things get done. Women, more than men, need to be asked to run for office. Running for office may not be easy, but asking someone else to run certainly is. Still, women are better citizens than men as measured by voter turnout. They have produced the gender gap—the difference between male and female voters as measured by political party. The gender gap has favored Democrats by as much as 11 percent in some contests. Women have voted in larger numbers than men in every presidential election since 1964, according to the Center for American Women and Politics.[14]

But there is much room for improvement. Among the most rapidly growing groups of voters we find a new cohort—unmarried women, according to Women's Voices. Women Vote, an advocacy organization that promotes voting among unmarried women. "We look at a segment of women: single, separated, divorced, or widowed, who tend not to vote," explains founder Page Gardner. Their research reveals that the marriage gap is much larger than the gender gap (except for women over the age of sixty-five): 34 percent.[15] These are the women who are, or will be, most affected by work/family policies. They are also the most mobile and disconnected segment of the population, who often feel both uninformed and disinterested. They make their decision late in the campaign. If single women voted in the same numbers as married women, the outcome of some elections would be reversed, Page believes. And if we added a higher voter turnout from Latinos and African-Americans, the impact of these growing constituencies could be decisive.

Staying Behind the Scenes

When women assume leadership roles they have an opportunity to reframe the debate and change the agenda. Are they ready? The answer should be yes, because there are more educated women than men, most women have benefited from participating in competitive sports, and most young women receive the same encouragement from their parents as their male siblings do—you can do anything. Yet college women do not strive for leadership positions at the same rate as men, according to a study published in 2011 by Princeton University president Shirley M. Tilghman. She noticed that women were visible in far fewer numbers than men in student government, for example, as class officers, editors of *The Daily Princetonian*, presidents of eating clubs, and recipients of academic awards and prizes. Tilghman wondered if this generation of Princeton women were less inclined to lead than their older sisters had been. The study concluded that "although some women run for elected office, many . . . choose less visible jobs behind the scenes. However, sometimes women who have expressed interest in more prominent posts have been actively discouraged by other students."

That didn't mean, though, that they weren't involved. "Despite being less likely than men to stand as candidates for a presidency or other more visible posts, undergraduate women do a large proportion of the important work in the organizations to which they belong," the report noted. It also concluded, "Women consistently undersell themselves, and sometimes make self-deprecating remarks in situations where men might stress their own accomplishments."[16]

The study, which could be replicated at other universities, indicates that the small numbers of women leaders in all fields are not due solely to women's caregiving responsibilities or to a hostile political climate. Something deeper is at work. Perhaps it is the anticipation of caregiving responsibilities that causes more women than men to stunt their leadership growth, even under safe conditions. When I asked a women's studies class whether they anticipated any conflicts between family and work, one student described her sister's recent experience: "Both she and her boyfriend were medical students. But my sister decided to drop out to become a physician's assistant because she thought it would be easier to raise a family." The student, expressing her disapproval, was determined to be different.

In another class about women and politics, I asked, "How many of you would consider running for office?" One woman tentatively raised her hand and said, "I would, but I'd rather work behind the scenes. I tend to be sarcastic." At that moment I happened to notice that a young man in the class was wearing a black T-shirt with orange Halloween-style lettering emblazoned across his chest: "Sarcasm, that's one of my strong points." It was a perfect teachable moment.

When I asked an undergraduate class at a Maryland university why the men were answering most of the questions, a woman replied, "Because we're not *sure* we're right." A male student volunteered, "Because we *know* we're right."

It begins even earlier than college, though. I once asked fourth- and fifth-graders at the Pomfret, Vermont, elementary school why the girls were not asking questions. A boy answered tentatively, "Because we're smarter?"

A loud chorus of "Nooo's" broke out from a small clique of girls in the front row who had been busy examining their fingernails. From that moment on, they were bursting with questions.

If we are to succeed in changing family/work policies, women and girls must learn to raise their hands, speak up, and risk rejection, both in the classroom and beyond, where the public debate will continue to be controversial. They must be encouraged to express their views from an early age right on to adulthood.

Time to Get Ready

It is time to get ready for battle to strengthen the American family and enable it to provide both economic security and loving care to all its members. Some observers have reached the conclusion that the battle has already been won. In "The End of Men," journalist Hanna Rosin, writing for *The Atlantic*, makes a case for economic forces favoring women. Male dominance, she says, "feels like the last gasp of a dying age rather than a permanent establishment."[17] Her optimism may be premature. Rosin applauds the fact that most of the new jobs—nursing, home health assistance, child care, food preparation—will be held by women but ignores the reality that many of these are low-wage jobs that keep families in or near poverty. Most women in these jobs cannot afford to pay for their own health insurance, or for the quality child care that could give their offspring a better chance.

The White House Council on Women and Girls' report *Women in America: Indicators of Social and Economic Well-Being* tells a different story. Packed with statistics, it backs up what we already know: that despite progress in education and participation in the workforce, women remain poorer than men, they live longer but have more health problems, and they are victims of violence at a higher rate.[18] Very few are in positions of real power.

In conclusion, I return to the three boxes I described in chapter 2: anger, imagination, and optimism. These are the ingredients that, when mixed carefully together, produce change.

Anger

"How can women be righteously angered?" Anita Hill asks me. She of all women has the right to be angry, having suffered humiliation at the hands of the US Senate during the confirmation hearings of Justice Clarence Thomas, whom she had accused of sexual harassment, only to be denounced herself as a "little bit nutty and a little bit slutty," by one commentator. Today this mild-mannered professor at Brandeis University answers her own question: "We have to be allowed to be angry."

Women are hesitant to be angry because "they don't want to be labeled femi-Nazis," she says. "Feminism has been caricatured to [such] a degree that it takes anger as a political tool away from them."

Most women want to distance themselves from anger; it's too dangerous. It is fair to ask: would those women who criticize an angry Bella Abzug and outspoken Betty Friedan have gotten to where they are if Bella and Betty hadn't raised voices, tinged with anger?

"We're all angry about something," Hill observes. "We all know how to get angry, but we've got to do it effectively to be able to tap into other people's anger." That is where political acumen is required, but there are many examples, including the Occupy Wall Street movement. There may not be a social change movement that has not been inspired by "righteous anger," as a prelude to activism. But we have to be careful—if anger is too severe, it may result in despair, the belief that nothing we can do will change anything. Or extreme anger may result in violence—the belief that the only way to change anything is tear the existing system down and start from scratch. There may be a place for violence, as we have seen demonstrated in protests against totalitarian regimes. But it is not likely to be effective in a present-day democracy. Change occurs best when we can express controlled, targeted anger focused on a new vision of society.

Imagination

Families, no doubt, are sometimes angry about their stressful lives, but they do not have time to even imagine what their lives would be like if they had access to affordable, dependable, quality child care that enabled them to work and their children to thrive. They cannot imagine that they would be able to take six months or a year off for family leave without losing a paycheck or a job. Without the ability to *imagine* a different future, it is impossible to bring it about. Working families remain convinced that not being able to integrate family and work successfully is *their* problem, nobody else's, and certainly not the government's. Our task is to provide the luxury of imagination to America's working families, not just as a daydream, but as the American dream.

If the Freedom Riders of the 1960s civil rights movement had submitted to the status quo and not imagined that whites and blacks could sit together at lunch counters in the South, there might still be "Whites Only" signs nailed to restroom walls. If disabled Americans had settled for being relegated to the attics of society, no mother would have encouraged her child to reach out and touch Judy Heumann's wheelchair. If gay and lesbian Americans had not come out of hiding and imagined that they could have the same rights as other Americans, they would have continued to live shadow lives, always in fear of rejection and persecution. Each group had the capacity to imagine a different world and their place in it. That vision inspired them to act.

Optimism

I admit, these are hard times to be an optimist. When I follow the news, I sometimes ask myself, why am I writing this book? How can we ask for more concern about others, more money, and more government at a time when the anti-government, anti-spending wave seems to be flooding the nation and drowning all new initiatives? Then I remind myself of the astounding figures that describe the level of American child poverty. I think of the women and men who are striving to be good parents and good caregivers. They want the very best for their children but often cannot provide it. We must listen to them.

We cannot allow ourselves to be conquered by despair. The hardest time to create change may be the best time to create change because the need for it is clear.

We must continue the work that feminism began. Earlier, feminism alerted us to fundamental gender inequities. These inequalities will persist until we address the conflicts families experience between their roles as wage earners and caregivers. It is unlikely that we will see a significant increase in the number of female elected officials, and female leaders everywhere, until we permit them to fulfill their dual roles. We will not stop the erosion of the middle class until we enable more mothers and fathers to work and provide decent, food, housing, and education for their families. Upward mobility, promised by the American Dream, will come to a full stop without fair policies that strengthen working families.

Government polices and private practices cannot solve all the daily dilemmas families face. But we *can* make their lives better.

The End of Patience: Reclaiming Family Values

Patience, silence, politeness—the characteristics that have won women praise in the past have to be set aside if women and their families want to achieve a different future.

We must snatch back the words "family values" and redefine them as the work/family policies necessary to sustain strong families. We may have not yet settled on the perfect catchwords to describe the twenty-first-century working family's needs, but we know what we must do to create change. The word "revolution" is once again appropriate. We have to organize, mobilize, and advocate with a fierce passion at all levels—from the grass-roots to the states to Washington, from east to west and north to south, leaving no constituency or person untouched. The well-being of the family must become a critical national concern that unites all constituencies—men, women, children; liberal, moderate, and conservative; the poor, middle class, and upper class; labor, the elderly, the disabled; employers and employees. The nation's economic security and moral integrity are at risk. It's time to ring the alarm bells and beat the drums to awaken the country up from its dormant state.

We, the richest, the most compassionate nation on earth, have the ability to respond to the call for action.

To succeed we have to jettison three firm beliefs:

- That we can't afford the expense
- That family policies impede job growth
- That the family is solely a private domain

Instead we must embrace these beliefs:

- That the cost to the nation of inaction is greater than the cost of action
- That investment in family/work policies fosters economic growth
- That we must share this investment for our children, our grandchildren, and the nation

It is time to strengthen the institution that all Americans—of every political persuasion—value most: the family. We cannot wait for the perfect moment. Now is the right time to begin.

NOTES

Chapter 1: Time for a New Revolution

1. Gail Collins, *When Everything Changed: The Amazing Journey of American Women from the 1960s to the Present* (Little, Brown and Company: New York, Boston, and London, 2009), 393.

Chapter 2: Back to the Family, After All

1. Maria Shriver and the Center for American Progress, *The Shriver Report: A Woman's Nation Changes Everything*, ed. Heather Boushey and Ann O'Leary (Center for American Progress and A Woman's Nation, October 2009), 19.
2. Kristin Rowe-Finkbeiner, *The F-Word: Feminism in Jeopardy—Women, Politics and the Future* (Emeryville, Calif.: Seal Press, 2004), 7, 104.
3. Tina Fey, "Confessions of a Juggler," *The New Yorker*, February 14, 2011, 64.
4. Joan C. Williams, *Unbending Gender: Why Family and Work Conflict and What to Do about It* (New York: Oxford University Press, 2001), 20.
5. Joan C. Williams, *Reshaping the Work-Family Debate: Why Men and Class Matter* (Cambridge, Mass., and London: Harvard University Press, 2010), 39.
6. Janet C. Gornick and Markus Jäntti, *Child Poverty in Upper-Income Countries: Lessons from the Luxembourg Income Study*, Luxembourg Income Study Working Paper, 509, May 2009, http://www.lisproject.org/publications/liswps/509.pdf, 7.
7. Dina Baskt, "Pregnant, and Pushed Out of a Job," *New York Times*, January 30, 2012, accessed February 7, 2012, http://www.nytimes.com/2012/01/31/opinion/pregnant-and-pushed-out-of-a-job.html.
8. "Remarks by Senator Hillary Rodham Clinton to the NYS Family Planning Providers," press release, January 24, 2005, posted on Nation-Building website, http://dean2004.blogspot.com/2005/02/transcript-hillary-clinton-speech-on.html.
9. Williams, *Reshaping*, 79.
10. Ellen Galinsky, Kerstin Aumann, and James T. Bond, *Times Are Changing: Gender and Generation at Work and Home*, 2008 National Study of the Changing Workforce (Families and Work Institute, 2009, revised August 2011), 19.
11. Lynda Laughlin, *Who's Minding the Kids? Child Care Arrangements: Spring 2005/Summer 2006*, Current Population Reports p70–121 (US Census Bureau, August 2010), http://www.census.gov/prod/2010pubs/p70-121.pdf.
12. Sam Dillon, "Top Test Scores from Shanghai Stun Educators," *New York Times*, December 7, 2010.
13. Michael Hirsh, "We're No. 11!" *Newsweek*, August 23/30, 2010.
14. Miriam Peskowitz, *The Truth Behind the Mommy Wars: Who Decides What Makes a Good Mother* (Emeryville, Calif.: Seal Press, 2005), 15.
15. Peskowitz, *The Truth*, 46.
16. "The G.I. Bill's History. Born of Controversy: The GI Bill of Rights," US Department of Veterans Affairs, http://www.gibill.va.gov/benefits/history_timeline/index.html.
17. US House of Representatives Office of the Clerk, "Women in Congress: Edith Nourse Rogers," http://womenincongress.house.gov/member-profiles/profile.html?intID=209#foot12, citing

Dorothy M. Brown, "Rogers, Edith Nourse," in *American National Biography*, vol. 18 (New York: Oxford University Press, 1999), 752–53.

Chapter 3: What Can We learn from the Rest of the World?

1. Sarah Fass, *Paid Leave in the States: A Critical Support for Low-Wage Workers and Their Families* (New York: National Center for Children in Poverty, March 2009), 3.
2. Tala Al-Hejailan, "Saudi Labor Law and the Rights of Women Employees," Arab News, January 24, 2010.
3. Francesca Levy, "Table: The World's Happiest Countries," Forbes.com, July 14, 2010, http://www.forbes.com/2010/07/14/world-happiest-countries-lifestyle-realestate-gallup-table.html.
4. Child poverty rates in the United States are between 20 and 22 percent, depending on the source.
5. Janet C. Gornick and Markus Jäntti, *Child Poverty in Upper-Income Countries: Lessons from the Luxembourg Income Study*, Luxembourg Income Study Working Paper 509, May 2009, http://www.lisproject.org/publications/liswps/509.pdf, 7.
6. Anne Lise Ellingsaeter and Arnlaug Leira, eds., *Politicizing Parenthood in Scandinavia: Gender Relations in Welfare States* (Bristol, UK: The Policy Press, 2006), 154.
7. Sam Dillon, "Top Test Scores from Shanghai Stun Educators," *New York Times*, December 7, 2010.
8. Gillian Witherspoon, Laura Gillen, and Megan Richardson, "Finland: Family Leave Policies," Tulane University, May 5, 2009, http://www.tulane.edu/~rouxbee/soci626/finland/familyleave.html.
9. Organisation for Economic Co-operation and Development , "Early Childhood Education and Care Policy in Finland," May 2000, http://www.oecd.org/dataoecd/48/55/2476019.pdf.
10. "Women in National Parliaments," Inter-Parliamentary Union, updated August 31, 2011, http://www.ipu.org/wmn-e/classif.htm.
11. The book *Raising the Global Floor* draws on the extensive research of the authors. More details can be found on the authors' website, www.raisingtheglobalfloor.org." McGill Institute for Health and Social Policy, "Raising the Global Floor: Adult Labour," World Legal Rights Database.
12. Randeep Ramesh, "Gender Gap Is Narrowing around the World, Report Claims," *The Guardian*, October 12, 2010.
13. Katrin Bennhold, "German Women Cast Off a Taboo on the Way to Work," *New York Times*, January 24, 2010.
14. Katrin Bennhold, "Where Having It All Doesn't Mean Having Equality," *New York Times*, October 12, 2010.
15. Organisation for Economic Co-operation and Development, "Labor Force Statistics by Sex and Age," OECD.Stat Extracts database, http://stats.oecd.org/Index.aspx?DataSetCode=LFS_D, accessed November 10, 2011.
16. *The World Factbook* 2009 (Washington, D.C.: Central Intelligence Agency, 2009), https://www.cia.gov/library/publications/the-world-factbook/index.html, accessed November 10, 2011.
17. Shari Roan, "Drop in US Birth Rate Is the Biggest in 30 Years," *Los Angeles Times*, March 31, 2011.
18. "Health Statistics: Teenage Pregnancy (Most Recent) by Country," NationMaster.com, http://www.nationmaster.com/graph/hea_tee_pre-health-teenage-pregnancy.
19. "Poverty in the United States: Frequently Asked Questions," National Poverty Center at the University of Michigan Gerald R. Ford School of Public Policy, http://www.npc.umich.edu/poverty, accessed December 14, 2011.
20. Katrin Bennhold, "Where Having It All Doesn't Mean Having Equality," *New York Times*, October 12, 2010.

21. Bennhold, "Where Having It All."
22. Bennhold, "German Women."
23. Ibid.
24. Katrin Bennhold, "The Good Mother, and Modern Politician," *New York Times*, January 18, 2010.
25. Alexis de Tocqueville, "How the Americans Understand the Equality of the Sexes," in Democracy in America, http://xroads.virginia.edu/-HYPER/DETOC/ch3_12.htm.
26. Maria Shriver and the Center for American Progress, *The Shriver Report: A Woman's Nation Changes Everything*, ed. Heather Boushey and Ann O'Leary (Center for American Progress and A Woman's Nation, October 2009), 19.
27. Ibid., 31, 33.
28. Katrin Bennhold, "In Sweden, Men Can Have It All," *New York Times*, June 10, 2010.
29. Ibid.
30. Katrin Bennhold, "Working (Part-Time) in the 21st Century," *New York Times*, December 30, 2010.
31. Bennhold, "Working (Part-Time)."
32. Ellen de Bruin, as cited in Bennhold, "Working (Part-Time)."
33. University of Leicester, "University of Leicester Produces the First-Ever 'World Map of Happiness'," press release, July 27, 2006, http://www.eurekalert.org/pub_releases/2006-07/uol-uol072706.php.
34. Organisation for Economic Co-operation and Development, *OECD Family Database* (OECD, Paris: OECD, 2011), www.oecd.org/social/family/database.

Chapter 4: What Can We learn from Similar Nations: England, Australia, and Canada?

1. "Parental Rights at Work," AdviceGuide, an online tool of the Citizens Advice Bureau (UK), http:/www.adviceguide.org.uk/index/life/employment/parental_rights_at_work.htm, accessed December 14, 2011.
2. Cathleen Benko and Molly Anderson, *The Corporate Lattice: Achieving High Performance in the Changing World of Work* (Boston: Harvard Business Review Press, 2010), 36.
3. Lew Daly, "The Case for Paid Family Leave: Why the United States Should Follow Australia's Lead," *Newsweek*, August 2, 2009, http://www.thedailybeast.com/newsweek/2009/08/03/the-case-for-paid-family-leave.html.
4. Ibid.
5. "The World Factbook," (updated weekly), Central Intelligence Agency, https://www.cia.gov/library/publications/the-world-factbook/rankorder/2091rank.html; Adam Liptak, "US Prison Population Dwarfs that of Other Nations," *New York Times*, April 23, 2008, http://www.nytimes.com/2008/04/23/world/americas/23iht-23prison.12253738.html?pagewanted=all.; Tamar Lewin, "Once a Leader, US Lags in College Degrees," *New York Times*, July 23, 2010, http://www.nytimes.com/2010/07/23/education/23college.html.
6. Michael Ignatieff, "Minor Differences Mean a Lot," review of *Continental Divide: The Values and Institutions of the United States and Canada*, by Seymour Martin Lipset, *New York Times*, May 13, 1990.
7. Eileen Trzcinski, "No Infant Left Behind: Public Finance Arguments for Mandated Leave and Income Supports for Parents," *Public Finance and Management 5*, no. 1 (2005): 34.
8. "Maternity Leave Benefits," table 5g of "Statistics and Indicators on Women and Men" (updated June 2011), United Nations Statistics Division, http://unstats.un.org/unsd/demographic/products/indwm/tab5g.htm.

9. Kate Zernike, "A Breast-Feeding Plan Mixes Partisan Reactions," *New York Times*, February 18, 2011.

Chapter 5: American Exceptionalism, Political Divisions, and the States

1. Mona Harrington, *Care and Equality: Inventing a New Family Politics* (New York: Routledge, 2000), 25–26.
2. Diane Stewart and Michael Lipsky, "Public Capacity and Public Trust," *The American Prospect*, February 1, 2010, http://prospect.org/cs/articles?article=public_capacity_and_public_trust.
3. Jeff Zeleny and Megan Thee-Brenan, "New Poll Finds a Deep Distrust of Government," *New York Times*, October 25, 2011.
4. The White House Press Release, accessed February 11, 2012, http://www.whitehouse.gov/the_press_office/President-Obama-Announces-White-House-Council-on-Women-and-Girls/.
5. Sheryl Gay Stolberg, "He Breaks for Band Recitals," *New York Times*, February 12, 2010.
6. National Partnership for Women and Families, *Key Findings from Nationwide Polling on Paid Family and Medical Leave* (conducted by Lake Research Partners), September 25, 2007, http://www.nationalpartnership.org/site/DocServer/WF_PaidLeave_PollResults_071002.pdf?docID=2521&autologin=true.
7. Heather Boushey, "It's Time for Policies to Match Modern Family Needs," Center for American Progress, March 29, 2010, http://www.americanprogress.org/issues/2010/03/work_survey.html.
8. *Domestic Violence & Employment Paid Family Leave Benefits: Your Legal Rights*, (San Francisco: The Legal Aid Society of San Francisco), http://www.las-elc.org/factsheets/dv-paid-leave.pdf, accessed December 9, 2011.
9. Rona Levine Sherriff, *Balancing Work and Family* (California Senate Office of Research, February 2007), http://www.paidfamilyleave.org/pdf/paidfamily07.pdf.
10. Tom Hester Jr., "In N.J., Offering Paid Leave Is an Emotional Debate," *Newsday*, March 15, 2008, http://www.njcitizenaction.org/news/pfl094.html.
11. New Jersey Business & Industry Association, "NJBIA Blasts Paid Leave Vote as Hurting an Economy Likely in Recession," news release, March 10, 2008, http://www.njbia.org/news_newsr_080310.asp.
12. Office of the Governor of New Jersey, "Governor Signs Historic Family Leave Insurance Legislation," press release, May 2008, http://www.njarch.org/images/Governor_signs_historic_family_leave_legislation.pdf.
13. *Paid Sick Days Legislation: A Legislators' Guide* (Washington, D.C.: Center for Law and Social Policy, November 2006), http://www.clasp.org/admin/site/publications/files/0326.pdf.
14. *Questions and Answers about Paid Sick Days: A Sloan Work and Family Research Network Fact Sheet* (Chestnut Hill, Mass.: Sloan Work and Family Research Network, April 2009), http://wfnetwork.bc.edu/pdfs/PaidSick.pdf.
15. DemFromCt [Greg Dworkin], "Interview with Jon Green, Connecticut Working Families," Daily Kos (blog), June 12, 2011, http://www.dailykos.com/story/2011/06/12/984309/-Interview-with-Jon-Green,-Connecticut-Working-Families.
16. Robert Drago and Vicky Lovell, *San Francisco's Paid Sick Leave Ordinance: Outcomes for Employers and Employees* (Washington, D.C.: Institute for Women's Policy Research, 2011).
17. Ibid., 1.
18. Ibid., 25.
19. Pat Garofalo, "Judge Upholds Wisconsin Paid Sick Leave Law—Will Republicans Move to Block It?" *ThinkProgress Economy* (blog), March 24, 2011.

20. "Send a Valentine to Congress," MomsRising.org, February 14, 2011, http://www.momsrising.org/blog/send-a-valentine-to-congress.

Chapter 6: Win–Win: Workplace Flexibility

1. Joint Economic Committee Majority Staff, *Paid Family Leave at Fortune 100 Companies: A Basic Standard but Still Not the Gold Standard* (Washington, D.C.: Joint Economic Committee, March 2008), http://jec.senate.gov/archive/Documents/Reports/03.05.08PaidFamilyLeave.pdf, 1, 3.
2. Joint Economic Committee, *Paid Family*, 15.
3. Vicky Lovell, Elizabeth O'Neill, and Skylar Olsen, *Maternity Leave in the United States*, Institute for Women's Policy Research Fact Sheet #A131 (Washington, D.C.: Institute for Women's Policy Research, August 2007).
4. Ibid.
5. 'Flexible Work Arrangements," Workplace Flexibility 2010, Georgetown Law, May 13, 2010, http://workplaceflexibility2010.org/index.php/policy_components/flexible_work_arrangements/.
6. Tucker Echols, "33.7 Million Now Telecommute," *Washington Business Journal*, February 17, 2009, http://www.bizjournals.com/washington/stories/2009/02/16/daily16.html.
7. Kate Lister and Tom Harnish, *Undress for Success: The Naked Truth about Making Money at Home* (Hoboken, N.J.: John Wiley & Sons, Inc., 2009).
8. "The Business Case for Telecommuting," WFC Resources, http://www.clalliance.net/EXPO/docs/The_Business_Case_for_Telecommuting-WFCResources.pdf.
9. For news about work and family research, Kossek refers readers to the News Feed of the new Work and Family Research Network (WFRN).
10. Eric Omer, "It Costs How Much to Replace an Employee?" EzineArticles.com, July 9, 2009, http://ezinearticles.com/?It-Costs-How-Much-to-Replace-an-Employee?&id=2555834.
11. "Employee Retention Seminar in South Africa," Cinncinati Press Coverage, April 30, 2003, http://www.sashacorp.com/press5.html.
12. Jody Heymann, *Profit at the Bottom of the Ladder: Creating Value by Investing in Your Workforce* (Boston: Harvard Business Press, 2010).
13. Jody Heymann, "Investing at the Bottom of the Ladder," *Stanford Social Innovation Review*, Winter 2011, http://www.ssireview.org/site/printer/investing_at_the_bottom_of_the_ladder/.
14. *Working Mother Best Companies for Hourly Workers: Executive Summary 2010*, http://www.wmmsurveys.com/HourlyWorkers2010_ExecutiveSummary.pdf, 16.
15. Helen Jonsen, "Flex Is the New Currency," *Working Mother*, January 28, 2010, http://www.workingmother.com/flex-new-currency.
16. Josh Dawsey and Rupali Arora, "15 Best New Cities for Business," CNNMoney, http://money.cnn.com/magazines/fortune/global500/2011/hottest_cities.
17. Joan Blades and Nanette Fondas, *The Custom-Fit Workplace: Choose When, Where, and How to Work and Boost Your Bottom Line* (San Francisco: Jossey-Bass, 2010), 8.
18. Cathleen Benko and Molly Anderson, *The Corporate Lattice: Achieving High Performance in the Changing World of Work* (Boston: Harvard Business Review Press, 2010), 3.
19. Benko and Anderson, *Corporate Lattice*, 6, citing a survey in Watson Wyatt, *Driving Business Results Through Continuous Engagement*, 2008/2009 WorkUSA Survey Report (New York: Watson Wyatt, February 3, 2009).
20. Joan Blades and Nanette Fondas, *The Custom –Fit Workplace: Choose When, Where, and How to*

Work and Boost Your Bottom Line (San Francisco: Jossey-Bass, 2010), 54.

21. Teresa Amabile and Steven Kramer, "Do Happier People Work Harder?" *New York Times*, September 3, 2011, http://www.nytimes.com/2011/09/04/opinion/sunday/do-happier-people-work-harder.html.
22. International Labor Comparisons, Charting International Labor Comparisons [2011 Edition] US Department of Labor, Bureau of Labor Statistics, http://www.bls.gov/fls/chartbook/section2.htm#chart2.7.

Chapter 7: The Early Years: Child Care and Early Education

1. Jennifer Cheeseman Day and Eric C. Newburger, *The Big Payoff: Educational Attainment and Synthetic Estimates of Work-Life Earnings*, Current Population Reports p23–210 (US Census Bureau, July 2002).
2. Tamar Lewin, "Value of College Degree Is Growing, Study Says," *New York Times*, September 21, 2010.
3. "Fast Facts," Institute of Education Sciences: National Center for Education Statistics, http://ed.gov/fastfacts/display.asp?id=76.
4. Richard Fry, "Education and Labor Market Status of Young Adults," a table in the executive summary of *College Enrollment Hits All-Time High, Fueled by Community College Surge*, (Washington, D.C.: Pew Research Center, October 29, 2009), http://pewresearch.org./pubs/1391/college-enrollment-all-time-high-community-college-surge.
5. Edward Zigler, Katherine Marsland, and Heather Lord, *The Tragedy of Child Care in America* (New Haven, Conn., and London: Yale University Press, 2009).
6. Gøsta Esping-Andersen, *The Incomplete Revolution: Adapting Welfare States to Women's New Roles* (Malden, Mass., and Cambridge, UK: Polity Press, 2009), 94.
7. Esping-Andersen, *Incomplete*, 104.
8. Sonya Michel, *Children's Interest/Mothers' Rights: The Shaping of America's Childcare Policies* (New Haven, Conn., and London: Yale University Press, 2000), 26.
9. Ibid., 72.
10. Ibid., 156.
11. Ibid., 73.
12. Ibid., 92.
13. Ibid., 189.
14. Zigler, Marsland, and Lord, *Tragedy*, 16.
15. Ibid., 6.
16. Ibid., 7.
17. Ibid., 10.
18. Ibid., 73.
19. Ibid., 11.
20. Jody Heymann, *Profit at the Bottom of the Ladder: Creating Value by Investing in Your Workforce* (Boston: Harvard Business Press, 2010), 130.
21. Michel, *Children's Interest*, 248.
22. Zigler, Marsland, and Lord, *Tragedy*, 18.
23. Ibid., 30.
24. Ibid., 37.
25. Ibid., 101.

26. "Highscope Perry Preschool Study: *Lifetime Effects: The HighScope Perry Preschool Study Through Age 40* (2005)," Highscope, http://www.highscope.org/content.asp?contentid=219.
27. Mission: Readiness, *Ready, Willing, and Unable to Serve: 75 Percent of Young Adults Cannot Join the Military: Early Education across America Is Needed to Ensure National Security* (Washington, D.C.: Mission: Readiness, 2009), 1.
28. "Early Education: Five Guiding Principles for Early Education," Committee for Economic Development, http://www.ced.org/issues/education/early-care-and-education/early-education.
29. William Christeson, Amy Dawson Taggart, and Soren Messner-Zidell, *Young Mississippians: Ready, Willing, and Unable to Serve* (Washington, D.C.: Mission: Readiness, 2010).
30. Institute for a Competitive Workforce, *Why Business Should Support Early Childhood Education* (Washington, D.C.: Institute for a Competitive Workforce, of the US Chamber of Commerce, 2010), 24.
31. Ibid.
32. Rachel Demma, *Building Ready States: A Governor's Guide to Supporting a Comprehensive, High-Quality Early Childhood State Systems* (Washington, D.C.: NGA Center for Best Practices, October 2010), 3.
33. William Gormley Jr., Ted Gayer, Deborah Phillips, and Brittany Dawson, *The Effects of Oklahoma's Universal Pre-K Program on School Readiness: An Executive Summary* (Washington, D.C.: Center for Research on Children in the US at Georgetown University, November 2004), http://www.crocus.georgetown.edu/reports/executive_summary_11_04.pdf.
34. William Carpluck, *Investments in Pennsylvania's Early Childhood Programs Pay Off Now and Later*, (Washington, D.C.: Pew Center on the States, March 2011), http://www.partnershipforsuccess.org/uploads/20110303_PAbriefFinal.pdf.
35. *The Science of Early Childhood Development: Closing the Gap Between What We Know and What We Do* (Cambridge, Mass.: National Scientific Council on the Developing Child, 2007), 1.
36. James Heckman, "Stimulating the Young," *The American*, August 7, 2009.
37. James Heckman, "Schools, Skills, and Synapses," *Economic Inquiry* 46, no. 3 (July 2008): 289–324.
38. "Heckman Equation," Heckman: The Economics of Human Potential, http://www.heckmanequation.org/heckman-equation, accessed December 9, 2011.
39. Nancy Duff Campbell, Judith C. Appelbaum, Karin Martinson, and Emily Martin, *Be All That We Can Be: Lessons from the Military for Improving Our Nation's Child Care System* (Washington, D.C.: National Women's Law Center, April 2000), http://www.nwlc.org/resource/be-all-we-can-be-lesson-military-improving-our-nations-child-care-system.
40. Ibid.
41. Based on an interview by Roger Neugebauer, "The US Military Child Care System: A Model Worth Replicating," *Exchange*, January/February 2005, 31-32.
42. Campbell, Appelbaum, Martinson, and Martin, *Be All That We Can Be*, 7.
43. Office of the Assistant Secretary of Defense, "DOD Announces School Year 2010/2011 Child Care Fee Policy," US Department of Defense, July 30, 2010, http://www.defense.gov/releases/release.aspx?releaseid=13765.
44. Ibid., 29–32.

Chapter 8: New Family Portraits

1. *The Shriver Report*, 19.
2. Ibid.

3. Tara Parker-Pope, "Surprisingly, Family Time Has Grown," *New York Times*, April 5, 2010, http://well.blogs.nytimes.com/2010/04/05/surprisingly-family-time-has-grown/.
4. Lisa Belkin, "When Mom and Dad Share It All," *New York Times Magazine*, June 15, 2008, http://www.nytimes.com/2008/06/15/magazine/15parenting-t.html?pagewanted=all.
5. *The Shriver Report*, 76.
6. Annie E. Casey Foundation, *2010 Kids Count Data Book*, http://datacenter.kidscount.org/DataBook/2010/OnlineBooks/2010DataBook.pdf, 36.
7. Janet C. Gornick and Marcia K. Meyers, *Gender Equality: Transforming Family Divisions of Labor*, the Real Utopias Project, vol. 6 (Brooklyn, N.Y., and London: Verso, 2009) 14.
8. Gornick and Meyers, *Gender*, 15.
9. Belkin, "When Mom and Dad."
10. Lisa Belkin, "Equal Workloads for Husbands and Wives," *New York Times*, July 25, 2011.
11. Belkin, "When Mom and Dad."
12. Shriver and the Center for American Progress, *The Shriver Report*, 36.
13. Ibid., 18.
14. Marc Vachon and Amy Vachon, *Equally Shared Parenting: Rewriting the Rules for a New Generation of Parents* (New York: Penguin, 2010), 165.
15. Ibid., 191.
16. Pam Belluck, "In Study, Fatherhood Leads to Drop in Testosterone," *New York Times*, September 1,2 2011
17. Lisa Belkin, "Why Dad's Résumé Lists 'Car Pool,'" *New York Times*, June 12, 2008.
18. Belkin, "Why Dad's."
19. Peter Baylies and Jessica Toonkel, *The Stay-at-Home Dad Handbook* (Chicago: Chicago Review Press, 2004), 3, 8.
20. Jeremy Adam Smith, *The Daddy Shift: How Stay-At-Home Dads, Breadwinning Moms, and Shared Parenting Are Transforming the American Family* (Boston: Beacon Press, 2009), xvi.
21. Smith, *Daddy Shift*, 22, 54.
22. Ibid., 57.
23. Ibid., 61.
24. Tanya Macramalla, "Men Who Help Clean Get More Sex?," *Limelife*, December 25, 2009, http://www.limelife.com/blog-entry/Men-Who-Help-Clean-Get-More-Sex/29319.html.
25. Vachon and Vachon, *Equally Shared*, 150.
26. Erin Anderssen, "Dads Happier When They Split Domestic Duties: Study," *The Globe and Mail*, November 9, 2010.
27. Derek Bok, *The Politics of Happiness, What Government Can Learn from the New Research on Well-Being* (Princeton, N.J.: Princeton University Press, 2010), 11, 13, 15.
28. Bok, *Happiness*, 61.
29. Ibid., 205.

Chapter 9: How Women Leaders Make a Difference

1. "Women in National Parliaments," Inter-Parliamentary Union, (updated monthly), http://www.ipu.org/wmn-e/classif.htm, accessed June 30, 2011.
2. "'Masculine Norms': Why Working Women Find It Hard to Reach the Top," Knowledge@Wharton, August 3, 2011, http://knowledge.wharton.upenn.edu/article.cfm?articleid=2821.
3. Jody Heymann, "Investing at the Bottom of the Ladder," *Stanford Social Innovation Review*, Winter

2011, http://www.ssireview.org/site/printer/investing_at_the_bottom_of_the_ladder/.
4. Catalyst Census, Catalyst@gmial.vresp.com Dec 14, 2011.
5. *Missing Pieces: Women and Minorities on Fortune 500 Boards* (Alliance for Board Diversity, 2011), http://theabd.org/Missing_Pieces_Women_and_Minorities_on_Fortune_500_Boards.pdf.
6. Nancy M. Carter, PhD, and Christine Silva, *Pipeline's Broken Promise: A Research Project on Highly Talented Employees in the Pipeline* (New York: Catalyst, 2010).
7. Ibid., 2.
8. Ibid., 3.
9. Ibid., 6.
10. The Wharton School, "'Masculine Norms' May Be Barriers for Women," *Human Resource Executive Online*, August 12, 2011.
11. Nadya A. Fouad and Romila Singh, *Stemming the Tide: Why Women Leave Engineering* (University of Wisconsin at Milwaukee, 2011).
12. *Targeting Inequity: The Gender Gap in US Corporate Leadership*, statement of Ilene H. Lang, president and chief executive officer of Catalyst, before the Joint Economic Committee, US Congress, September 28, 2010, http://jec.senate.gov/public//index.cfm?a=Files.Serve&File_id=d5ae8b33-f762-4cf2-850b-84d2ded6218d.
13. Ibid.
14. Georges Desvaux, Sandrine Devillard-Hoellinger, and Pascal Baumgarten, "Women Matter: Gender Diversity, a Corporate Performance Driver," Mckinsey&Company, 2007, http://www.mckinsey.com/locations/swiss/news_publications/pdf/women_matter_english.pdf.
15. Beth Brooke and Billie Williamson, *Groundbreakers: Using the Strength of Women to Rebuild the World Economy*, Ernst & Young, 2009, http://www.ey.com/GL/en/Issues/Driving-growth/Groundbreakers---Executive-Summary.
16. Sharon Reier, "In Europe, Women Finding More Seats at the Table," *New York Times*, March 22, 2008.
17. Michael Collins, "Gender Impacts Approach to Business in the Boardroom," Diversity Best Practices, October 20, 2010, http://www.diversitybestpractices.com/news-articles/gender-impacts-approach-business-boardroom.
18. Ken Auletta, "A Woman's Place," *The New Yorker*, July 11, 2011, http://www.newyorker.com/reporting/2011/07/11/110711fa_fact_auletta#ixzzIU4TTINCK.
19. *Duke.Fact.Checker Blog*; "Obituary—Juanita Kreps, James B. Duke professor of economics," July 8, 2010, http://dukefactchecker.blogspot.com/2010/07/obituary-juanita-kreps-james-b-duke.html.
20. Claire Cain Miller, "For Incoming I.B.M. Chief, Self-Confidence Is Rewarded," *New York Times*, October 27, 2011.
21. Julia Werdigier, "Fund Plans to Invest in Companies with Women as Directors," *New York Times*, October 26, 2009.
22. Nicola Clark, "Getting Women into Boardrooms, by Law," *New York Times*, January 27, 2010.
23. Reier, "In Europe."
24. Robert Goddard, "UK: Women on Boards—Lord Davies' Report," Corporate Law and Governance (blog), February 24, 2011, http://corporatelawandgovernance.blogspot.com/2011/02/uk-women-on-boards-lord-davies-report.html.
25. As quoted in a letter from Joseph F. Keefe, president and CEO of Pax World, on behalf of the "Say No to All Male Boards" campaign, available on the Pax World website at http://paxworld.s3.amazonaws.com/22/f1/9/700/ltr_to_re_board_diversity_and_pvgs__040511.pdf.

26. Werdigier, "Fund Plans."
27. Ibid.
28. As quoted by Kelly Wallace, "Does Wall Street Need More Women?" CBSNews.com, September 10, 2009, http://www.cbsnews.com/stories/2009/09/10/eveningnews/main5301487.shtml.
29. Sheelah Kolhatkar, "What If Women Ran Wall Street?" *New York Magazine*, March 21, 2010, http://nymag.com/news/businessfinance/64950.
30. Letter from Joseph F. Keefe.
31. Ibid.
32. "Towards a Level Playing Field: The Business Case for Gender Diversity," (event package for panel discussion, New York City, September 23, 2009), http://static.85broads.com/documents/Towards-A-Level-Playing-Field.pdf.

Chapter 10: What Women Need to Create Equal Opportunities in the Workplace

1. Del Jones, "Often, Men Help Women Get to the Corner Office," *USA Today*, August 5, 2009, http://www.usatoday.com/money/companies/management/2009-08-04-female-executives-male-mentors_N.htm.
2. Michael S. Dahl, Cristian L. Dezsö, and David Gaddis Ross, *Like Daughter, Like Father: How Women's Wages Change When CEOs Have Daughters* (Catalyst, 2011), http://www.catalyst.org/blog/2011/05.
3. Elizabeth Gudrais, "Family or Fortune," *Harvard Magazine*, January-February 2010, http://harvardmagazine.com/2010/01/family-or-fortune.
4. Roni Caryn Rabin, "Patterns: Pediatricians Turning to Part-Time Work," *New York Times*, December 14, 2009.
5. Douglas O. Staiger, David I. Auerbach, and Peter I. Buerhaus, "Trends in the Work Hours of Physicians in the United States," Journal of the American Medical Association, (n. d.), http://jama.ama-assn.org/content/303/8/747.full?home.
6. Barbara Bein, "Physicians Working Fewer Hours a Week," AAFP, http://www.aafp.org/online/en/home/publications/news/news-now/professional-issues/20100315jamaworkinghours.html.
7. Geraldine Fabrikant, "Where Are the Women on Wall Street?", *New York Times*, January 27, 2010.
8. *The Economic Impact of Women-Owned Businesses in the United States*, (McLean, Va.: Center for Women's Business Research, October 2009), http://www.womensbusinessresearchcenter.org/Data/research/economicimpactstud/econimpactreport-final.pdf.
9. Ibid.
10. "Sone Facts about Women Entrepreneurs," Go4Funding, (n. d.), http://www.go4funding.com/Articles/Entrepreneur/Some-Facts-About-Women-Entrepreneurs.aspx.
11. Media Kit, (Washington, D.C.: National Association of Women Business Owners, 2010), http://nawbo.org/pdfs/NAWBOMediaKit.pdf.
12. "Paycheck Fairness Act Coalition: New Polling Data Shows Voters *Overwhelmingly Support* the Paycheck Fairness Act," describing the results of a poll taken by Lake Research Partners, May 21–24, 2010, on behalf of the National Partnership for Women and Families.
13. Tanya Senanayake, "The Wage Gap: Women Still Make Less Than Men," National Women's Law Center, September 13, 2011, http://www.nwlc.org/our-blog/wage-gap-women-still-make-less-men.
14. James Sherk, "Paycheck Fairness Act," Heritage Foundation, February 22, 2011, http://www.heritage.org/research/reports/2011/02/paycheck-fairness-act.

15. Linda D. Hallman, "Exclusive: The Paycheck Fairness Act: Now an Economic Imperative," April 20, 2010, Women's Media Center, http://womensmediacenter.com/blog/2010/04/exclusive-the-paycheck-fairness-act-now-an-economic-imperative/.
16. Barbara A. Mikulski, US Senate floor speech, November 17, 2010, http://mikulski.senate.gov/media/speeches/11-17-2010-Ledbetter.cfm.
17. Christina Hoff Sommers, "Fair Pay Isn't Always Equal Pay," *New York Times*, op-ed, September 21, 2010.
18. Stacy Blackman, "Study Examines Male–Female Wage Gap, Post-.B.A." *MBA Admissions: Strictly Business* (blog), August 26, 2011, http://www.usnews.com/education/blogs/MBA-admissions-strictly-business/2011/08/26/study-examines-male-female-wage-gap-post-mba.
19. Adam Liptak, "Justices Rule for Wal-Mart in Class-Action Bias Case," *New York Times*, June 20, 2011.
20. Peter Lattman, "3 Women Claim Bias at Goldman," *New York Times*, September 15, 2010.
21. Bob Van Voris and Christine Harper, "Goldman Sachs Sued over Alleged Gender Discrimination," Bloomberg News, September 15, 2010, http://www.bloomberg.com/news/2010-09-15/goldman-sachs-sued-by-three-women-over-alleged-gender-discrimination.html.
22. Sarah Pierce, "Novartis Settles Gender Discrimination Lawsuit," Legafi, July 20, 2010, http://legafi.com/lawsuits/news/464-novartis-settles-gender-discrimination-lawsuit.
23. John W. Curtis, "Persistent Inequity: Gender and Academic Employment," remarks prepared for "New Voices in Pay Equity," a panel convened by the American Association for University Professors for Equal Pay Day, April 11, 2011.
24. Judy Goldberg Dey and Catherine Hill, *Behind the Pay Gap* (Washington, D.C.: American Association of University Women Educational Foundation, 2007), 2.
25. Nancy Hopkins, in a keynote address at the for MIT150 Symposium *Leaders in Science and Engineering: The Women of MIT*, March 28, 2011.
26. Claire Cain Miller, "Out of the Loop in Silicon Valley," *New York Times*, April 18, 2010.
27. Miriam Peskowitz, *The Truth Behind the Mommy Wars: Who Decides What Makes a Good Mother* (Emeryville, Calif.: Seal Press, 2005), 67.
28. Joan C. Williams, *Reshaping the Work-Family Debate: Why Men and Class Matter* (Cambridge, Mass., and London: Harvard University Press, 2010), 28–29.
29. Family responsibilities discrimination, as described by the Center for WorkLife Law, University of California Hastings College of the Law, http://www.uchastings.edu/centers/worklife-law.html.
30. Williams, *Reshaping*, 28.

Chapter 11: Building a Coalition

1. "Union Members Summary," Economic News Release from Bureau of Labor Statistics, US Department of Labor, January 27, 2012, http://www.bls.gov/news.release/union2.nr0.htm.
2. Kerstin Aumann, Ellen Galinsky, Kelly Sakai, Melissa Brown, and James T. Bond, *The Elder Care Study: Everyday Realities and Wishes for Change*, Families and Work Institute 2008 National Study of the Changing Workforce (Families and Work Institute, 2010), http://www.familiesandwork.org/site/research/reports/elder_care.pdf.
3. "About the Program" (AARP Best Employers for Workers over 50), AARP, August 2011, http://www.aarp.org/work/employee-benefits/info-09-2009/about_the_best_employers_program.html.
4. Stephen Miller, "Caregivers in the 'Sandwich Generation; Face Double Worries," *Society for Human Resource Management*, November 20, 2010.
5. Aumann et al., *Elder Care Study*, 2.

6. Marcie Pitt-Catsouphes, Christina Matz-Costa, and Elyssa Besen, *Age & Generations: Understanding Experiences at the Workplace*, Research Highlight 6 (Sloan Center on Aging & Work at Boston College, March 2009), 3.
7. Marcie Pitt-Catsouphes, Stephen Sweet, and Kathy Lynch, with Elizabeth Whalley, *2009 Talent Management Study* Issue Brief 23 (Sloan Center on Aging & Work at Boston College, October 2009), 1.
8. Williams, *Reshaping*, 80.
9. Brad Harrington, Fred Van Deusen, and Beth Humberd, *The New Dad: Caring, Committed and Conflicted* (Boston College Center for Work & Family, 2011), 10.
10. Ibid., 13.
11. Maria Shriver and the Center for American Progress, *The Shriver Report: A Woman's Nation Changes Everything*, ed. Heather Boushey and Ann O'Leary (Center for American Progress and A Woman's Nation, October 2009), 242.
12. James Martin, "60 Women's Religious Orders Support Health Care Bill," *In All Things (blog) of America: The National Catholic Weekly*, March 17, 2010.
13. Helene Cooper, "Nuns Back Bill Amid Broad Rift over Whether It Limits Abortion Enough," *New York Times*, March 19, 2010, http://www.nytimes.com/2010/03/20/health/policy/20abortion.html.
14. Ibid.
15. Frank Bruni, "To Know Us Is to Let Us Love," *New York Times*, June 26, 2011.
16. Susan Page, "Gay Candidates Gain Acceptance," *USA Today*, July 20, 2011, http://www.usatoday.com/news/politics/2011-07-19-gay-candidates-politics_n.htm.
17. Bruni, "To Know Us."

Chapter 12: Child Poverty

1. Janet C. Gornick and Markus Jäntti, *Child Poverty in Upper-Income Countries: Lessons from the Luxembourg Income Study*, Luxembourg Income Study Working Paper 509, May 2009, http://www.lisproject.org/publications/liswps/509.pdf, 7. Poverty rates vary depending on who is measuring them and the criteria used. This study compares the United States to other developed countries. But no matter how child poverty is measured, the rate in the United States is exceedingly high and rising.
2. Kristin Anderson Moore, Zakia Redd, Mary Burkhauser, Kassim Mbwana, and Ashleigh Collins, *Children in Poverty: Trends, Consequences, and Policy Options*, Child Trends research brief 2009-11 (Washington, D.C.: Child Trends, April 2009), http://www.childtrends.org/files/child_trends-2009_04_07_rb_childreninpoverty.pdf, 2.
3. Hope Yen, "Census Shows 1 in 2 People Are Poor or Low-Income," Bloomberg Businessweek, December 15, 2011, http://www.businessweek.com/ap/financialnews/D9RL00K00.htm.
4. Charles M. Blow, "Hard-Knock (Hardly Acknowledged) Life," *New York Times*, op-ed, January 29, 2011.
5. Sabrina Taverinse and Robert Gebeloff, "New Way to Tally Poor Recasts View of Poverty," *New York Times*, November 7, 2011.
6. Monica Davey, "Families Feel Sharp Edge of State Budget Cuts," *New York Times*, September 7, 2011.
7. Charles M. Blow, "Failing Forward," *New York Times*, op-ed, August 26, 2011.
8. Gornick and Jäntti, *Child Poverty*, 10.
9. Ibid., 11.

10. Ibid., 7.
11. Ibid., 34.
12. Children's Defense Fund, "Child Poverty," in *The State of America's Children* (Children's Defense Fund, 2011), B-4. B-2, F-2.
13. "New Report Shows Alarming Rates of Poverty among US Children," *PBS Newshour*, August 18, 2011, http://www.pbs.org/newshour/bb/business/july-dec11/childrenpovert_08-18.html.
14. Charles M. Blow, "The Decade of Lost Children," *New York Times*, op-ed, August 5, 2011.
15. Gornick and Jäntti, *Child Poverty*, 4.
16. Blow, "Lost Children," August, 5, 2011.
17. Poverty rates, depending on the source, range from 20 to 22 percent.
18. Carmen DeNavas-Walt, Bernadette D. Proctor, Jessica C. Smith, *Income, Poverty and Health Insurance Coverage in the United States: 2009,* US Census Bureau Current Population Reports p60–238 (Washington, D.C.: US Government Printing Office, September 2010), 62–67.
19. Donald G. McNeil Jr., "Broad Racial Disparities Seen in Americans' Ills," *New York Times*, January 14, 2011.
20. "Ten Important Questions about Child Poverty and Family Economic Hardship," National Center for Children in Poverty, http://www.nccp.org/faq.html.
21. Blow, "Lost Children," August 5, 2011.
22. Moore et al., *Children in Poverty*, 5.
23. Gøsta Esping-Andersen, *The Incomplete Revolution: Adapting Welfare States to Women's New Roles* (Malden, Mass., and Cambridge, U.K.: Polity Press, 2009), 78.
24. Andrew Romano and Tony Dokoupil, "Men's Lib," Newsweek, September 27, 2010, 46–47.
25. Isabel V. Sawhill and John E. Morton, *Economic Mobility: Is the American Dream Alive and Well?* (Washington, D.C.: Economic Mobility Project, 2007), 5.
26. Ibid., 4.
27. Ibid., 5, 6.
28. Ibid., 7.
29. "Americans Like Occupy Wall Street More Than Congress," *Say It Ain't So Already* (blog), October 25, 2011, http://sayitaintsoalready.com/2011/10/25/americans-like-occupy-wall-street-more-than-congress.

Chapter 13: How Do We Win?

1. MomsRising, "Send a Letter to Your Member of Congress Now Telling Them to Put Our Kids First!" http://action.momsrising.org/letter/budget_cuts_2012_V2.
2. "Hard Times Generation: Families Living in Cars," *60 Minutes*, November 27, 2011, http://www.cbsnews.com/video/watch/?id=7389750n.
3. Thomas B. Edsall, "The Distorted View from Capitol Hill," Campaign Stops (blog), *New York Times*, January 1, 2012, http://campaignstops.blogs.nytimes.com/2012/01/01/the-distorted-view-from-capitol-hill/.
4. Eric Lichtblau, "Economic Slide Took a Detour at Capitol Hill, *New York Times*, Dec. 27, 2011.
5. David Brooks, "Free-Market Socialism," *New York Times*, January 23, 2012, accessed February 7, 2012, http://www.nytimes.com/2012/01/24/opinion/brooks-free-market-socialism-.html?_r=1&ref=davidbrooks.
6. Mona Harrington, *Care and Equality: Inventing a New Family Politics* (New York: Routledge, 1999), 80.

7. Raymond Hernandez, "A Gillibrand Campaign: More Women in Politics," *New York Times*, July 5, 2011.
8. Devin Dwyer, "Okla. Governor Candidates Debate Marital Status, Parenting Experience," ABC News website, October 26, 2010, http://abcnews.go.com/Politics/vote-2010-oklahoma-governors-debate-motherhood-prerequisite-office/story?id=11971580.
9. Jonathan Alter, "Woman of the World," *Vanity Fair*, June 2011, 143.
10. "Nobel Peace Prize recognises women rights activists," BBC News, October 7, 2011, http://www.bbc.co.uk/news/world-europe-15211861.
11. Barry Neild and Moni Basu, "'Be Not Afraid to Denounce Injustice,' Sirleaf Says in Accepting Nobel Peace Prize," News in Black, December 10, 2011, http://www.newsinblack.com/world/Be-not-afraid-to-denounce-injustice-Sirleaf-says-in-accepting-Nobel-Peace-Prize-135375208.html.
12. Tony Dokoupil, "Why Female Politicians Are More Effective," *The Daily Beast*, January 22, 2011.
13. LZ Granderson, "Would Female Leaders Solve Debt Crisis?" *CNN Opinion*, July 19, 2011.
14. Center for American Women and Politics, "Facts," http://www.cawp.rutgers.edu/index.php.
15. From Greenberg Quinlan Rosner Research: GQRR, http://gqrr.com/.
16. *Report of the Steering Committee on Undergraduate Women's Leadership* (Princeton, N.J.: Princeton University, March 2011), 5.
17. Hanna Rosin, "The End of Men," *The Atlantic*, July/August 2010, http://www.theatlantic.com/magazine/archive/2010/07/the-end-of-men/8135/.
18. US Department of Commerce Economics and Statistics Administration and Executive Office of the President Office of Management and Budget, *Women in America: Indicators of Social and Economic Well-Being*, a report prepared for the White House Council on Women and Girls (March 2011), 3–4.

INDEX

PAUL BOISVERT

Madeleine M. Kunin was the first woman governor of Vermont and the first woman in the United States to serve three terms. She served as Deputy Secretary of Education and Ambassador to Switzerland in the Clinton administration. Kunin is the author of *Pearls, Politics & Power* and *Living a Political Life*. She is also a Marsh professor at the University of Vermont and a commentator on Vermont Public Radio, as well as founder of the global Institute for Sustainable Communities (ISC), a nongovernmental organization focused on climate change and civil society. She lives in Burlington, Vermont, with her husband, John Hennessey.

"This logo identifies paper that meets the standards of the Forest Stewardship Council®. FSC® is widely regarded as the best practice in forest management, ensuring the highest protections for forests and indigenous peoples."

Chelsea Green Publishing is committed to preserving ancient forests and natural resources. We elected to print this title on 30-percent postconsumer recycled paper, processed chlorine-free. As a result, for this printing, we have saved:

28 Trees (40' tall and 6-8" diameter)
11 Million BTUs of Total Energy
2,763 Pounds of Greenhouse Gases
12,459 Gallons of Wastewater
790 Pounds of Solid Waste

Chelsea Green Publishing made this paper choice because we and our printer, Thomson-Shore, Inc., are members of the Green Press Initiative, a nonprofit program dedicated to supporting authors, publishers, and suppliers in their efforts to reduce their use of fiber obtained from endangered forests. For more information, visit: www.greenpressinitiative.org.

Environmental impact estimates were made using the Environmental Defense Paper Calculator. For more information visit: www.papercalculator.org.

the politics and practice of sustainable living

CHELSEA GREEN PUBLISHING

Chelsea Green Publishing sees books as tools for effecting cultural change and seeks to empower citizens to participate in reclaiming our global commons and become its impassioned stewards. If you enjoyed reading *The New Feminist Agenda*, please consider these other great books related to workplace policy, politics, and the economy.

PEARLS, POLITICS AND POWER
How Women Can Win and Lead
MADELEINE M. KUNIN
9781933392929
Paperback • $14.95

DIARY OF AN ECO-OUTLAW
An Unreasonable Woman Breaks the Law for Mother Earth
DIANE WILSON
9781603582155
Paperback • $17.95

LOCAL DOLLARS, LOCAL SENSE
How to Shift Your Money from Wall Street to Main Street and Achieve Real Prosperity
MICHAEL SHUMAN
9781603583435
Paperback • $17.95

REINVENTING FIRE
Bold Business Solutions for the New Energy Era
AMORY LOVINS
9781603583718
Hardcover • $34.95

For more information or to request a catalog, visit **www.chelseagreen.com** or call toll-free **(800) 639-4099**.